DECONSTRUCTING SPORT HISTORY

SUNY series on Sport, Culture, and Social Relations
CL Cole and Michael A. Messner, editors

Deconstructing
Sport History

A Postmodern Analysis

Edited by
Murray G. Phillips
with a
Foreword by
Alun Munslow

STATE UNIVERSITY OF NEW YORK PRESS

Published by
State University of New York Press, Albany

© 2006 State University of New York

For information, address State University of New York Press,
194 Washington Avenue, Suite 305, Albany, NY 12210-2384

Production by Marilyn P. Semerad
Marketing by Michael Campochiaro

Library of Congress Cataloging in Publication Data

Deconstructing sport history : a postmodern analysis / edited by Murray G. Phillips ;
foreword by Alun Munslow.
    p. cm. — (SUNY series on sport, culture, and social relations)
    Includes bibliographical references and index.
    ISBN 0-7914-6609-4 (hardcover : alk. paper) — ISBN 0-7914-6610-8 (pbk. : alk.
paper)
    1. Sports—Sociological aspects. 2. Sports—History. I. Phillips, Murray G. (Murray
George) II. Series.

GV706.5.D395 2005
306.4'83—dc22

                                                              2004030963

10 9 8 7 6 5 4 3 2 1

Contents

Foreword

As a history undergraduate, in the United Kingdom in the 1960s, I was told that only through an unrelenting diligence in the archive could I move toward better, balanced, and justified explanations about what happened in the past. And, of course, only through rational inference might I be able to tell what it most likely meant. In this way I learned that the logic of history was empiricism, analysis, and hypothesis testing. I was also schooled to accept that the basis of history was the single statement of justified belief. Moreover, an important corollary to this was also dinned into me. It was that as long as historians are reasonable people, disinterested in their accounts, even-handed and not judgemental in their inferences, and are happy with tiny incremental advances in knowledge, then the discipline does not merely hold to objectivity and truth as regulatory ideals, but they can be achieved. So it is the natural state of affairs, I was also informed, that historical explanations are always provisional and that this provisionality is of a particularly worthy kind, indeed, the only kind of provisionality worth having. It was and is the provisionality of interpretation. History is an interpretation because it is always conditional on the estimable triad of new evidence, better inference, and the application of improved conceptualization/theory that explains the widest possible range of available evidence. This virtuous circle is, therefore, the ultimate shield against mendacity and partiality. Briefly, but sternly, I was warned not to confuse provisionality with relativism. In other words, the possibility of truthful historical knowledge is there, but only if you do not step outside the empirical-analytical pentacle.

It was only later—after I had become a professional historian and possessed a hard-core social science PhD—that I read Hayden White's *Metahistory*. I then lapsed. I began to wonder if the logic of history that I had been taught might not, in fact, exhaust its nature. Inevitably I began to wonder if provisionality in historical interpretation could have something to do with the possibility of historical knowledge itself. In other words, was the ontology of history even more complicated than I had been led to believe? What I got from White (and other philosophers of history such as Mink, Ankersmit, Danto, Carr, Jenkins, and Ricoeur in their own ways) was a profound uncertainty about history as some kind of reconstruction or facsimile or something that was even better: an explanation of what the past really meant! Although the "linguistic turn" now sounds faintly old hat in the face of many new "history turns" it is worth recalling that it was not so long ago that it was briefly fashionable to criticize reconstructionist naïve empiricism. But now that particular stalking horse has gone the way of all horseflesh (surely I am not being too optimistic here?) I still harbor doubts that we are yet, as a profession, self-conscious enough to label our constructionist history with a poststructuralist and antinarrativist health warning. But, as this collection so clearly reveals, history is as much about the historian and the present and its own future as it is about the past itself. Happily, history will always have a future as long as we do not forget to debate the nature of its provisionality and the relationship between interpretation and explanation.

Epistemological skepticism is not intellectual irresponsibility. It is, rather, an honest and, perforce, a demanding ethical excursion into that dangerous territory we call "uncertainty"—uncertainty about knowledge of the real, the (im)possibility of objectivity, how we create "historical concepts" that purport to offer an explanatory match with what happened and, not least, the indeterminacy of our representations. Arguably, the past is only as fixed as our images of it and the metaphors we substitute for it. What we constitute as "the past" is no more rigid than our present practices of classification and description. Once we understand that we can free ourselves of the belief that the past is over and done with: that the past does not change. As this collection so clearly reveals, we can usefully and fully engage with "the-past-as-history," we can do it "meaningfully," but only once we let go of the certainties in which I, for one, was trained. This is a collection that I strongly commend to everyone who has an open mind about his or her engagement with the time before now.

Alun Munslow

Introduction

Sport History and Postmodernism

MURRAY G. PHILLIPS

In our contemporary or postmodern world, history conceived of as an empirical research method based upon the belief in some reasonably accurate correspondence between the past, its interpretation and its narrative representative is no longer a tenable conception of the task of the historian.

—Alun Munslow, Deconstructing History

In *Deconstructing History*, Alun Munslow offers a critique of the empirical research method that provides a direct challenge to sport history and a glimpse into the wider turmoil in the historical profession. Disagreements, dissention, and controversy are certainly nothing new to the historical profession, but the last couple of decades have witnessed a growing critique of fundamental historical practices that have characterized the discipline. The creation of specific journals, such as *Rethinking History*, and an increasing range of books from the 1980s by prominent historians and philosophers indicate both an expanding interest in and, as Munslow mandates above, a growing skepticism of historical practices. As E. H. Carr was more than well aware, the perennial question "what is history?" refuses to go away.[1]

What is specifically pertinent for this book is that the interest in historical practices has not been reflected in the subdiscipline of sport history. An analysis of English-language historical journals including *Sport History Review*, the *Journal of Sport History*, *The International Journal of the History of Sport*, and *Sporting Traditions* illustrate minimal interest in critiquing the ways in which sport history has been created and produced.[2] As Table I.1

1

Table I.1.
"State of the Subdiscipline" Articles in Sport History Journals (1974–2000)

Journal	Number of Published "State of the Subdiscipline" Articles	Total Number of Published Articles	Percentage of "State of the Subdiscipline" Articles
Sport History Review (1970–)	9	321	2.8
Journal of Sport History (1974–)	12	297	4
International Journal of the History of Sport (1984–)	20	470	4.3
Sporting Traditions (1984–)	10	169	5.9

indicates, these attempts to evaluate, summarize, or critique the subdiscipline in the major journals have been miniscule in comparison to the total number of published articles. In addition to these articles, there are synopses in other discipline-based journals,[3] several chapters in books[4] and at least four books that have examined methodological issues or problems in sport history.[5] This survey, over three decades of the life of sport history, indicates that the cupboard is not bare in terms of internal analysis, but it seems reasonable to conclude that self-reflection has not been a defining characteristic of the subdiscipline.

The relatively small number of articles, chapters, and books written about the "state of the subdiscipline" are informative in a number of ways. They show that sport history has not been a stagnant or static subdiscipline. New topics, issues, and methodologies have arisen. Topics have ranged from Greek and Roman sports, to medieval tournaments, to Communist sporting activities, to college and professional sports, to Olympic history as well as historical analysis of specific sports and sportspeople. Some of these topics have been examined with specific focus on class, commercialism, ethnicity, gender, imperialism, nationalism, race, and regionalism, and a small number of sport historians have employed Eliasian, feminist, Marxist, modernization, Gramscian and Weberian theories in their work. In this regard sport history, as several authors have indicated, has taken "its philosophical, theoretical, and methodological cues from social history."[6]

As informative as the state of the subdiscipline synopses are, with the exception of a few instances, they do not raise questions about the fundamental practices of producing sport history. Precious few of these state of the subdiscipline articles critique the underlying assumptions on which sport history has been built or, as Munslow has contended, "the foundational way historians 'know' things about the past has been unchallenged."[7] Very rarely do sport scholars, for instance, modify the perennial question, "what is history?" to ask, "what is sport history?" or extend this question, following the insights of a range of historians and philosophers, to ask, "what are the methodological, epistemological and ontological premises of sport history?" Nor have scholars queried why sport historians are failing to engage with debates that have questioned practices in many historical disciplines or, for that matter, the issues that have unsettled, destabilized, and reconstituted much of the humanities. The limited acknowledgement of these issues in sport history has been the catalyst for this collection.

SPORT HISTORY'S MOMENTS

One of the few sport historians who has addressed the methodological, epistemological, and ontological foundations of sport history is Douglas Booth.[8] In his chapter in this collection, entitled "Sport Historians: What Do We Do? How Do We Do It?," Booth dissects sport history according to both models of historical inquiry and the popular explanatory paradigms. He identifies seven major explanatory paradigms that have included traditional narrative, advocacy, contextual, comparative, causal, social change, and linguistic. Providing rich examples from the sport history archives, he discusses specific objectives and epistemologies pertinent to the range of explanatory paradigms. As diverse as these objectives and epistemologies are, Booth concludes that sport historians "structure their work to place sport within a broader social, economic or political context, or to explain some issue of social change."

In terms of models of historical inquiry, Booth has utilized Munslow's framework and identifies three basic models of historical inquiry: reconstruction, construction, and deconstruction, which conceptualize history in accordance with different objectives, epistemologies, and modes of presentation. Booth's application and summary of Munslow's framework, particularly Table I.1, are detailed, precise, and informative. I will not replicate Booth's analysis but for the purposes of this introduction point to some key fault lines between the basic models of historical inquiry: reconstruction, construction, and deconstruction.

Reconstructionist history promotes a rational, objective, and purportedly impartial investigation of the past that focuses on resolving historical issues by examining unique events. This form of history is evidence based, and it is overtly nonphilosophical and atheoretical. Reconstructionist historians reject the use of social theory or any form of preconceived theories of explanation. It is on this point that reconstructionist and constructionist history diverge. Constructionist history attempts to understand historical events by placing them in preexisting frameworks, which involves a range of theories, ideologies, and social categories, in a way that still allows for human agency, intentionality, and choice. Constructionist histories have often been ideologically selfconscious advocating the political agendas of marginalized groups from women to blacks to immigrants to colonized peoples to the working classes. Deconstructionist histories are distinct from reconstructionist and constructionist histories on at least two issues. First, the emphasis on the divinity of the sources in reconstructionist and constructionist history is undermined because deconstructionists understand sources as "texts" that potentially provide a range of realities and possible alternatives. Second, deconstructionists argue that historians do not automatically discover a narrative story in the past; rather they have no choice but to impose a narrative on events that is intended to resemble the past. Textuality of the sources and the unavoidable, impositionalist role of the historian create a relativism of meaning and elevate the importance of form, a neglected issue in both reconstructionist and constructionist history, over content.[9]

This synopsis of the key fault lines between the different forms of history are considerably expanded by Booth in his chapter. Munslow's model of historical inquiry can also be used to create a temporal map of the contours of the subdiscipline of sport history. By adapting Norman Denzin and Yvonna Lincoln's concept of "moments," a heuristic term used to depict the emergence of new paradigms in research, it is possible to recognize reconstructionist, constructionist, and deconstructionist moments in sport history. The reconstructive history moment (1974 onwards) for sport history typified the early years of subdiscipline. Booth sees Gerry Redmond's history of women's golf in Canada as a typical example of reconstructionist history, and a glance at the early editions of all the major journals reveals the subdiscipline was replete with historians attempting to be nontheoretical, nonphilosophical, and representing the past "as it was."

The constructionist historical moment (1978 onward) was initiated by Allen Guttmann's *From Ritual to Record* (1978) which evaluated Marxist, Neo-Marxist, and Weberian theories in the context of American sport and explicitly utilized Weberian "ideal types" to differentiate modern from premodern sport.[10] Guttmann's work was followed by Richard Gruneau's *Class, Sports and Social Development* (1983), Melvin Adelman's *A Sporting Time* (1986) and John Hargreaves' *Sport, Power and Culture* (1986).[11] As Booth points out, these sources are exceptional as most sport historians have not been heavily involved in theory development, preferring instead to utilize organizing concepts such as "urbanism," "nationalism," "gender," "class," "race," "ethnicity," and "hegemony." Sport history, like history more generally, came under the methodological and theoretical influence of the social sciences.[12]

The deconstructive history moment (1998 onwards) is represented by Synthia Sydnor's "A History of Synchronized Swimming." Using the work of Walter Benjamin, Sydnor's history of synchronized swimming provides the readers with fragments, snapshots, and montages with little explanation, minimal analysis, and no closure. As she suggests to her readership: "You can swim in circles, above and below, without having to gulp a linear argument."[13] There is little doubt that Sydnor's original presentation at the North American Society for Sport History and the article subsequently published in a special edition of the *Journal of Sport History* received a less than welcoming reception. Her article, however, remains the best example in sport history of the "disobedient" postmodern attitude "which disregards convention, disobeys the authoritative voice and which replaces any definitive closure with an interminable openness, any exhaustive ending with an et cetera, and any full stop with an ellipsis."[14]

In many ways, the above classifications are artificial and selective creations as I grafted Denzin and Lincoln's concept of moments in qualitative research onto the subdiscipline of sport history. No doubt other historians would see sport history differently, perhaps objecting to the inclusion of Gruneau and Hargreaves on the grounds of discipline boundaries between sociology and history. Sydnor's piece could be rejected for failing to abide by established historical practices with her work pigeonholed in some other academic discipline, outside history, perhaps cultural studies. Other problematic issues with Denzin and Lincoln's concept are that new moments imply the replacement of earlier moments. However, it is important to recognize that the emergence of constructionist history does not indicate that reconstructionist history has ceased. New moments do not signal the demise of previous moments.[15] Taking all these problematic and relativistic aspects into account, moments help create a temporal map of the subdiscipline and enable me to make this crucial point: the deconstructive moment in sport history is relatively recent, and the contribution is extremely modest. There have been major works that have utilized some selective aspects of deconstructive history—through discourse analysis as in Patricia Vertinsky's *The Eternally Wounded Woman*, through multiple voices and perspectives as in Michael Oriard's *Reading Football* and *King Football*, through monument and memory as in Patricia Vertinsky and Sherry McKay's *Disciplining Bodies in the Gymnasium*, through representation, narrative and collective memory as in Daniel Nathan's *Saying It's So*—but I am hard pressed to find examples that sit alongside Sydnor's journal article.[16] This book explicitly seeks to add to the limited understanding of the deconstructionist approach in sport history, or what I will refer to as "postmodern sport history," and in the process provide examples from historians who challenge the assumptions that underpin reconstructionist and constructionist history.

SPORT HISTORY AND POSTMODERNISM

Postmodernism should be embraced critically and with great caution.[17] Acerbic criticisms of postmodernism are easy to find. Protagonists contend that postmodernism is constructed in a way that represents it as popular, chic, and even heroic; whereas modernism is portrayed as outdated, contaminated, and even tyrannical. As Mats Alvesson argues, modernism "is easily constructed in ways that make postmodernism the option for anyone but bad and boring people."[18] Similarly, postmodernists assail the grand narratives and totalizing discourses of modernism yet, in their places, provide a different intellectual imperative with other grand narratives. Postmodernism is also seen as negative, condemning, and antithetical to knowledge creation, offering instead a pluralism leading to anarchic nihilism. Finally, postmodernism's lofty ideals are both self-contradictory and self-defeating. How, for example, can scholars contribute to our understanding of the social world, if language does not reflect an extra linguistic reality?[19]

In sport history circles, I have certainly witnessed rejections of postmodernism at a number of conferences where the term has been used to deride challenges to "traditional" history, to mock theoretical approaches to the historical process, or to jibe at the apparent pandering to contemporary trends in other academic disciplines. Sport historians are not alone in these negative reactions to postmodernism. Beverley Southgate cites a raft of prominent historians from either side of the Atlantic including G. R. Elton, Richard Evans, Elizabeth Fox-Genovese, Gertrude Himmelfarb, and Elisabeth Lasch-Quinn who have all rallied against postmodernism. He contends they suffer from "pomophobia" which "is quite literally a dis-ease—an unease, or lack of ease with postmodernism, an anxiety about it, or . . . an actual *fear* of it."[20] Fox-Genovese, for example, contends that postmodernism actually "repudiates the idea of history as an intellectual practice or a collegial profession."[21] Some historians have gone as far as drawing parallels between postmodern analysis and the Nazis. Holocaust historian, Deborah Lipstadt, has contended that postmodern history "fosters deconstuctionist history at its worst. No fact, no event, and no aspect of history has any fixed meaning or content. Any truth can be retold. Any fact can be recast. There is no ultimate historical reality . . . Holocaust denial is part of this phenomenon."[22] Lipstadt raises an incredibly important point: does postmodernism lead down the path to anarchic nihilism? No it does not. I agree with Munslow who contends that postmodernism does not "open the flood gates to historians who lie and cheat. Such arguments are merely the last refuge of historians who can't respond openly to epistemological scepticism."[23] This issue will be addressed in more detail in the conclusion to this book.

All of this negative critique is heavy baggage for any term to wear, but I will persist with postmodernism and hope readers do not turn off at this point, because the term serves some useful purposes. I will use the general rubric of postmodernism because it encapsulates a wide range of beliefs that have challenged traditional history over the last three decades. What has variously been referred to as the "cultural turn,"[24] the "rhetorical attitude,"[25] the "linguistic turn,"[26] the "poetics of history,"[27] "relativist history" or "deconstructive history,"[28] and the "narrative-linguistic character of history,"[29] have all critiqued the "traditional" model of history as an examination of the past for "its own sake."[30] Even though these approaches critique traditional history from slightly different vantages, postmodernism encompasses many of them as Munslow argues:

> Postmodernism as an approach to understanding thus produces, among other things, tentative beliefs, playfulness, style and vogue, neo-pragmatism in philosophy, the linguistic turn, presentism, relativism, the reality-effect, deconstructionism and self-reflexivity in history and literature, doubts about referentiality, and the ultimate failure of narrative as an adequate model of representation.[31]

As this definition indicates, there are many strands of postmodernism, and it is probably more accurate to discuss postmodernisms in the plural rather than in the singular. Genevieve Rail has identified five postmodernisms: a style typically found in artistic representation, an artistic practice in performance arts, an epochal transition, a method centering on literary theory, and, finally, postmodernism as theoretical reflection.[32] Andrew Sparkes is astute when he suggests that one does not have to buy into every dimension of postmodern positions to extract something useful from them.[33]

The central virtues of postmodernism that are grasped with both hands in this book are in line with those expressed by Laurel Richardson:

> The core of postmodernism is the *doubt* that any method or theory, discourse or genre, tradition or novelty, has a universal and general claim as the "right" or the privileged form of authoritative knowledge. Postmodernism *suspects* all truth claims as masking and serving particular interests in local, cultural, and political struggles. But it does not automatically reject conventional methods of knowing and telling as false and archaic. Rather, it opens those standard

methods of inquiry and introduces new methods, which are also,
then subject to critique.[34]

Postmodernism is essentially a way of critiquing the methodological, epistemological and ontological status of sport history. I do not employ postmodernism in the same way as Jenkins who argues that postmodern insights can
not be grafted onto traditional history and that the difference between
modernity and postmodernity is insurmountable, incommensurate and permanent.[35] My application of postmodernism is in the optimistic, and perhaps
naïve according to Jenkins, spirit of encapsulating the varieties of aforemen-
tioned approaches—the cultural, rhetorical and linguistic turns, the poetics
of history, and relativistic, deconstructive and narrative-linguistic history—
employed by philosophers and practitioners of history.

The emphasis on *doubt*, as stressed by Richardson, is precisely the thrust
of Steven W. Pope's chapter entitled "Decentering 'Race' and (Re)present-
ing 'Black' Performance in Sport History." Pope, like several other scholars,
recognizes that sport historians have modeled themselves on social history
and, as a consequence, have endorsed, championed and practiced the
empiricist tradition. Sport historians have privileged archival research,
"data" and "facts" over the postmodern self-reflexive model of historical production. Pope challenges sport historians to consider adopting a postmodern
sensibility and provides his own comparative analysis of stylized performances of black basketball players and jazz musicians. Following Richardson's
interpretation of postmodernism, Pope raises epistemological questions. He
discards the notion of "race" on the basis that there is more difference within
"racial" groups than between them, in favor of a "more nuanced, interdisciplinary, cultural aesthetic" and concludes "that we can theorize such embodied practices without resorting to the essentializing concept of 'race.'" From
Foucault, Pope takes the idea of historicizing history in terms of analyzing
the production of history of basketball and jazz. From Bourdieu he utilizes
concepts of "capital" and "habitus" to understand the embodied practices
that exemplify these activities. He concludes: "the future of a more vibrant
scholarship mandates a more active (less insular, defensive) engagement
with postmodern methods and sensibilities." Pope's chapter exemplifies the
key postmodern dimensions that characterize this collection.

SPORT HISTORY AS TRADITIONAL HISTORY

Before the *doubts* that are raised by postmodernism are more fully addressed,
it is important to define what postmodern history most commonly critiques—traditional history. As much as both Michael Oriard and Robert E.

Rinehart in their chapters warn against establishing false dichotomies in analyzing sports historiography, I will use traditional history as an "ideal type" in a Weberian sense for two reasons. First, it is against this model that the postmodern position on history is revealed at its starkest. Second, presenting two ends of the spectrum—traditional versus postmodern—is a deliberate device employed here to push the key issues for debate to the forefront. In essence, creating a false dichotomy is intended as a heuristic aid to reflect upon popular, contemporary practices and new, challenging approaches to the production of sport history.

What constitutes traditional history, or what others have referred to as "modernist,"[36] "normal,"[37] "proper,"[38] or "reconstructive"[39] history, or studying the past "as it was,"[40] or examining the past "for its own sake"[41] or the "empirical-analytical approach,"[42] is as slippery as defining postmodernism. Traditional history displays many features of the nineteenth-century novel: stories with clearly articulated beginnings, middles and ends presented in a linear fashion—usually centering on cause and effect—and narrated in the third person.[43] As Keith Jenkins continues with a specific epistemological focus, traditional history has several defining features:

- it promotes realism, empiricism and documentarism all under the supervision of the objective, impartial historian
- it is anti-theoretical, anti-a priori and non-present centered
- it employs a commonsense, communication style of historical writing that attempts to avoid rhetoric.[44]

Admittedly Jenkins' synopsis does fall into the trap of painting traditional history in a dark and gloomy hue and postmodernism in bright, vivid colors. Nevertheless, its value to this introduction is that Jenkins identifies the prevalent characteristics of traditional historical assumptions.

Realism is the ontological position many sport historians assume as they purport not only to have access to the past, but what they describe is the knowable reality of the past rather than impressions constructed by historians.[45] As Robert Berkhofer summarizes, "realism enters historical practice to the extent that historians try to make their structure of factuality seem to be its own organizing structure and therefore conceal that it is structured by interpretation represented as (f)actuality."[46] Realism is often conflated with empiricism in historical practice. Detailed, meticulous and critical examination of the evidence, usually in the form of the document, is used inductively to provide access to the past. Fuelled by the correspondence theory of truth, the content of the past allows historians "to discover *the* most likely cause(s), *the* hidden story and, hence, *the* most likely meaning."[47] As Jenkins suggests, all this is achieved under the careful scrutiny of the unified, rational, and knowing historian who acts in a disinterested, even-handed, and unbiased way by prioritizing the sovereignty of the sources and letting "the facts speak for themselves."[48] Content defines form in historical work, not the other way around.

Catriona M. Parratt in her chapter "Wasn't It Ironic? The Haxey Hood and the Great War" directly challenges realism, empiricism, and objectivity in history by explicitly weaving her personal experiences into her work. She explains her family's ironies: the expected death of an uncle on or near Parratt's birthday and the annual mourning that frequently flowed into the deaths of other relatives, including her great uncle who was killed in the Great War and whose body, like those of many other young soldiers, was never recovered. These personal ironies of the Great War live through her analysis of the Haxey Hood, a version of folk football played annually in the Isle of Axholme.

By exploring her family's personal Great War experiences, Parratt works against the grain of established practices in history by writing herself into the story.[49] Under the influence of the heroic model of science, traditional historians have taken themselves out of their work by positioning themselves as dispassionate observers writing in passive voices or in the third person. Historians have produced what has been termed "author evacuated texts" where they are simultaneously nowhere, but everywhere. The analogy is made with Victorian school children: "to be seen (in the credits) but not heard (in the text)."[50] Historians writing themselves out of their work have been a deliberate attempt to provide the aura of objectivity, truthfulness, and realism.

By explicitly placing herself in her work, Parratt builds on the insights of Hayden White. White is a central figure in postmodern history and has had a similar impact on the theory and practice of the field, as did Clifford Geertz on anthropology.[51] White's position is that history is essentially a literary or poetic enterprise in which all historical texts are framed by deep-seated tropes, and more superficial modes of emplotment, modes of argument, and modes of ideology.[52] Parratt explores how her personal experiences determined her troping of the folk football of the Isle of Axholme: irony of her family's experience of the Great War prefigured her ironic troping of the Haxey Hood. She concludes her chapter with one final irony: "the Great War was exactly the right event at the right moment in history for keeping the Hood safe and ensuring its longer term survival."

Parratt's chapter also questions those who believe that history can be written from antitheoretical, anti–a priori, and antipresent centered positions. Letting the "facts speak for themselves" may be an admirable goal, but postmodern historians and sport sociologists alike recognize this as unattainable. Sport sociologists have chastised the antitheoretical basis of sport history and have recommended that historians move beyond their apprehensions and reservations to include theory in their work, especially if they wish to avoid antiquarianism.[53] Sport historians have retorted that theoretical approaches suffer from making the empirical evidence fit the theory and from applying arbitrary theories to the past.[54] Other detractors argue that historians do not have the option of either buying into or out of theory, that they are intermeshed in theoretical propositions. Even if historians do not borrow theories from disciplines such as anthropology, cultural studies, geography, economics, or sociology, they engage in theoretical work. All historians make assumptions about the historical process. What constitutes common knowledge? What questions are asked of the evidence, and how do these questions shape the story? Where do historians look, and what do they look for? Who are the key historical actors, and what are the seminal historical events? These are all questions that historians have to answer. As Mary Fulbrook argues: "These often hidden, implicit assumptions are as much bodies of theory as are the concepts and strategies of those operating within an explicitly theoretical '-ism.'"[55] In essence, historians—antitheoretical, atheoretical, and theoretical—all work with theoretical assumptions whether they acknowledge it or not.

Explicitly theory-laden history also grates against traditional history because it frequently works against the communication model of historical writing. Tony Mangan, one of the most prominent figures in sport history and long-time editor of *The International Journal of the History of Sport*, in his contribution to the "End of Sport History?" debate[56] highlights the importance of jargon-free writing. Citing the work of Peter Gay on the importance of "style," Mangan contends that the historian must "appreciate elegance and depreciate clumsiness, to decipher obscure passages, to expose verbal ambiguities" Mangan adds that "too much writing in the history of sport, as more than one journal editor can bear witness, is clumsy, simplistic, turgid and unclear. It earns brickbats rather than wins esteem. Clarity of exposure, elegance of presentation, subtlety of perspective are worthy ambitions for the new millennium."[57] As this influential sport historian mandates, clear and lucid writing has been a benchmark on which the quality of sport history has been assessed.

As admirable and worthy as the desire to write clearly and lucidly in the communication style is, it eschews the poststructuralist-inspired crisis in representation. Poststructuralism has drawn attention to the unproblematic way in which many sport historians have assumed that the written word represents reality. Very rarely have sport historians asked questions related to the representational status of the written word. For example, does language directly reflect the world? Or is language a self-contained set of signs with internal coherence only that does not reflect an external reality? Douglas Booth in his analysis of discourse, textualisation, and narrative in sport history contends that most practitioners have uncritically accepted language as a transparent medium, a few have pursued discourse analysis as a supplementary analytical tool, and even fewer have treated language as an epistemological issue.[58]

One of the few writers in sport studies, and a contributor to this collection, who has at least approached the epistemological issues of language and representation is John Bale. In *Writing Lives in Sport*, Bale and collaborators Mette Christensen and Gertrude Pfister examine (auto)biography with a critical eye focused on literary analysis dealing with, in specific chapters, layers of "truth," discourse, poetics, voice, textualization, and reality.[59] With a similar orientation on representation, Bale and Mike Cronin examine sport histories through the lens of postcolonialism. They point out that written and photographic representations are neither copies of the original text nor transparent replicas of reality nor accurate and unambiguous. Instead representations are nothing more than metaphors of what they purport to portray. From the postcolonial perspective, issues of representation encourage the evaluation of the complexity of sport, sporting experience as resistance, interrogation of those engaged in colonial representations of sport and body cultures, and the discovery and recovery of hidden sporting spaces.[60] Like many postmodern historians, postcolonial studies see the ambiguity of language as both challenging and liberating, opening up new ways of examining the past in all its complexity.

Brett Hutchins in his chapter "Sport History between the Modern and Postmodern" adds some additional components to Jenkins' dimensions of traditional history. In a very informative, comparative table contrasting "ideal types" of traditional with postmodern history (see table 2.1), he contends that Enlightenment project ideals have driven traditional history into representing the past as a linear master narrative built around progress, reason, and rationality. Furthermore traditional historians, in contrast to structuralist and poststructuralist views of language, see language as directly reflecting the world or an extralinguistic reality. Language in traditional history is an effective vehicle to create the past. Finally, the concept of "power" is mostly neglected in the production of traditional history. Power is downplayed in the way professional historians work in institutional settings under regimes imposed by governments, universities, publishers, and funding agencies. The world according to "white men, privilege and cultural domination" is promoted as *the* perspective of history at the expense of the "experiences of subordinated, ethnic and gendered groups." Power is also deemphasized through the concept of the unified, rational and knowing subject, a central figure in Enlightenment humanism, that enables historians to not only control the past but ensures knowability of that past.[61]

The issue of power is the central theme in Patricia Vertinsky's chapter entitled "Time Gentlemen Please: The Space and Place of Gender in Sport History." Vertinsky is skeptical of postmodernism and its application to history on a number of grounds. From her perspective, postmodernism has not comprehensively theorized agency, has not developed strategies commensurate with feminist ideals, runs the risk of excluding the lives of real women, and, most alarmingly, remains within a patriarchal framework: "in the current debate about modernism and postmodernism, feminists cannot help but point out how both modernism and postmodernism remain so frequently, so unimaginatively, patriarchal." This is a point well made. Even taking these well grounded concerns into account, Vertinsky values the postmodernist contribution to historical analysis. Postmodernist thought has resulted in a more reflexive sport history that embraces previously banished topics such as women, gender, and the body. Sport history has moved from writing women into the sporting record, to gender studies, to depictions of the body in action. In particular, the conflation of postmodernism and feminism has stimulated interest in the construction of the gendered subject, investigation of plural viewpoints of women and multiple gendered identities, and analysis of the representations of the sporting body. The consequences, according to Vertinsky, are marked: ". . . the inclusion within sport history of a focus on gender—which in turn forces a focus on the body and bodily practices—has pressed an increasing number of sport historians to pay attention to a much wider and deeper version of the history of sport and physical education." While Vertinsky is wary of some dimensions of postmodernism, she sees more positives than negatives. What Vertinsky values in the postmodernist contribution to history is the ". . . potential of incorporating multiple voices and perspectives into the study of sport history and encouraging challenges to the long standing notion of science and society as a patriarchal hierarchy with a claim to truth."

Hutchins, like Vertinsky, values postmodern history because it exposes epistemological and ontological issues with the result encouraging and forcing "critical reflection on the processes and methods involved in writing about the past." His main contention is that a growing band of historians situate themselves between traditional and postmodern history. Donald Bradman, the famous Australian and international cricketer, is the case study that Hutchins uses to negotiate postmodern issues of meaning and representation. Employing cultural sociology, particularly the concepts of "collective memory," "articulation," and "dialogic reading," Hutchins promotes a practical approach to the modern-postmodern conundrum. The major ideological sites of power in the representation of Bradman are examined to highlight that while meanings are not permanently fixed or uncontested, dominant or preferred meanings are still evident. In the case of the iconic cricketer, dominant and competing constructions of Bradman included "the relentless run-machine, the boy from the bush, the brave fighter facing up to bodyline bowling, the businessman and administrator, the nation-builder, the devoted husband, the apolitical sportsman, the solitary man, the trademark, the unseen hero living in retirement, and the deceased Australian hero."

THE EPISTEMOLOGICAL FRAGILITY OF SPORT HISTORY

So what are the *doubts* that are raised by postmodernism about traditional history? These *doubts* are both epistemological and ontological. Postmodernism raises specific epistemological doubts about the nature, theory, and foundations of how traditional history creates knowledge and ontological doubts by questioning the assumptions of the traditional historians who contend that the past is a knowable reality. Jenkins states the epistemological and ontological link exposed by the postmodern position: "Epistemology shows we can never really know the past; that the gap between the past and history (historiography) is an ontological one, that is, in the very nature of things such that no amount of epistemological effort can bridge it."[62]

Jenkins' point is that the past/history distinction is a key issue in the postmodern position. Postmodernism clearly recognizes that the past/history distinction cannot be diminished. The past is what actually occurred in some previous era; history is the stories we tell about the past. The two are related but are not the same for a number of well-acknowledged reasons. History cannot cover all of the past because of its sheer enormity and, therefore, can only represent a selection of the past. The past is not an account as is history, but it is simply events, situations, and reactions, and these qualities of the past make it very difficult to evaluate histories. We cannot, as Eaglestone illustrates, check a history like we can a map of a city by walking out the areas it covers.[63] Sure sources can be checked, or other historical accounts can be compared, but because the past is gone, "there is no fundamentally correct 'text' of which other interpretations are just variations; variations are all there are."[64] Another fundamental difference between the past and history is that the events of the past happened forward, yet history happens in reverse by analyzing, explaining, and representing the past backward. History is created retrospectively. Related to this retrospective reading, historians know far more about the past than those who lived in it. They not only know the ending of specific events of the past; they have access to new documents, ideas, and concepts. Because of these insurmountable differences between the past and history, as well as a number of other issues as postmodern historians argue, the epistemology of history is extremely fragile.[65] Even the magic of empiricism can not transform the past "as it was" onto the page.[66]

Both Jeffrey Hill and John Bale in their chapters in this book highlight the fragility of the epistemology of history by critically examining different types of evidence: newspapers and photographs. Hill in "Anecdotal Evidence: Sport, the Newspaper Press, and History" reiterates the crucial role of the newspaper in sport history: "Press reports have become a staple—perhaps *the* staple—source in the task of reconstructing the history of sport and games." His critique, however, questions the "correspondence theory of truth" in which newspapers, as well as other sources, such as press reports, personal letters, and government minutes, are seen as providing untrammeled access to the past. Hill advocates replacing the term source with that of text, as the latter implies that the traces of the past can be "read" in a number of ways as opposed to uniformly consumed, understood, and controlled. By taking into account the poststructuralist critique of language, Hill maintains that sources are not simple reflections of the past. His case study is the 1914 Cup Final played at Crystal Palace, London, when a visitor from the North, after seeing the famous glass edifice at the venue, claimed "By gum, aw wouldn't like to go and mend a brokken pane up theer." Hill argues that this statement can be read at many different levels and concludes sources are not passive texts as they work on the historian as much as the historian works on them. This sporting example makes the larger point "that any meaning the historian ascribes to 'the past' can only be achieved through the imaginative and representational process characteristic of narrative discourse."[67]

As much as written sources can be read in a number of ways, John Bale's chapter, "Partial Knowledge: Photographic Mystifications and Constructions of 'the African Athlete,'" makes a very similar conclusion in respect to another historical text, the photograph. Bale's focus is on one particular photograph taken in the small central African nation of Rwanda in 1907 of the body-cultural activity of *gusimbuka-urukiramende* by the anthropology party led by the Duke of Mecklenburg. The major theme of this chapter is the ambiguity of the photograph in terms of what it both denotes and connotes. Bale contextualizes the photograph, deconstructs its spatial aspects, and interprets the incorporation of the photograph in a range of historical discourses. The photograph is examined as a European production, and its spatial dimensions on a macro level—as a sport photograph in travel writing and in track and field magazines—and on a micro level, in terms of the composition of the photograph. Another focal point of this chapter is the construction of meanings of the photograph influenced or dictated by the captions and the juxtaposition with other photographs and texts. Bale concludes that the photograph of the body-cultural activity of *gusimbuka-urukiramende* portrayed the "Tutsi" male as a European high jumper, and this image contributed to the construction of the athletically superior "black athlete" as well as stereotyping the Tutsi in Rwandan history. These conclusions, however, should be seen in the context of Bale's explicit message that stresses "the instability of visual images and considerable slippage in the ways in which a photograph may be used and read during its existence."

Hill and Bale's contributions are very important because they expose the epistemological attachment to evidence in traditional history. Three central aspects of traditional history—realism, empiricism, and documentarism—are all reliant on evidence, and it is evidence that is used to show the inadequacies of theoretical history, to highlight historians do not work with a-priori or present-centered practices and to evaluate historical narratives. With these notions in mind, evidence is gathered, sifted, and analyzed by the unified, rational and knowing historian, and the reliability of the evidence is assessed by attempting to understand the perspective of the author of the source and is used inductively to provide the best possible explanations for events or the purposeful actions of people in specific circumstances. Evidence provides the bond between history and the past. Munslow sums up the epistemological significance of evidence to traditional history: "Without evidence, therefore, history would be just fiction." He challenges historians to consider: "Can we write proper history, or non-fictional history if we reconsider the nature of this bond?"[68] Both Hill and Bale's analysis of newspapers and photographs highlight the problematic dimensions of the bond between the past and history.

Michael Oriard also challenges this bond in his chapter, "A Linguistic Turn into Sport History," by examining the past, in his case American football, as a cultural text that, he argues, provides multiple and often conflicting meanings. Unlike many sport historians, Oriard is prepared to concede that his work involves a considerable amount of a priori deductive reasoning rejecting specific theoretical approaches—including the myth-and-symbol school as well as those who contend sport is a microcosm of society—in favor of a textual analysis of sport history. Summarizing his approach to his recent major works, *Reading Football* and *King Football*, Oriard does not accept the poststructuralist argument that words are so removed from an extralinguistic reality that any meanings are possible. The textual analysis he practices, similar to Hutchins' approach, contends that producers and consumers within material, social, political, and economic contexts create meanings. A real recoverable past exists, according to Oriard, even though "sport history at its best can only be an art of approximation." Where his approach differs again to many sport historians is that he prefers dialogic over monologic readings of evidence. Oriard eschews allegorical or totalizing readings of American football, such as interpreting the specific, brutal practice of the "flying wedge" as an allegory for American imperialism, preferring multiple readings reflecting class, gender, race, ethnicity, religion, and community interests among other issues.[69] Football, as presented through the lenses of the mass media, is understood as a cultural text capable of different interpretations by its audiences. In this way, Oriard's work clearly emphasizes meaning rather than causation epitomizing, as David Cannadine has recently recognized, the major recent shift in historiography.[70] As Oriard summarises: "the textual approach to football attends to the full range of often conflicting narratives that are attached to the game."

ALTERNATIVE PARADIGMS FOR SPORT HISTORY

The solution put forward by Synthia Sydnor in her chapter entitled "Contact with God, Body, Soul" is the postmodern theological approach "radical orthodoxy." The philosophically grounded, radical orthodoxy has been clearly articulated since the 1990s and is understood to have emerged out of the postmodern world, extending postmodern themes and fulfilling the postmodern project. It provides, according to Sydnor, a theological sensibility and stresses the centrality of the sacred to all knowledge, including sport history: "I think that sport history, any discipline—all earthly activities and practices for that matter—can only aim toward honoring God, of journeying toward God and the sacred." Sydnor recognizes that sport historians have critiqued the nihilism in contemporary sport practices but contends that the subdiscipline has been obsessed with empty transcendental yearnings and urban mythologies such as the cult of superstar athletes, Eastern and Western bodily practices, and immortality through extreme sports and back-to-nature sports. Sport historians have rarely pushed their analyses to "the level of theological reflection, which have redemptive qualities and build analogical worldviews." Drawing on postmodern and postcolonial theory, central concepts including "nothingness," "voidness," "liminality," the "other," the "hypen," and "alterity" are used to envision sport history as a cultural site with transformative sacramental qualities. For Sydnor, sport history is an avenue that "humans voice, become conscious of, and journey to union with the infinitely perfect God."

What is striking about Sydnor's contribution is that she explicitly states her worldview: a postmodern theological trajectory for the subdiscipline of sport history. Many sport historians, I assume, will object to her position that radical orthodoxy provides the future pathway for sport history. Nevertheless, one of the many important issues that Sydnor brings to the forefront is the importance of worldviews or ideology, as Hayden White has articulated, to the production of history. If Sydnor's promotion of radical orthodoxy worries sport historians, the pressing question that follows is: can history be written free from the philosophical worldview or ideology of the historian? Can, for example, those who use empiricism as their guiding methodology/epistemology guarantee an ideologically pure historical process? Certainly Fulbrook makes a strong case that those historians using empiricism as their guiding methodology/epistemology are staking out some ideological turf.[71] Similarly, postmodern historians answer this question in the negative: "History is always *history from* a certain worldview."[72] As Eaglestone explains: "A Marxist historian is a Marxist because he or she believes that Marxism is the best way to bring about social justice; liberal historians believe that tolerance is the greatest virtue; a conservative believes that traditions can teach us how to live best."[73] If all history is written from either an implicit worldview, which has characterized a great deal of sport historiography, or from an explicitly stated worldview, as in Sydnor's contribution, is there such a thing as an objective worldview? Again postmodernists answer in the negative: "If there were, everybody would share it, and philosophers would stop arguing."[74]

If an objective worldview and an ideologically free historian are illusions, if narrative is not simply a transparent form of communication, if words do not necessarily reflect an extra linguistic world, and if the past/history divide highlights the epistemological fragility of history, then many of the taken-for-granted assumptions underpinning traditional history seem precarious. Cumulatively these issues seriously challenge traditional history. Nevertheless, as Rosenstone summarizes, "no writers have clung more firmly (desperately, even) to traditional forms than those academic historians whose professed aim is to accurately reconstruct the past."[75]

Robert E. Rinehart addresses some of these challenges in his chapter entitled "Beyond Traditional Sports Historiography: Toward a Historical 'Holograph.'" He is very critical of the subdiscipline of sport history that suffers from historical nostalgia, dwelling in fond remembrance rather than critical analysis, and most disturbingly for Rinehart, suffers from a static, unchanging, and uncontested approach in the tradition of the historical grand narrative. The alternative according to Rinehart is to represent history as a "holograph" in which its production is understood as self conscious, reflexive, relativist, malleable, and contested. Accordingly, a "historical holograph" is a "more amorphous, fluid descriptor that comes closer to what my worldview sees as the reality of sport history research." Like Sydnor, Rinehart realizes the centrality of the historian's worldview to what they produce.

The holograph highlights the personal, subjective nature of historical production initially from the research questions asked, to the types of answers pursued and the modes of reporting the final product. The questions asked not only drive the research process but the final form of the writing, and the issues selected for investigation are shaped by the richness of sources, the presumed audience, and the predilections of the historian. This is a far cry from history as grand narrative. Borrowing from sociology, anthropology, and cultural studies, Rinehart challenges us to encourage new experimental ways to find a voice for historical actors and their experiences in the form of poetic representations, ethnodrama, and fictional representations. These are certainly approaches rarely used in sport history, and his rationale is that "experimentation with different genres does ensure a re-look at fundamental questions of research, at point of view, at representational practices (both failures and successes), at verisimilitude and authenticity, and at a variety of research problems that many traditional researchers learn in graduate school and then rarely interrogate again." Rinehart seeks historians to realize the conscious choices made in their work from the initial research questions to the finished work, and to develop some semantic control over the process and production of history. The analogy of the holograph fits neatly with a central tenet of postmodern history: "neither the past nor its traces can present themselves as history, historians do it for them; if 'the before now' is to enter—transformed—into our consciousness as a history then . . . it has to do so by way of a textual substitution, a simulacrum."[76]

ORGANIZATION OF THE BOOK

In soliciting contributions for this collection, I gave the authors a very broad brief to write something that examines and/or challenges the production of knowledge in sport history. As indicated in my synopsis, the responses to this brief vary considerably from narrow and penetrating analyses that address specific issues to wider critical analyses of the methodological, epistemological, and ontological basis of sport history. The contributions also vary on their applications of the tenets of postmodern history, and it would be inappropriate to categorize all contributors as postmodern writers. What I have *chosen* to amplify in this introduction are the dimensions of the contributors' work that illustrate postmodernist approaches to history. My rationale is that because sport historians, as indicated by the major journals and books, have rarely articulated postmodernism, because its key tenets have only been selectively debated, because the postmodern "moment" is relatively recent in sport history, some extended analysis of postmodernism is needed even if it only serves as a stance for historians to rationalize their own future work.

Organization of the authors' contributions in this book was difficult. Topics, writing styles, emphases, and interests all differ among the contributors, but I positioned the contributions under the following headings: "On Theory," "On Practice," and "On the Future." Booth's, Hutchins', and Oriard's chapters are positioned in the section "On Theory"; Bale's, Hill's, Parratt's, and Pope's chapters are collated under the section "On Practice"; Rinehart, Sydnor, and Vertinsky are in the final section "On the Future." This is obviously a very subjective division. As has been argued previously, all history is underpinned by theoretical paradigms, all contributors discuss practice either implicitly or explicitly, and each chapter has implications for the future of sport history. My division is based on my reading of their work: Booth, Hutchins, and Oriard deal with more theory than practice; Bale, Hill, Parratt, and Pope more practice than theory; and Rinehart, Sydnor, and Vertinsky explicitly address future directions for the subdiscipline of sport history.

NOTES

My thanks to John Bale, Brett Hutchins, Gary Osmond, and Richard Tinning for their constructive comments.

1. Edward H. Carr, *What is History?* (Harmondsworth: Penguin, 1980 [1961]).

2. Since the inception of the *Canadian Journal of Sport History* in 1970 (renamed *Sport History Review*) there have been nine articles published that have examined the state of the subdiscipline. Since its incarnation in 1974, the *Journal of Sport History* has published two special editions (1983 and 1998) as well as five articles, a total of twelve articles. (Not included in this total are special editions on specific issues like sport and race, gender, or class). Tackling similar issues, the *British Journal of Sports History* (renamed *The International Journal of the History of Sport*) has published twenty articles, and *Sporting Traditions* produced one special edition in 1999 that contains ten articles focusing on general issues in sport history.

3. Roberta J. Park, "Research and Scholarship in the History of Physical Education and Sport: The Current State of Affairs," *Research Quarterly for Exercise and Sport* 54, no. 2 (1983): 93–103; Nancy L. Struna, "In 'Glorious Disarray': The Literature of American Sport History," *Research Quarterly For Exercise and Sport* 56, no. 2 (1985): 151–60; Douglas Booth and Annemarie Jutel, "The Death of Sports History?" *Sporting Traditions* 16, no. 1 (1999); Douglas Booth, "Sport History: What Can Be Done?" *Sport, Education and Society* 2, no. 2 (1998): 189–204.

4. Nancy L. Struna, "Sport History," in *The History of Exercise and Sport Science*, eds. J. D. Massengale and R. A. Swanson (Champaign, IL: Human Kinetics, 1996), 143–80; Nancy L. Struna, "Social History and Sport," in *Handbook of Sport Studies*, ed. J. Coakley and E. Dunning (London: Sage, 2000), 187–203.

5. Lindsay Day and Peter Lindsay, *Sport History Research Methodology* (Edmonton: University of Alberta, 1980); Steven W. Pope, *The New American Sport History: Recent Approaches and Perspectives* (Urbana: University of Illinois Press, 1997); Steven A. Riess, *Major Problems in American Sport History: Documents and Essays* (Boston: Houghton Mifflin, 1997).

6. Catriona M. Parratt, "About Turns: Reflecting on Sport History in the 1990s," *Sport History Review* 29, no. 1 (1998): 4.

7. See ihr.sas.ac.uk/ihr/Focus/Whatishistory/.

8. See Douglas Booth, "Escaping the Past? The Cultural Turn and Language in Sport History," *Rethinking History* 8, no. 1 (2004): 103–25 and Douglas Booth, *The Sports Historian: Models, Paradigms and Themes* (London: Routledge, forthcoming).

9. Munslow, *Deconstructing History*, 18–26. For a recent detailed analysis and specific examples of reconstructive, constructive and deconstructive genres see Keith Jenkins and Alun Munslow, eds., *The Nature of History Reader* (London: Routledge, 2004).

10. Allen Guttmann, *From Ritual to Record: The Nature of Modern Sports* (New York: Columbia University Press, 1978).

11. Richard S. Gruneau, *Class, Sports, and Social Development* (Amherst: University of Massachusetts Press, 1983); Melvin L. Adelman, *A Sporting Time: New York City and the Rise of Modern Athletics, 1820–70* (Urbana: University of Illinois Press, 1986); John Hargreaves, *Sport, Power and Culture—A Social and Historical Analysis of Popular Sports in Britain* (Cambridge: Polity, 1986).

12. For a detailed discussion of the relationship between history and social theory see Alun Munslow, *The New History* (Harlow, England: Pearson, 2003), 101–17.

13. Synthia Sydnor, "A History of Synchronized Swimming," *Journal of Sport History* 25, no. 2 (1998): 254.

14. Keith Jenkins, *Refiguring History: New Thoughts on an Old Discipline* (London: Routledge, 2003), 6.

15. Andrew C. Sparkes, *Telling Tales in Sport and Physical Activity: A Qualitative Journey* (Champaign, IL: Human Kinetics, 2002), 3–9.

16. Patricia A. Vertinsky, *The Eternally Wounded Woman: Women, Doctors, and Exercise in the Late Nineteenth Century* (Manchester: Manchester University Press, 1990); Michael Oriard, *Reading Football: How the Popular Press Created an American Spectacle* (Chapel Hill: University of North

Carolina Press, 1993); Michael Oriard, *King Football: Sport and Spectacle in the Golden Age of Radio and Newsreels, Movies and Magazines, the Weekly and the Daily Press* (Chapel Hill: University of North Carolina Press, 2001); Patricia Vertinsky and Sherry McKay, eds., *Disciplining Bodies in the Gymnasium: Memory, Monument, Modernism* (London: Routledge, 2004); Daniel A. Nathan, *Saying It's So: A Cultural History of the Black Sox Scandal* (Urbana: University of Illinois Press, 2003).

17. For critical applications of postmodernism to sport, physical education, and human movement see JuanMiguel Fernandez-Balboa, *Critical Postmodernism in Human Movement, Physical Education, and Sport* (Albany: State University of New York Press, 1997) and Genevieve Rail, *Sport and Postmodern Times* (Albany: State University of New York Press, 1998).

18. Mats Alvesson, *Postmodernism and Social Research* (Buckingham: Open University Press, 2002), 38.

19. Alvesson, *Postmodernism and Social Research*, 37–43.

20. Beverly Southgate, *History, What and Why? Ancient, Modern, and Postmodern Perspectives* (London: Routledge, 1996), 148–49.

21. Elizabeth Fox-Genovese, "History in a Postmodern World," in *Reconstructing History: The Emergence of a New Historical Society*, eds. E. Fox-Genovese and E. Lasch-Quinn (New York: Routledge, 1999), 54.

22. Robert Eaglestone, *Postmodernism and Holocaust Denial* (Cambridge: Icon, 2001), 7.

23. Munslow, *The New History*, 195.

24. Victoria E. Bonnell and Lynn A. Hunt, eds., *Beyond the Cultural Turn: New Directions in the Study of Society and Culture* (Berkeley: University of California Press, 1999).

25. Brian Fay, Philip Pomper and Richard T. Vann, eds., *History and Theory: Contemporary Readings* (Malden, Mass.: Blackwell, 1998).

26. Richard Rorty, ed., *The Linguistic Turn: Recent Essays in Philosophical Method* (Chicago: University of Chicago Press, 1992 [1967]).

27. Robert F. Berkhofer, *Beyond the Great story: History as Text and Discourse* (Cambridge: Belknap Press of Harvard University Press, 1995).

28. Munslow, *Deconstructing History*; Alun Munslow, *The Routledge Companion to Historical Studies* (London: Routledge, 2000).

29. Munslow, *The New History*.

30. Keith Jenkins, *The Postmodern History Reader* (London: Routledge, 1997).

31. Munslow, *Deconstructing History*, 187.

32. Genevieve Rail, "Postmodernism and Sport Studies," in *Theory, Sport, and Society*, eds. J. Maguire and K. Young (Oxford: JAI, 2002), 179–207.

33. Sparkes, *Telling Tales in Sport and Physical Activity*, 11.

34. Laurel Richardson, "Writing," in *Handbook of Qualitative Research*, eds. N. Denzin and Y. Lincoln (London: Sage, 2000), 928.

35. Jenkins, *Refiguring History*, 60–70.

36. Gertrude Himmelfarb, "Postmodernist History," in *Reconstructing History: The Emergence of a New Historical Society*, eds. E. Fox-Genovese and E. Lasch-Quinn (New York: Routledge, 1999), 71–93.

37. Berkhofer, *Beyond the Great Story*, 28–31.

38. Jenkins, *The Postmodern History Reader*, 16–21.

39. Munslow, *Deconstructing History*, 20–22, 36–56, 99–119.

40. Beverley Southgate, *History: What and Why? Ancient, Modern, and Postmodern Perspectives* (London: Routledge, 2001), 12–29.

41. Jenkins, *The Postmodern History Reader*, 2.

42. Munslow, *The New History*, 180–95.

43. Robert A. Rosenstone, "Introduction: Practice and Theory," in *Experiments in Rethinking History*, eds. A. Munslow and R.A. Rosenstone (New York: Routledge, 2004), 1.

44. Jenkins, *The Postmodern History Reader*, 16.

45. Alun Munslow, "Introduction: Theory and Practice," in *Experiments in Rethinking History*, 8.

46. Robert Berkhofer, "The Challenge of Poetics to (Normal) Historical Practice," *Poetics* Today 9, no. 2 (1988): 449, cited in Jenkins, *The Postmodern History Reader*, 20.

47. Munslow, "Introduction," in *Experiments in Rethinking History*, 9 (emphasis in original). For a detailed discussion of reality and correspondence see Munslow, *The New History*, 45–60.

48. Jenkins, *The Postmodern History Reader*, 20.

49. See, for example, "Round Table: Self and Subject," *Journal of American History* 89, no. 1 (2002) (my thanks to Steve Pope for directing me to this debate).

50. Sparkes, *Telling Tales in Sport and Physical Activity*, 89.

51. Bonnell and Hunt, *Beyond the Cultural Turn*, 2.

52. For an application of White's ideas in sport history see Murray G. Phillips, "A Critical Appraisal of Narrative in Sport History: The Surf Lifesaving Debate" *Journal of Sport History* 29, no. 1 (2002): 25–40.

53. John Horne, Alan Tomlinson, and Gary Whannel, *Understanding Sport: An Introduction to the Sociological and Cultural Analysis of Sport* (London: E & FN Spon, 1999), 77; Eric Dunning, Joseph A. Maguire and Robert E. Pearton, eds., *The Sports Process: A Comparative and Developmental Approach* (Champaign, IL: Human Kinetics, 1993), 4.

54. Richard Holt, *Sport and the British: A Modern History* (Oxford: Clarendon, 1989), 357–58; Dunning, Maguire, and Pearton, *The Sports Process*, 4.

55. Mary Fulbrook, *Historical Theory* (London: Routledge 2002), 4.

56 Booth and Jutel, *Sporting Traditions*.

57. J. A. Mangan, "The End of History Perhaps? But the End of the Beginning for the History of Sport! An Anglo-Saxon Autobiographical Perspective," *Sporting Traditions* 16, no. 1 (1999): 63, 64–65.

58. Booth, "Escaping the Past?"

59. John Bale, Mette K. Christensen, and Gertrude Pfister, eds., *Writing Lives in Sport: Biographies, Life-histories and Methods* (Langelandsgade: Aarhus, 2004).

60. John Bale and Mike Cronin, "Introduction: Sport and Postcolonialism" in *Sport and Postcolonialism*, eds. J. Bale and M. Cronin (New York: Berg, 2003), 1–13.

61. Munslow, "Introduction," in *Experiments in Rethinking History*, 9.

62. Keith Jenkins, *Re-thinking History* (London: Routledge, 1991), 19.

63. Eaglestone, *Postmodernism and Holocaust Denial*, 25.

64. Jenkins, *Re-thinking History*, 11.

65. For good summaries of the past/history distinction see Eaglestone, *Postmodernism and Holocaust Denial*, 24–26; Jenkins, *Re-thinking History*, 5–20. For a more detailed analysis see D. Lowenthal, *The Past Is a Foreign Country* (Cambridge: Cambridge University Press, 1985).

66. Munslow, "Introduction," in *Experiments in Rethinking History*, 7.

67. Munslow, *The New History*, 23.

68. Alun Munslow, *The Routledge Companion to Historical Studies* (London: Routledge, 2000), 92–95.

69. Oriard, *Reading Football*, 1–20.

70. David Cannadine, *What Is History Now?* (New York: Palgrave, 2002).

71. Fulbrook, *Historical Theory*, 3–11.

72. Eaglestone, *Postmodernism and Holocaust Denial*, 34.

73. Eaglestone, *Postmodernism and Holocaust Denial*, 34.

74. Eaglestone, *Postmodernism and Holocaust Denial*, 35.

75. Rosenstone, "Introduction," in *Experiments in Rethinking History*, 1.

76. Jenkins, *Refiguring History*, 54.

PART ONE

On Theory

CHAPTER 1

Sport Historians

What Do We Do? How Do We Do It?

DOUGLAS BOOTH

Sport historians have no difficulty recognizing the content of their field. Any study of bygone events, individuals, groups, practices, and institutions with a sporting flavor constitutes sport history. But ask historians of sport to formally define the objectives, assumptions, methods, and modes of presentation of their discipline, and they talk in vague terms about facts, narratives, context, and theory. More likely, they will twist the question and describe the sources of their own esoteric research, whether it be the biography of a deceased sport star, the leisure tastes of working-class coalminers in mid-Victorian Northumberland, women's intercollegiate basketball in the Midwest at the turn of the twentieth century, social changes experienced by Jewish-American sportswomen, or the culture of teenage Australian surfers in the 1960s. Against this background of prevarication, it comes as no surprise that scholars working in other disciplines consider such histories deficient.[1]

This chapter dissects the philosophy of sport history. It explains what sport historians do and how they do it, in a survey of historical knowledge and the application of that knowledge to the field. The first part investigates the general nature of historical knowledge using a framework developed by Munslow.[2] He discerns three basic models of historical inquiry: reconstruction, construction, and deconstruction. Reconstructionism and constructionism dominate sport history. Reconstructionists and constructionists privilege empirical methods, accept historical evidence as proof that they can recover the past, and insist that their forms of representation are transparent enough to ensure the objectivity of their observations. The key difference between reconstructionists and constructionists is the extent to which they engage a priori knowledge. The latter willingly embrace the concepts and theories of others as tools to propose and explain relationships between events; reconstructionists oppose theory on the grounds that it subjects historians to "predetermined explanatory schemes" and reduces them to "tailoring evidence."[3] Skeptical of objective empirical history, deconstructionists view history "as a constituted narrative" devoid of "moral or intellectual certainty."[4] Slow to penetrate sport history, deconstructionism nonetheless poses some major challenges for reconstructionism, which places inordinate confidence in the cognitive power of narratives that are held to emanate naturally from historical facts.

The second part examines more explicit applications of historical knowledge in sport history under the heading "explanatory paradigms." An "interactive structure of workable questions and the factual statements which are adduced to answer them,"[5] an explanatory paradigm carries quite specific philosophical assumptions and constitutes the framework used by historians to orientate their arguments. Sport history comprises seven basic explanatory paradigms: traditional narrative, advocacy, contextual, comparative, causal, social change, and linguistic.

MODELS

Historians disagree about much: the objectives of history, the meaning of facts, the construction of facts, methods of procedure, the role of theory, the basis of theory, the form of presentation. But they also agree that history is an evidence-based discipline and that evidence imposes limits on interpretation. The philosophical and epistemological agreements and disagreements within sport history are examined below using Munslow's three models of historical inquiry. Sport history supports reconstructionists, constructionists, and a lesser number of deconstructionists; each group conceptualizes history around a different set of objectives, epistemology, and mode of presentation (see table 1.1).

Reconstruction

Operating under the assumption that they can discover the past as it actually happened (table 1.1, box 1), reconstructionists promote history as a realist epistemology in which knowledge derives from empirical evidence and forensic research into primary sources (table 1.1, boxes 5 and 7). Forensic research means interrogating, corroborating, and contextualizing sources to verify them as real and true. Reconstructionists maintain that history exists

Table 1.1.[6]

Models of History

	Reconstruction	Construction	Deconstruction
Objective	Discovers *the* past as it actually was (1)	Interprets how, why, and trends (2)	Discovers *a* past (3)
Epistemology	• Evidence-based • Evidence imposes limits on interpretations • Acknowledge that distance ensures detachment (4)		
	• Privilege empiricism • Accept historical evidence as proof that the past can be recovered • View the past as fixed • See the past as yielding knowledge about the development of the present • Regard the present as an unproblematic platform from which historians look back into the past • Assume that traditional forms of representation are transparent and preserve the objectivity of observations (5)		• Begins analysis with linguistic / discursive characterization of the historical account • Holds the past as a slave to the present (6)
	• Craft-like discipline • Facts precede interpretation • Limits on interpretation imposed by institutional and professional conventions • Iterative activity (7)	• Theoretical discipline • a priori knowledge precedes facts • Limits on interpretation imposed by concepts and theory (8)	• Craft-like discipline • Historical knowledge always relative • Limits on interpretation imposed by epistemology (9)
Presentation	• Opposes technical language • Narrative is the unquestioned form of history • Narrative produces close approximations to the truth • De-emphasizes the text in favour of the world it purports to represent (10)	• Employs technical language • Narratives are not in themselves explanations • Presented as arguments, models, logical propositions • Contains an implicit narrative presented as the past (11)	• Employs technical language • Narrative is not epistemologically self-assured • Emphasizes the construction of sources and texts (12)

independently of the historian and that discovering the past is an objective process, uncontaminated by ideology. "The historian is permitted only one attitude, that of impartial observer, unmoved equally by admiration or repugnance," say reconstructionists who insist that real historians are obliged to "simply relate the facts" and to avoid dictating readers' responses.[7] Rejecting any notion that ideological considerations might influence their histories, reconstructionists are particularly vigilant of colleagues who mesh ideology with sources: this amounts to subjectivity and distorts history. Boulongne accuses "feminist leagues," "radical political groups," and the "sporting-counter-society" of misconstruing Pierre de Coubertin, the founder of the International Olympic Committee, by ignoring his encouragement of women and girls whom he wanted to partake in physical activity. These "malicious detractors," Boulongne rails, "abbreviate quotations" and remove evidence from its historical context.[8]

Narrative is the medium of reconstructionism that adherents assume is essentially transparent (table 1.1, box 10). In evaluating good representations of sport history, reconstructionists gauge the structure, unity and coherence of the narrative. Reconstructionists place maximum emphasis on the narrative as a whole process and the way it informs the structure of the argument, although they also assess relationships between individual statements and sources. Cross-examination of evidence involves interrogation of language to ascertain the tone and accuracy of sources and to clarify what particular sources say and what they leave out. More specifically, interrogation entails questions about word usage, figures of speech, and stylistic cadence and the way that these articulate ideas and sympathies.[9] Reconstructionists maintain a strong vigilance over style and rhetoric in their sources and especially in colleagues' texts. Style has "enormous evidential value, both in getting and in giving evidence"; rhetoric is a "mechanical trick" associated with propaganda, poetics, and oratory.[10] Yet, for all their talk about careful scrutiny of colleagues' language, reconstructionists rarely take their evaluations beyond banal observations about grace of expression and clarity of writing. Sport historians will be all too familiar with book reviewers who refer to "wooden prose," "mechanical prose," "dull prose," "hyperbolic prose," "lively prose," "sharp prose," "witty prose," and every other type of prose. At the heart of these comments lies the trite notion that readability is integral to good history.[11]

Construction

Like reconstructionists, constructionists believe that empirical evidence provides the ultimate source of knowledge about the past. In this sense reconstructionism and constructionism are evidence-based, objectivist-inspired models in which historians aspire to build accurate, independent, and truthful reconstructions of the past (table 1.1, box 4). Both also distinguish the representation of history from fiction and value judgement: history means attempting to discover what actually happened in the past. Where these models diverge is with respect to acceptance of a priori knowledge, particularly theory. Real historical phenomena, according to conservative reconstructionists, are unique configurations and one-off occurrences: history consists of the "stories of . . . individual lives or happenings, all seemingly individual and unrepeatable."[12] A form of methodological individualism emphasizing human actions and intentions, or what sociologists call agency,[13] conservative reconstructionism casts theory into the realm of speculation. Theory, argues Elton "infuses predestined meaning" into history:

> All questions are so framed as to produce support for the theory, and all answers are predetermined by it. Historians captured by theory may tell you that they test their constructs by empirical research, but they do nothing of the sort; they use empirical research to prove the truth of the framework, never to disprove it . . . [A]dherents of theory do not allow facts to disturb them but instead try to deride the whole notion that there are facts independent of the observer.[14]

In short, theory is antithetical to the objectives and practices of conservative reconstructionism.

Not all reconstructionists are so averse to theory; not all reconstructionists consider the investigation of unique events as the litmus test of historical knowledge. They acknowledge that historians also discern patterns of behavior across time, societies, and social groups and that they categorize different forms of human action and place them into general molds. Such approaches compel historians to think "in terms of abstraction" and theory.[15] For example, collective identities such as nationalities, religions, occupational groups and social classes are invaluable and indispensable historical abstractions. While "no two individuals are entirely alike," how they think and act in certain situations—as members of a sporting fraternity or fans of a national sporting team—will typically "follow a highly regular pattern," even "to the point where their response can be predicted." Moreover, while theories alert historians to regularities and patterns, they can also reveal "aspects which resist categorization and which give the event or the situation its unique qualities."[16]

Constructionists deem theory integral to historical research (table 1.1, box 8): "The writer of history who desires to be more than a mere antiquarian must have a thorough *theoretical* training in those fields of inquiry with which his work is concerned."[17] While not denying that historians require an intimate and technical knowledge of their sources, Sombart derided such attributes as the skills of the "hodman." "Theoretical training alone makes the true historian," he believed.[18]

Constructionists claim that theory is fundamental in history for at least three reasons. First, the range and volume of evidence bearing on many historical problems is so large that historians cannot avoid selection, and theory is a critical tool. It provides frameworks and principles for selecting evidence and thus steers practitioners away from contradictions in their explanations. Second, theory brings to the fore interrelations between the components of human experiences at given times and in so doing enriches historical accounts. Third, as already mentioned, identifying historical patterns invariably involves some form of abstract thinking and connections to theoretical explanations and interpretations. Responding to the conservative reconstructionist charge that theory predetermines history, constructionists counter that theories enhance understanding and that no one can "approach their evidence innocent of presupposition."[19]

Where do sport historians sit in this debate between reconstructionists and constructionists over theory? The reconstructionist position holds minimal sway, but this does not mean that sport historians have embraced "complex social science constructionism."[20] On the contrary, sport historians have not employed the historical record to construct formal theories of sport, nor have they used it to apply, test, or confirm theories. Hardy probably comes closest of any sport historian to producing a formal theory of sport. At the heart of his work is the Sportgeist, the spirit of sport consisting of four transhistorical values—physicality, competition, creativity, and achievement. Each value begets its own set of tensions—between moderation and aggression, victory and fair play, freedom and regimen, and community and individual respectively—which "connect sports to their historical surroundings."[21] Hardy's Sportgeist falls well short of the positivist definition of a theory as a set of ordered propositions incorporated into a deductive system.[22] Far from proffering predictions about sport, Hardy places the meaning of sport at any historical conjecture within "three interrelated contexts: the Sportgeist, the sport structure, and general structure."[23] The vast majority of sport historians utilize "organizing concepts," as distinct from fully fledged theories, to "fine focus" their interpretations of the evidence.[24] Perhaps better recognized as classes of objects (e.g., amateur sports, extreme sports), general notions (e.g., hegemony, gender), themes (e.g., urbanization, democratization), periods (e.g., Victorian era, late capitalism), and constellations of interrelated traits (e.g., sporting gentlemen, manliness), concepts abound in sport history. However, they remain descriptive labels and do not in themselves provide explanations for how something came about or changed. Nonetheless, by identifying recurrent features and patterns,[25] concepts expose new realms of observation, enabling historians to move past the "single instance" and to "transcend immediate perceptions."[26]

The proliferation of concepts in sport history raises the question, where do they come from? Most sport historians simply appropriate concepts from outside the field, too often without critical reflection or analysis. Hoberman is one exception. His concept of "idealistic internationalisms" derives from a comparison of four international organizations: the Red Cross, the Esperanto movement, the Boy Scouts, and the olympic movement.[27]

By examining "analogies between historical instances," Hoberman follows Stinchcombe's recommendation for inventing "fruitful concepts."[28] His idealistic internationalisms also fulfils Stinchcombe's notion of a "profound concept": its invention emanates from "comparison of [the] actions and sentiments" of the agents who create international movements.[29] (In this sense, Hoberman extols agency.) However, Hoberman's idealistic internationalisms slips and slides. It is not clear how far he wants to extend the analogies between the movements that comprise the concept. Only the olympic movement appears as a twentieth-century idealistic internationalism. The Red Cross, formed in 1863, hardly rates a mention, even in discussions of nineteenth-century internationalism; the Esperanto and Boy Scout movements receive scant attention in the interwar age of fascism and completely disappear from the discussion relating to the post–Second World War era. Indeed, idealistic internationalisms becomes increasingly irrelevant to the argument.

Stinchcombe and Denzin regard concepts as the major units of theory; concepts define the shape and content of theory, especially when linked together.[30] The fact that Hoberman makes no attempt to link idealistic internationalisms to other concepts and thus develop a fully fledged theory is reflected in the title of his article: "*Toward* a Theory of Olympic Internationalism."[31]

Deconstructionism

Deconstructionists have abandoned all pretexts of objectivity:[32] historical understanding involves unavoidable relativism (the belief that there are no overarching rules or procedures for precisely measuring bodies of knowledge, conceptual schemes, or theories and that without fixed benchmarks the only outcome can be difference and uncertainty).[33] Thus deconstructionists do not promote the single interpretation associated with *the* history, for example, *the* history of women olympians. Rather, they examine

different perspectives within *the* history, for example, successful women
olympians, women excluded from the olympics, black female olympians,
Islamic female olympians, and so forth. In this sense, deconstructionists
acknowledge that each group has its own unique perspective and faces its
own struggles. Proceeding from the premise that nothing written can be
read as meaning, deconstructionists attempt to discover the intentions of
the author of each and every source or text. While reconstructionists claim
that their process of interrogating or conversing with sources is tantamount
to deconstruction, deconstructionists insist that the differences are substantial. According to deconstructionists, historians necessarily impose themselves on the reconstruction process, and any notion that they can isolate
themselves is erroneous.[34]

Deconstructionism deems interpretation an act of linguistic and literary
creation (table 1.1, box 12).[35] Historical material does not naturally organize, let alone write, narratives; nor are decisions about emplotments simple
technical matters.[36] White, who more than any other scholar has directed
attention to the nature and role of historical narratives, argues that modes of
emplotment involve ontological and epistemological choices. "History as a
plenum of documents that attest to the occurrence of events," writes White,
"can be put together in a number of different and equally plausible narrative
accounts."[37] Moreover, these choices carry distinct ideological and political
implications: historians and their readers may reach quite "different conclusions" from these narratives "about 'what must be done' in the present."[38]

Sport historians have overwhelmingly ignored White's work. Phillips
is the sole exception. Attempting to shed light on the processes of historical production in sport history, Phillips employs White's model to compare
two sets of historical narratives, produced by Douglas Booth and Ed Jaggard, about the Australian surf lifesaving movement.[39] Essentially drawing
on the same evidence, Booth and Jaggard frame remarkably different narratives, which Phillips, following White, attributes to the way that they
trope (prefigure their discourses), use emplotment and argument to construct their explanations, and incorporate ideology into their narratives
(table 1.2). According to Phillips, Booth's account of female surf lifesavers
unfolds as a tragedy, whereas Jaggard's history of women's involvement in
surf lifesaving follows a romantic plot. In Booth's narrative women fight
for, and gain, access to the masculine domain of surf lifesaving, although
full admission does not alleviate their "suffering" and "agony." Booth's
story line is one of enduring tragedy exemplified by frequent "buts," which
serve as a literary device to amplify women's pain. "Women were admitted
as full members *but . . .* ; women gained administrative positions *but . . .* ;
and discrimination has been tempered *but . . .*"[40] Unlike "Booth's tortured
souls," Jaggard's women are "heroes."[41] Female triumphs and achievements

Table 1.2.
Locating Booth and Jaggard in Hayden White's Model of Historical Explanation[43]

Trope	Emplotment	Argument	Ideological Implication
Metaphor	Romantic (Jaggard)	Formist (Jaggard)	Anarchist
Metonymy (Jaggard)	Tragic (Booth)	Mechanistic	Radical (Booth)
Synecdoche (Booth)	Comic	Organicist	Conservative
Irony	Satirical	Contextualist (Booth / Jaggard)	Liberal (Jaggard)

shape Jaggard's story. In the face of "barriers, discrimination and abuse," women "persisted with dogged determination" to become "involved," "admitted" and "accepted," in surf lifesaving.[42]

Different emplotments (and tropes and arguments) in the works of Jaggard and Booth, Phillips argues, fuse with their ideological perspectives. The two sport historians reveal their respective liberal and radical ideologies in discussions about social changes within surf lifesaving and in particular the pace and desirability of change. Jaggard agrees that surf lifesaving is a "conservative, masculine institution." Yet, notwithstanding these "warts," he believes surf lifesaving deserves its place on the beach and that the movement's governing council needs merely to fine tune its policies to preserve what is ultimately a well-earned iconic status in Australia. Booth, by contrast, demands "structural transformations" to "reconstitute" the movement.[44]

Phillips' analysis is profound; he clearly demonstrates the need for sport historians to better familiarize themselves with deconstructionism as a model of historical enquiry. This is all the more important as linguistic elements of deconstructionism diffuse from other quarters, notably cultural studies, into sport history. We will examine some of these elements at the end of the next section, which addresses the question, how do sport historians do history?

EXPLANATORY PARADIGMS

More specific than a model, yet less prescriptive than a method, an explanatory paradigm is an "interactive structure of workable questions and the factual statements which are adduced to answer them."[45] Sport historians structure their arguments, or frame their questions and answers, within seven distinct explanatory paradigms: traditional narrative, advocacy, contextual, comparative, causal, social change, and linguistic (see table 1.3, column 1).

Table 1.3.
Explanatory Paradigms in Sport History

	Objectives	*Epistemology*
Traditional Narrative (Reconstruction)	• Instruct (tell a moral story) through an authoritative work • Suppress historian's voice (especially personal pronouns, "I" in favor of third-person narrative)	• Past recoverable with evidence • Traditional representations are transparent and preserve the objectivity of observations • Texts are referential (refer to worlds outside their own linguistic systems) • Non-reflexive • Omniscience
Advocacy (Reconstruction)	• Debunking popular sporting myths • Find the facts	• Facts the basis of truth • Historians' primary allegiance is to truth and the profession • History analogous to law • Historians adopt various roles: judge, partisan eyewitness, expert witness, leading counsel
Contextual (Reconstruction/ construction)	• Situate subject in the entirety of events to which it is bound • Stress the interrelationship between part (sport) and whole (society)	• Historical events constitute a single process • Broader social, economic, and political contexts "explain" sport • Broader social, economic and political contexts "legitimize" the study of sport
Comparative (Reconstruction/ construction)	• Identify and analyze historical similarities • Identify and analyze historical differences	• Comparisons are tools of explanation
Causal (Reconstruction/ construction)	• Identify the causes of events • Distinguish between contingent and structural causes of events	• History is either contingent *or* determined
Social Change (Construction)	• Specific historical situations help historians understand diversity and change • Empirical generalizations refer to theoretical issues • Theorize about processes of change over time	• History is a process
Linguistic (Deconstruction)	• Reveal how the processes that constitute texts also provide meaning for their producers and different audiences • Reveal the subtexts of topics explored • Emphasize multiple perspectives • Reflexive	• Sources are sites of intersecting meanings that receive diverse readings and interpretations • Texts are read as structures of meaning flowing from semiotic, social, and cultural processes by which they are constructed / textualized • Sources are not concrete objects with fixed meanings • Narrative is not epistemologically self-assured

Of course, most historians embrace two or three paradigms, although the philosophical assumptions that undergird any one piece of work will determine the specific combination and range of paradigms. Generally speaking, the traditional narrative, advocacy, and contextual explanatory paradigms fall within the ambit of reconstructionism, the comparative, causal, and social change paradigms align with constructionism, and the linguistic paradigm parallels deconstructionism. As shall become clear, the contextual, comparative, and causal paradigms can also support the philosophies of both reconstructionism and constructionism (see table 1.3, column 1).

Traditional Narrative

The subject of vigorous debate, historians nonetheless agree that at the heart of narrative lies "some sense of story"[46] and that it is the overwhelmingly dominant form of representing the past. Conservative reconstructionists assume a high degree of correspondence between narrative and the past and promote the view that a narrative is simply the medium of their histories, the shape and structure of which closely resemble actual events in the past. In other words, reconstructionists hold that narrative language is mimetic or referential, that is, unproblematic or, at the very least, adequate to the job of describing the past. Reconstructionists believe that a historical explanation materializes "naturally from the archival raw data, its meaning offered as interpretation in the form of a story related explicitly, impersonally, transparently, and without resort to any of the devices used by writers of literary narratives, viz., imagery or figurative language."[47]

The idea that historical material organizes itself naturally is consistent with "scissors-and-paste" history. Scissors-and-paste historians choose a topic and then search for "statements about it, oral or written, purporting to be made by actors in the events concerned, or by eyewitnesses of them, or by persons repeating what actors or eyewitnesses have told them, or have told their informants, or those who informed their informants, and so on." After locating these statements, historians "excerpt" and "incorporate" them into their own histories, which they cast as simple technical recoveries of the past by discoveries of the facts.[48] Redmond's narrative of women's golf in Canada illustrates scissors-and-paste history.

Catalogs of facts buttress Redmond's conclusion that Canadian women achieved gender equality in golf by the late nineteenth century. The facts include lists of women's golf clubs, names of female golf administrators, newspaper journalists' comments about women's enthusiasm for the game, and details of the hours and competitions that women played. At first glance Redmond's factual narrative is a technical, pristine recovery of the past, but impositions intrude in both the sources and the narrative. Comments by journalists about women's passion for golf do not constitute facts. By the late nineteenth century sport reporting was an entertainment genre similar to "popular storytelling," "ancient epics," "medieval folktales," and "penny-paper serials."[49] Redmond's narrative describing women's access to golf is also a clear example of imposition that whitewashes gender relations and requires no political explanation for what amounted to restricted access. "Lady members could use the links every morning except Saturday," and they could use the links "Monday, Tuesday, Thursday and Friday afternoons." Almost in passing Redmond adds, "this practice was not uncommon, because it reserved the links for men's weekend use."[50] Alternatively, he could have written something like "men banished women from the links on Wednesday afternoons and all day Saturday." Of course, such a representation was no option for a historian eager to bestow credit on the Scots "for having introduced [golf and curling] into Canada which could be played by both sexes, at all levels and almost all ages."[51]

Traditional reconstructionist narratives have virtually disappeared from the leading academic sport history journals (although this has not stopped practitioners from submitting them for review). Their demise, however, appears more connected to the lack of contextualization (see below) than any unease about unreflective uses of source material and a failure to interrogate sources. One form of reconstructionism, the advocacy paradigm, makes a virtue of forensic interrogation of sources and retains an important place in sport history.

Advocacy

Reconstructionists charge advocates with undermining the objectivity of history and destroying the credibility of the historian as a "neutral, or disinterested, judge" whose "conclusions . . . display . . . judicial qualities of balance and evenhandedness."[52] But as Berkhofer reminds us, "there is a difference between arguing *for* a point of view" and "arguing *from* a point of view" (emphasis added) and by definition all historians are advocates for particular cases, stances, or interpretations.[53] In this chapter the term *advocate* refers exclusively to those historians whose basic objective is to debunk sporting myths. Advocates include Collins who debunks William Webb Ellis as the founder of rugby,[54] Henderson, who exposes the false claim that Abner Doubleday invented baseball,[55] and Young, who reveals the myth of the ancient Greek amateur Olympian.[56]

Advocates combine two approaches: forensic interrogation of the evidence and examination of the motives and interests of myth builders. In the case of the Doubleday myth, Henderson interrogates the evidence of Abner

Graves. In a letter (subsequently destroyed by fire) written to a private commission appointed to investigate the origins of baseball early in the twentieth century, Graves advised that "Abner Doubleday invented baseball in
Cooperstown, New York, in the year 1839."[57] Henderson finds that "Doubleday was not in Cooperstown in 1839 . . . He entered West Point Military
Academy on September 1st, 1838, and was not in Cooperstown on leave or
otherwise in 1839."[58] Henderson identifies the beneficiaries and key propa-
gators of the Doubleday myth as the sporting goods magnate Albert Spalding
and the Cooperstown Chamber of Commerce. Spalding established the special commission in the hope that "publicity might accrue to the firm" whose
owner "unraveled the mystery" of baseball's beginnings, while the Cooperstown Chamber of Commerce rushed to "exploit" the "historical association," purchasing the local Doubleday Field, which it developed to include
the National Baseball Museum and Hall of Fame.[59]

What criteria should historians use to assess the neutrality or objectivity of advocates? Smith classifies advocates according to how they handle the
relationship between involvement (the capacity to empathize with and
evoke the situation of particular participants in specific historical situations)
and detachment (the capacity to observe processes and relationships objec-
tively, discounting political/moral commitments and emotion-laden
responses).[60] On this basis Smith recognizes four types of advocate. Avoiding
theory and trying to "give coherence to as much empirical complexity as possible," *judges* "achieve a creative balance between involvement and detachment, each complementing the other."[61] Usually involved with a particular
viewpoint, *partisan eyewitnesses* "can achieve detachment" although they
find it difficult; the *expert witnesses*, by contrast, achieve a high degree of
detachment at the expense of all involvement. Last, *leading counsels* express
a high degree of involvement at the expense of detachment. Leading counsels often "identify strongly with the interests of the subordinate groups they
have researched."[62] Collins, Henderson, and Young are judges. Henderson,
for example, empathizes with Spalding and the Cooperstown Chamber of
Commerce—"the development of the Doubleday Field and the Baseball
Museum and Hall of Fame were both done in the best of good faith"[63]—and
makes objective recommendations—"there is no reason why the Museum
should not be maintained at Cooperstown" providing it "functions . . . to
teach the truth."[64]

Contextualization

Nothing is more fundamental in the lexicon and methodology of history
than context. "Although historians may differ among themselves about

what constitutes a proper context in any given case," observes Berkhofer, "they do not question the basic desirability of finding one as the appropriate background for understanding past ideas, behaviours and institutions."[65] Among the first generation of sport historians, contextualization was a critical explanatory paradigm: by placing sport in its broader economic, political, and social context sport historians hoped to earn intellectual credibility from peers who dismissed the subject as trivial and irrelevant. Olson confirms the continued centrality of contextualization in sport history. The "best" sport histories, he says, "successfully analyze a particular topic and then shed light on much broader issues."[66] Olson praises John Watterson in this regard. Watterson's *College Football*, Olson continues, "effectively places college football in the larger context of American social, economic, cultural and political life, and in doing so transcends the narrow confines of sport history."[67]

Despite the importance of contextualization, "historians rarely discuss what [this] involves" or "the larger implications . . . for the profession or its audience."[68] The general consensus is that contextualization establishes patterns that share relationships beyond a temporal juxtaposition. Walsh elaborates: Historians

> initially confront what looks like a largely unconnected mass of material, and . . . then go on to show that sense can be made of it by revealing certain pervasive themes or developments. In specifying what was going on at the time, [historians] both sum up individual events and tell us how to take them. Or . . . they pick out what [is] significant in the events they relate, [that is,] what points beyond itself and connects with other happenings as phases in a continuous process.[69]

Historians may agree that temporal contiguity meets the criteria for contextualization, however contextual relationships are not necessarily well integrated. On the contrary, the contextualist "impulse is not to integrate all the events and trends that might be identified in the whole historical field, but rather to link them together in a chain of provisional and restricted characterizations of finite provinces of manifestly 'significant' occurrence."[70]

Marwick delineates contextual relationships using a model comprising four principal components:

1. Major forces and constraints
  - *structural* (geographical, demographic, economic and technological),

- *ideological* (what is believed and is possible to be believed, existing political and social philosophies), and
- *institutional* (systems of government, justice, policing and voting, educational, religious and working-class organizations, and the family).

2. **Events** (Great Depression, Second World War).
3. **Human agencies** (politicians, presidents, prime ministers, protest movements).
4. **Convergences and contingencies** (interrelationships between events and human agencies that generate unforeseen events and circumstances).[71]

Gorn's contextualization of a brutal form of fighting involving maximum disfigurement of one's opponents in early American frontier societies illustrates Marwick's model. Eye-gouging, as this fighting was sometimes known, flourished within a peculiar combination of structural, ideological, and institutional "forces." Geographically and socially isolated, the male-dominated backwoods supported a semisubsistence economy and weak legal and political institutions. It was a harsh impoverished world that nurtured a strong sense of fatalism among populations who assumed pain and suffering to be their lot. In a world where "aggressive self-assertion and manly pride were the real marks of status . . . brutal recreations toughened men for a violent social life."[72] Gorn identifies two types of events: unsuccessful attempts by different legislatures to stem "the carnage," and tales of heroic encounters that passed into folklore and legend and thus contributed to the reproduction of gouging culture. The key agents in the backwoods were not political leaders but legendary gougers, "tested gang leaders who attained their status by being the meanest, toughest, and most ruthless fighters, who faced disfigurement and never backed down."[73] Gouging eventually declined as new forces emerged and introduced new agents: market-orientated staple crop production replaced hunting; and improved transport systems, towns, schools, churches, and families gradually smothered the backwoods. "Modern" men turned to alternative means to display their status and defend their honor, and in this they were assisted by contingent technology: the revolver. Gunplay, rather than fighting tooth and nail, offered a cleaner and more dignified method by which to settle disputes and confirm one's social position.

Contextualization is vulnerable to sinking into vague holism[74] and Marwick's model does not ameliorate this tendency. Gorn neatly side steps this problem by analyzing eye-gouging as a phenomenon with its own rituals and meanings associated with the attainment and preservation of masculine culture.[75]

Although reconstructionists and constructionists both utilize the contextual paradigm they conceptualize it differently. Reconstructionists stress the "nonrepetitive elements" and the "individuality of the overall network of relationships";[76] constructionists insist that contextualization is a matter of theory.[77] The reconstructionist perspective prevails in sport history, and this has particular relevance for the comparative paradigm. As Berkhofer explains, where "contextualism renders the unit of study and its context unique . . . comparative history practically becomes an oxymoron."[78] Comparisons in sport history usually assume a simple form where the practitioner alludes to similarities or differences in particular instances.

Comparison

Comparisons involving allusions to another case in order to illustrate or highlight aspects of a particular case abound in sport history. Comparisons include instances of similar or different kinds, and they range across space, time, practices, ideologies, institutions, groups, and individuals. For example, to exemplify the rigid codes of conduct and peculiar masculinity associated with German pistol dueling in the late nineteenth century, McAleer compares it with British boxing.[79]

Conservative reconstructionists judge comparison "wrong in principle" on the grounds that "history is about unique entities" and that "nothing in the past can be compared with anything else."[80] Sport historians have generally ignored this position, yet they seem strangely undaunted by the practical problems that beset even simple comparisons. Historical research is not conducive to comparative approaches that require primary sources from different regions, spanning long time periods, or that demand high competence in different languages.[81] In practice, historical competence and expertise are typically confined to precise time periods and geographical regions that become smaller as the number of sources increases. The fact that so many sport historians ultilize mismatches of primary and secondary sources to make comparisons confirms the extent of the problem.

As noted earlier, some historians consider drawing comparisons as the means by which to formulate concepts (e.g., Hoberman), and others deem them integral to the construction of causal, and ultimately theoretical, historical explanations (e.g., Stinchcombe). Notwithstanding Carr's view that identifying the causes of phenomena constitutes a major problem in history,[82] sport historians have generally shied from placing their arguments into an explicit causal paradigm and have tended to conflate causation with contextualization.

Causation

As in the two preceding explanatory paradigms, conservative reconstructionists and constructionists conceptualize causation in radically different ways. The former assume direct relationships been causes and effects: if event B (e.g., the formation of the New South Wales Rugby League) happened immediately after event A (e.g., Alex Burdon breaking his collarbone while playing a representative match for the New South Wales Rugby Union) then it must have happened because of A (i.e., players formed a new competition, the New South Wales Rugby League, when the union refused to compensate the incapacitated Burdon for his medical expenses and lost income). In this case a set of purely fortuitous or contingent (and, as expected, agent driven) circumstances led to the formation of the New South Wales Rugby League.

The majority of reconstructionists and constructionists regard contingent factors as superficial, or secondary, causes and search elsewhere. Many allude to social structures, unquestionably the most common concept in sport history. In preference to structure, historical sociologist Theda Skocpol has developed a rigorous test for causation based on systematic comparison. Her approach involves analyzing cases of agreement and disagreement.

> First, one can try to establish that several cases having in common the phenomenon one is trying to explain also have a common set of causal factors, although they vary in other ways that might have seemed causally relevant. Second, one can contrast the cases in which the phenomenon to be explained and the hypothesized causes are both absent, but which are otherwise as similar as possible to the positive cases.[83]

Given that sport historians are as suspicious of historical sociology as they are of mainstream sociology, it is hardly surprising that they have ignored Skocpol's comparative method of agreement and disagreement.[84] Elsewhere I suggest that it has potential to explain why professional rugby emerged and prospered in England and Australia around the turn of the twentieth century yet failed to take hold in other rugby nations such as New Zealand, South Africa, and Wales.[85]

Rather than systematic comparisons, sport historians typically integrate causal explanations into their histories by alluding to social structures. Often used to describe simple patterns identified in observations, in social history implicit assumptions usually underpin the term *structure*:

> first, that the phenomenon under inspection can be analyzed as a series of component units of a specified type (e.g. roles, classes,

value-commitments, genders, societies); second, that these units are related to each other in quite definite ways; third, that the relationships between units connect together to give the phenomenon under observation a characteristic pattern which needs to be understood as a totality; and fourth, that the pattern of relationships is relatively stable and enduring over time.[86]

These four assumptions shine through in the structurally inclined explanations of the formation of the New South Wales Rugby League.[87] First, the Rugby Union and the Rugby League subscribed to specific class-based ideologies; second, the ideologies of the union and the league shaped their respective actions especially how they dealt with the amateur problem; third, the ideologies and actions of the two rugby organizations were symptomatic of broader antagonistic social relations between the middle and working classes in Australia; and fourth, the social antagonisms between the middle and working classes that emerged in the second half of the nineteenth century endured well into the twentieth century.

Opponents of structural causation launch two predictable objections: that it ignores agency and the actors who make choices and shape their own situations for their own ends by exercising their rationality and that it conceptualizes structures as purely "determining factors." Sport historians in the 1970s and 1980s found the latter highly problematic especially where practitioners adopted a cavalier attitude toward historical facts. In light of these well-documented concerns, sport historians have been wary of assigning causal weight to abstract structures.[88] Hardy displays particular sensitivity to this issue and emphasizes the importance of understanding structures as intentional and unintentional human creations.[89] Hardy's Sportgeist lays bare the roles of intentional and unintentional agency in the production of structures as well as the problems for historical practice posed by attempting to marry agency and structure.

On the one hand, individuals "invigorate" the Sportgeist with their own meanings: "players, fans, and coaches constantly make their own decisions on physicality, achievement, competition and creativity."[90] On the other hand, while "every participant has . . . a measure of agency" in making the Sportgeist,[91] individuals can only make history within a framework of external constraints that they cannot change. Hardy identifies two basic external constraints in sport: "the sport structure and the general structure."[92] The former comprises "the ensemble of specific rules, tactics, organizations, facilities, records and equipment through which individuals animate the Sportgeist"; the general structure includes "climate, topography, economic systems, class, gender and race relations."[93] The interaction between agency and structural constructs finds its clearest expression in Hardy's examination of sport entrepreneurs Henry Chadwick, Albert Spalding, James Sullivan, and Senda Berenson. Each had a "profound influence on the structure of American sport" and were "extremely successful" in cementing a new sport structure as they attempted to "harness a personal vision of the Sportgeist." Yet their agency had limits: "it is one thing to fashion a game form," quite "another to control the spirit that people animate within the game form."[94]

It is in those works dealing with social change that concepts and structures find their clearest expression.

Social Change

Like other social historians, sport historians "spend most of their time explaining change—or its absence."[95] Questions about the emergence of sport, its increasing commercialization, its appropriation as a tool of national identity, and the integration of women and racial and ethnic minorities occupy many sport historians. The very breadth of these questions typically "invites the application of theory,"[96] but sport historians have generally shied from theory, neither constructing it nor employing it as a heuristic device. (As influential and oft cited as Allen Guttman's *From Ritual to Record* [1978] and Melvin Adelman's *Sporting Time* [1986] may be, as examples of theory development and application respectively, they remain exceptions in sport history.) For the vast majority of sport historians, organizing concepts, such as "urbanization," "rationalization," "nationalism," "gender," "class," and "hegemony," rather than fully fledged theories, provide the instruments to fine focus their interpretations. Scholars working in other disciplines typically find this approach "conceptually confused and unacceptable."[97] For Holt it is perfectly consistent with historical logic and practice that seeks to throw light on "loosely related activities" that change their "forms and meanings over time."[98] Social change, in other words, is a collection of phenomena as opposed to a "single phenomenon," and historians improve their understanding by drawing on a range of concepts that may appear incongruent from a strict theoretical perspective.[99]

The first part of this chapter raised a question about the origins of concepts and noted that most sport historians appropriate them from other disciplines rather than building their own. This should not be taken to mean that the field adopts a willy-nilly eclectic approach to concepts. The concepts that prevail in sport history at any one time—and hegemony is one current vogue—overwhelmingly derive from the contemporary intellectual *Zeitgeist*, which itself is a response to social, political, and economic conditions.[100] Three primary blocks of concepts have dominated sport history: modernization (e.g., "urbanization," "rationalization," "specialization," "bureaucraticization," "democratization"), Marxism ("capitalism," "class," "hegemony," "social control," "subordination," "alienation," "resistance"), and, to a lesser degree, postmodernism ("culture," "identities," "globalizaton," "niche markets," "individualism"). Support for each of these blocks comes from specific quarters. Concepts associated with modernization initially found favor in North American sport history where the modernization model dominated American social science after the Second World War; sport historians living in Western welfare states (Britain, Canada, Australia, New Zealand) preferred Marxist concepts, and postmodern concepts enjoy most appeal among second and third generation sport historians skeptical of traditional objective empiricism.

Sport historians working in the social change explanatory paradigm (which includes accounts of the absence of change) place no less store in agency than in concepts. Tygiel, Vertinsky, Cahn, Cronin, and Grundy, for example, assign enormous importance to the details of individual actors.[101] Football player Jack Charlton "created an atmosphere where soccer could become the national game" of Ireland.[102] Psychologist Granville Stanley Hall was instrumental in cementing in popular opinion negative "biologically deterministic views about women's physical and mental capabilities."[103] Conversely, tennis star Billie Jean King's 1973 on-court victory over Bobby Riggs perhaps constituted "the ultimate victory against sexism in sport."[104] Nonetheless, sport historians have largely overlooked the problems of marrying structure and agency.

The Linguistic Explanatory Paradigm

Associated with discourse and textual analysis, and the revival of narrative, the linguistic explanatory paradigm emerged along with postmodernism, poststructuralism, literary criticism, and deconstruction in the humanities. The following outline of the linguistic paradigm in sport history focuses only on textual analysis and contemporary narratives.

Deconstructionist historians apply the same rigor to interrogating sources and documents as critics who read literary texts. Some deconstructionists advocate expanding the conceptualization of texts to include nonliterary forms such as paintings, films, television programs, clothing styles, sports spectacles, political rallies, and even societies and cultures.[105] Oriard captures well the idea of sport as an interpretative text in his discussion of a violent on-field collision between two American football players.[106] Spectators will read this text, Oriard says, in different ways depending on their personal circumstances and the social circumstances of the players. And as he reminds us, the options are virtually limitless. Oriard's example demonstrates the key objectives of textual analysis: to restore what people actually experienced and to eliminate master narratives that impose predetermined meanings.[107]

Narrative increasingly joined the lexicon of sport history in the 1990s, although few practitioners have clarified their understanding or application of the term. Parratt and Mewett are notable exceptions.[108] Whereas Oriard conceptualizes early American football as a set of texts, Parratt and Mewett approach their subjects—the Haxey Hood (a folk-football-type game played at Haxey village in Lincolnshire), and the dying Australian sport of professional running respectively—as sets of narratives. Mewett, for example, describes professional running as replete with stories of coaches protecting their runners from "snoopers" representing competing stables of information leaked from within stables, and of public surveillance of runners. These are neither arbitrary narratives nor the tall tales of live theater; they are "models of how to win, and strategies to combat threats to winning."[109] Indeed, these narratives constitute professional running by informing runners and trainers of how they should behave and act.

In a critique of textual analysis, Rorty discusses the approach as one where scholars seek truth, or reality, via the secret codes of language. They want to "stay within the boundaries of a text, take it apart, and show how it works" and in so doing debunk "the myth of language as mirror of reality."[110] Bloom is a case in point in sport history. Reading the transcript of an interview between two anthropologists and a Native American who graduated from a special Indian School in the early twentieth century, Bloom claims to have found "hidden transcripts." Bloom argues that these hidden transcripts provide clues into the real nature of race and racism in the United States and the ability of subordinate classes to shape their own identities. In the end, the power of Bloom's argument relies on contextualizing evidence external to the transcript interview.[111] Thus he falls back on traditional historical practice, particularly the historical guild's understanding of context. A similar issue arises in contemporary narratives.

Just as Bloom attempts to break from the notion of master narrative and restore peoples' actual experiences, he—like Mewett, Oriard, and Parratt—also strives to give voice to others. Allowing people to tell their own stories is a simple matter; historians have been doing this for aeons by putting voices in full quotations. The real problem for historians is that they do not just reclaim past voices; they also contextualize those voices. And contextualization means making decisions about the relationships among multiple viewpoints. Ultimately, no matter how diverse the subjects' voices in the represented world of the text, the historian's narrative will consider one perspective best or right.[112] In short, the linguistic paradigm has not changed the reality that historians are still narrators who subordinate subjects' viewpoints to their own. Thus, it remains a moot point as to whether the linguistic paradigm constitutes a radical departure from reconstructionist and constructionist approaches to the past, their representations of the past, and their presentations of findings. Certainly in sport history, little has changed beyond some vocabulary and the introduction of a few new subjects. Sydnor is, to my knowledge, the sole sport historian to have attempted to present subject matter in a radically new way.[113]

CONCLUSION

Sport historians today mostly work at the epistemological intersection of reconstruction and construction which Appleby, Hunt, and Jacob label practical realism.[114] While practical realism acknowledges the very real gap between words and reality, it does not consider the distance sufficient cause to abandon the search for accuracy. Rarely are words arbitrarily connected to objects. *Sportsman*, for example, connotes a specific set of behaviors. The meaning of the term changed over time as different groups appropriated it for themselves, but the community of sport historians has built up a strong consensus on the different meanings. Practical realism emphasizes that historical facts derive from tangible material documents and hard supporting evidence. The olympic charter, for example, is a knowable, usable document, ultimately separable from whatever language historians use to describe it. Similarly, the charter limits the factual assertions that historians can extract from it and hence the interpretations they put forward. Practical realists concede that all histories begin from the personal interests and cultural attributes of the historian, that no knowledge is neutral, that all knowledge is contentious, and that its production involves struggles between different interest groups. Nonetheless, they reject the view that historical narratives are forms of literature. Likewise, they dismiss the charge that constant reassessment of the past is proof that the field lacks objectivity: reassessment reflects attempts by successive generations to give new meaning to the past.

With respect to explanatory paradigms, most historians structure their work to place sport within a broader social, economic, or political context or to explain some issue of social change. Concluding that American sport is simultaneously "radical and conservative," both "challenging some aspects of . . . society while underpinning others," Grundy explains this "dual function" by recourse to "social context": "The most effective efforts to employ athletics in the service of social change have generally been linked with broader social shifts; young women started playing varsity basketball during the heady atmosphere of the woman suffrage campaigns, while African American athletes made the greatest national strides amid the liberalizing racial attitudes of the post-War II era."[115]

Contextualization and social change ironically pose the greatest technical hurdles for sport historians. A fine line separates over- and undercontextualization. The former overlooks sport as a relatively autonomous social practice; the latter assigns a significance to sport that far exceeds its social influence. Grundy expresses this dilemma well. On the one hand, sport is a "powerful realm for demonstrating individual potential—the reason why outstanding female, African American, and other athletes have been able to make meaningful impressions on both fans and doubters." On the other hand, "sports offer far less room for questioning the rules under which athletes compete, let alone the larger meaning of competition itself." Similarly, reconciling agency and structure remains a thorny issue for sport historians working within the paradigm of social change. Again Grundy articulates the problem. While success at a sport can "promote" individual confidence and collective endeavor to address social issues and concerns, "when it comes to the details of forging plans for a more diverse society," structural notions of "competition and individual effort embodied in [sport] offers limited guidance and could even prove an obstacle."[116] The only fact remaining is that sport historians desiring respect from peers in other disciplines will have to better attune themselves to these issues.

NOTES

1. Edward P. Thompson, *The Poverty of Theory: Or an Orrery of Errors*, 2 ed. (London: Merlin, 1995), 51.

2. Alun Munslow, *Deconstructing History* (London: Routledge, 1997).

3. Geoffrey R. Elton, *Return to Essentials: Some Reflections on the Present State of Historical Study* (Cambridge: Cambridge University Press, 1991), 27.

4. Munslow, *Deconstructing History*, 14, 15.

5. David H. Fischer, *Historians' Fallacies: Toward a Logic of Historical Thought* (New York: Harper and Row: 1970), xv.

6. Key sources include Munslow, *Deconstructing History*, and Robert F. Berkhofer, *Beyond the Great Story: History as Text and Discourse* (Cambridge, MA: Harvard University Press, 1995).

7. Michael Stanford, *A Companion to the Study of History* (Oxford: Blackwell, 1994), 91.

8. Yves-Pierre Boulongne, "Pierre de Coubertin and Women's Sport," *Olympic Review* (2000): 23–6.

9. Louis Gottschalk, *Understanding History: A Primer of Historical Method*, 2 ed. (New York: Knopf, 1969), 149–50.

10. Peter Gay, *Style in History* (New York: Basic Books, 1974), 3. See also Gottschalk, *Understanding History*, 17–19.

11. John Tosh, *The Pursuit of History: Aims, Methods and New Directions in the Study of Modern History*, 2 ed. (London: Longman, 1991), 113; J. A. Mangan, "The End of History Perhaps—But the End of the Beginning for the History of Sport! An Anglo-Saxon Autobiographical Perspective," *Sporting Traditions* 16, no. 1 (1999): 62–63. See Philippe Carrard, *Poetics of the New History: French Historical Discourse from Braudel to Chartier* (Baltimore: Johns Hopkins University Press, 1992), 141–46 for a critical comment.

12. Michael M. Postan, *Fact and Relevance: Essays on Historical Method* (Cambridge: Cambridge University Press, 1971), 62.

13. Steven Lukes, *Individualism* (Oxford: Blackwell, 1973).

14. Elton, *Return to Essentials*, 15, 19.

15. Munslow, *Deconstructing History*, 22–23; Tosh, *The Pursuit of History*, 154–55.

16. Tosh, *The Pursuit of History*, 160–61.

17. Werner Sombart, "Economic Theory and Economic History," *The Economic History Review* 2, no. 1 (1929): 3.

18. Sombart, "Economic Theory and Economic History," 3.

19. Munslow, *Deconstructing History*, 23, 40.

20. Munslow, *Deconstructing History*, 48.

21. Stephen Hardy, "Entrepreneurs, Structures, and the Sportgeist: Old Tensions in a Modern Industry." In *Essays on Sport History and Sport Mythology*, ed. Donald G. Kyle and G. Stark (College Station: Texas A and M Press, 1990), 47–51.

22. Norman Denzin, *The Research Act*, 3 ed. (Englewood Cliffs, NJ: Prentice Hall, 1989), 49.

23. Hardy, "Entrepreneurs, Structures, and the Sportgeist," 47.

24. Munslow, *Deconstructing History*, 46.

25. Peter Burke, *History and Social Theory* (Cambridge: Polity, 1992), 29.

26. Denzin, *The Research Act*, 13.

27. John Hoberman, "Toward a Theory of Olympic Internationalism," *Journal of Sport History* 22, no. 1 (1995): 1–37.

28. Arthur L. Stinchcombe, *Theoretical Methods in Social History* (New York: Academic, 1978), 17.

29. Stinchcombe, *Theoretical Methods in Social History*, 22.

30. Stinchcombe, *Theoretical Methods in Social History*, 17–19; Denzin, *The Research Act*, 53, 59–60.

31. Hoberman, "Toward a Theory of Olympic Internationalism."

32. Munslow, *Deconstructing History*, 71.

33. Munslow, *Deconstructing History*, 188.

34. Munslow, *Deconstructing History*, 118.

35. Munslow, *Deconstructing History*, 74.

36. Munslow, *Deconstructing History*, 100–01.

37. Hayden White, *Metahistory: The Historical Imagination in Nineteenth-century Europe* (Baltimore: Johns Hopkins University Press, 1983), 283.

38. White, *Metahistory*, 283.

39. Murray G. Phillips, "A Critical Appraisal of Narrative in Sport History: Reading the Surf Lifesaving Debate," *Journal of Sport History* 29, no. 1 (2002): 25–40.

40. Phillips, "A Critical Appraisal of Narrative in Sport History," 30, emphasis added.

41. Phillips, "A Critical Appraisal of Narrative in Sport History," 32.

42. Phillips, "A Critical Appraisal of Narrative in Sport History," 31.

43. Key sources include White, *Metahistory*, 29; Munslow, *Deconstructing History*, 154; Phillips, "A Critical Appraisal of Narrative in Sport History," 28, 35.

44. Phillips, "A Critical Appraisal of Narrative in Sport History," 33–34.

45. Fischer, *Historians' Fallacies*, xv.

46. Berkhofer, *Beyond the Great Story*, 37.

47. Munslow, *Deconstructing History*, 10.

48. Robin G. Collingwood, *The Principles of History* (Oxford: Oxford University Press, 1999), 12–13.

49. Michael Oriard, *Reading Football: How the Popular Press Created an American Spectacle* (Chapel Hill: University of North Carolina Press, 1983), 89.

50. Gerald Redmond, *The Sporting Scots of Nineteenth-Century Canada* (Toronto: Associated University Presses, 1982), 232.

51. Redmond, *The Sporting Scots of Nineteenth-Century Canada*, 233–34.

52. Peter Novick, *That Noble Dream: The "Objectivity Quest" and the American Historical Profession* (Cambridge: Cambridge University Press, 1988), 2.

53. Berkhofer, *Beyond the Great Story*, 165.

54. Tony Collins, *Rugby's Great Split: Class, Culture and the Origins of Rugby League Football* (London: Cass, 1998).

55. Robert H. Henderson, *Ball, Bat and Bishop: The Origin of Ball Games* (Urbana: University of Illinois Press, 1947/2001).

56. David Young, *The Olympic Myth of Greek Amateur Athletics* (Chicago: Ares Publishers, 1984).

57. Henderson, *Ball, Bat and Bishop*, 176.

58. Henderson, *Ball, Bat and Bishop*, 186.

59. Henderson, *Ball, Bat and Bishop*, 173, 190, 192–93.

60. Dennis Smith, *The Rise of Historical Sociology* (Cambridge: Polity, 1991), 163.

61. Smith, *The Rise of Historical Sociology*, 165.

62. Smith, *The Rise of Historical Sociology*, 165.

63. Henderson, *Ball, Bat and Bishop*, 193.

64. Henderson, *Ball, Bat and Bishop*, 193–4.

65. Berkhofer, *Beyond the Great Story*, 31.

66. J. Olson, *Testimonial on the Cover of John Watterson, College Football: History, Spectacle, Controversy* (Baltimore: Johns Hopkins University Press, 2000).

67. Olson, *Testimonial on the Cover of John Watterson, College Football*.

68. Berkhofer, *Beyond the Great Story*, 32.

69. William H. Walsh, "Colligatory Concepts in History," in *The Philosophy of History*, ed. Patrick Gardiner (Oxford: Oxford University Press, 1974), 136.

70. White, *Metahistory*, 18–19.

71. Arthur Marwick, *The Sixties: Cultural Revolution in Britain, France, Italy, and the United States, c.1958–c.1974* (Oxford: Oxford University Press, 1998).

72. Elliot Gorn, "'Gouge and Bite, Pull Hair and Scratch,' The Social Significance of Fighting in the Southern Backcountry," *American Historical Review* 90 (1985): 22.

73. Gorn, "'Gouge and Bite, Pull Hair and Scratch,'" 36.

74. Berkhofer, *Beyond the Great Story*, 34.

75. Gorn, "'Gouge and Bite, Pull Hair and Scratch.'"

76. Berkhofer, *Beyond the Great Story*, 34.

77. Bryan Palmer, Review of Roy Rosenzweig, "Eight Hours for What We Will and Francis Couvares, the Remaking of Pittsburgh," *Social History* 10, no. 3 (1985): 400–04.

78. Berkhofer, *Beyond the Great Story*, 34.

79. Kevin McAleer, *Dueling: The Cult of Honor in Fin-de-Siècle Germany* (Princeton: Princeton University Press, 1994), 77–78.

80. Miles Fairburn, *Social History: Problems, Strategies and Methods* (New York: St. Martin's, 1999), 92.

81. Jeremy Black and Donald MacRaild, *Studying History* (London: Macmillan, 1997), 102.

82. Edward H. Carr, *What is History*, 2 ed. (Harmondsworth: Penguin Books, 1990), 104–05.

83. Theda Skocpol, *States and Social Revolutions: A Comparative Analysis of France, Russia and China* (Cambridge: Cambridge University Press, 1979), 35.

84. See for example, Bernard Whimpress, "Sporting Traditions X: The Debate Continues," *Victorian Bulletin of Sport and Culture* 6 (1996): 12–13.

85. Douglas Booth, "From Allusion to Causal Explanation: The Comparative Method in Sports History," *International Sports Studies* 22, no. 2 (2001): 5–25.

86. Malcolm Waters, *Modern Sociological Theory* (London: Sage, 1994), 92.

87. See for example, Murray G. Phillips, "Football, Class and War: The Rugby Codes in New South Wales, 1907–1918," in *Making Men: Rugby and Masculine Identity*, eds. John Nauright and Tim Chandler (London: Frank Cass, 1996): 158–80.

88. See for example, Richard Gruneau, *Class, Sports and Social Development* (Amherst: University of Massachusetts Press, 1983): 48.

89. Hardy, "Entrepreneurs, Structures, and the Sportgeist"; Stephen Hardy and Alan Ingham, "Games, Structures, and Agency: Historians on the Americal Play Movement," *Journal of Social History* 17 (1983): 285–301.

90. Hardy, "Entrepreneurs, Structures, and the Sportgeist," 54.

91. Hardy, "Entrepreneurs, Structures, and the Sportgeist," 54.

92. Hardy, "Entrepreneurs, Structures, and the Sportgeist," 54.

93. Hardy, "Entrepreneurs, Structures, and the Sportgeist," 53.

94. Hardy, "Entrepreneurs, Structures, and the Sportgeist," 54–55.

95. Tosh, *The Pursuit of History*, 154–55.

96. Tosh, *The Pursuit of History*, 154.

97. Richard Holt, *Sport and the British: A Modern History* (Oxford: Claredon, 1989), 362.

98. Holt, *Sport and the British*, 362.

99. Holt, *Sport and the British*, 362.

100. Jeffrey Alexander, "Modern, Anti-, Post and Neo," *New Left Review* 210 (1985): 63–101.

101. Jules Tygiel, *Baseball's Great Experiment: Jackie Robinson and His Legacy* (New York: Vintage Books, 1984); Patricia Vertinsky, *The Eternally Wounded Woman: Women, Doctors, and Exercise in the Late Nineteenth Century* (Urbana: University of Illinois Press, 1994); Susan Cahn, *Coming on Strong: Gender and Sexuality in the Twentieth Century* (Cambridge, MA: Harvard University Press, 1994); Mike Cronin, *Sport and Nationalism in Ireland: Gaelic Games, Soccer and Irish Identity since 1884* (Dublin: Four Courts, 1999); and Pamela Grundy, *Learning to Win: Sports, Education, and Social Change in Twentieth-Century North Carolina* (Chapel Hill: University of North Carolina Press, 2001).

102. Cronin, *Sport and Nationalism in Ireland*, 132.

103. Vertinsky, *The Eternally Wounded Woman*, 25.

104. Cahn, *Coming on Strong*, 251.

105. Berkhofer, *Beyond the Great Story*, 11.

106. Oriard, *Reading Football*, 2–3.

107. Oriard, *Reading Football*, 15.

108. Peter Mewett, "History in the Making and the Making of History: Stories and the Social Construction of Sport," *Sporting Traditions* 17, no. 1 (2000): 1–17; and Catriona Parratt, "Of Place and Men and Women: Gender and Topophilia in the 'Haxey Hood,'" *Journal of Sport History* 27, no. 2 (2000): 229–45.

109. Mewett, "History in the Making and the Making of History," 2, 14–15.

110. Richard Rorty, *Consequences of Pragmatism (Essays: 1972–1980)* (Brighton: Harvester Press, 1982), 152.

111. John Bloom, *To Show What an Indian Can Do: Sports at Native American Boarding Schools* (Minneapolis: University of Minnesota Press, 2000).

112. Berkhofer, *Beyond the Great Story*.

113. Synthia Sydnor, "A History of Synchronized Swimming," *Journal of Sport History* 25, no. 2 (1998): 252–67.

114. Joyce Appleby, Lyn Hunt, and Margaret Jacob, *Telling the Truth about History* (New York: Norton, 1994).

115. Grundy, *Learning to Win*, 300.

116. Grundy, *Learning to Win*, 301.

CHAPTER 2

Sport History between the Modern and Postmodern

BRETT HUTCHINS

In dealing with the challenge of postmodern historiography and theory to traditional modes of history, most of us will keep doing what we have always done—attempting to understand the past from the present. The contribution of postmodern thought, however, has been to encourage critical reflection on the processes and methods involved in writing about the past. In an age variously described as late modernity, radical modernity, liquid modernity, globalized, postfeminist, postcolonial and postindustrial, it is practical to engage with the giddying effect of postmodern thinking on the practice and understanding of history. Many of the challenges issued by this school of thought (if it can be thought of in these terms) are relevant and are irreducible to the ambivalence, uncertainty, risk, and anxiety that are central to contemporary social experience. Postmodern thought represents the interrogation of the self, a social and cultural order attempting to dissect former certainties that no longer hold or occasionally even make sense, and as part of this, a past that no longer speaks for itself. It is a traditional order turned upside down and hostile to the maintenance of illusions.

Postmodern thinkers ask useful questions about the epistemological and ontological foundations of the historical enterprise. They seek to bring into sight what would otherwise remain hidden in the assumptions of traditional historical approaches, particularly surrounding notions of objectivity, subject position, and truth. Keith Jenkins, Alun Munslow, Robert F. Berkhofer, Patrick Joyce, and F. R. Ankersmit have all supplied demanding and thought-provoking books and articles addressing how and why we write history.[1] The study of the past can no longer be an end in itself, if it ever was.

None of what has been said so far implies that postmodern historiography has or can devour traditional historical approaches or understanding. Debates between empiricist-cum-scientific historians and advocates of postmodern thinking have been unfolding for the past twenty-five years or more. These dialogues regularly end in deadlock and disengagement, often due to the assertions made and intemperate language used by antagonists. Stereotypically, the "corrosive logic" of the dreaded postmodernists is cast against the "naivety" of the uptight traditionalists.[2] This antipathy has created a seemingly unbridgeable divide that I argue is a false one, in that it fails to reflect the diversity of historical practice and the myriad approaches to the study of the past.

Only a small number of sport historians have addressed the issues introduced by "postist" theories.[3] Journals such as *The International Journal of the History of Sport* appear to farm out explicitly theoretical articles to sociology and cultural studies publications such as *Culture, Sport, Society*. The implication of this practice is that postmodern and theoretical approaches to the past are not considered proper or authentic history. Australia's *Sporting Traditions* has lately published the occasional article, but this has come after a protracted and regressive debate over "history" versus "theory." *Journal of Sport History* and *Sport History Review* appear open to the publication of the occasional article on postmodern historiography, which indicates a grudging engagement with the issues raised by an attempted reconfiguration of the historical project.

Sport history's lack of engagement with postmodern concepts and theories is disappointing as what is proposed *in practice* is not necessarily destructive to an understanding of the past. Jenkins, one of the most prolific practitioners among the postmodern brigade, is only half right when he claims that the traditional approaches of E. H. Carr and Geoffrey R. Elton are irrelevant in our "new times."[4] There is little doubt that history as a discipline has moved on from Carr and Elton, but any postmodern replacement is intrinsically reliant on modernist orthodoxies for its analysis and arguments. It is difficult to make a definitive break from modernist conceptions of history in the current social milieu. The postmodern needs the modern to award it conceptual, theoretical, and practical coherency. It is this dialectical interaction between the modern and postmodern that has become a guiding principle of historical practice.

This chapter argues that most historians analyze, research, and write in the crosscurrent of postmodern historiography and traditional empiricist modes of writing history. The contested relationship between these positions has resulted in searching questions on what can be known about the past via historical texts, examination of the structures and vagaries of language, and critique of representation. There is an increased awareness that "the foremost achievement of interpretation is keeping the job of interpretation going,"[5] and that the stories we tell about the past are also about the present and future. While I do not necessarily agree with or apply many postmodern theories and arguments, they do aid in critical reflection upon practice—the formation of research questions, the building of arguments, and the collation and critical use of texts. In the next section, I argue that this dialectic is not dissimilar to the long-running disputes over the respective positions of Elton and Carr. The case is made that the majority of historians unavoidably exist between the modern and postmodern and that this situation is a healthy one.

Discussion in the remainder of the chapter comments on the so-called acids of postmodernity and how they are not as threatening to collective understanding of the past as has been made out by some staunch traditionalists. I also explain that cultural sociology has been analyzing the role and validity of history in the structuring of social life since the interwar years and provides some useful pointers in negotiating the modern-postmodern divide. Finally, I supply an example of how I have dealt with the epistemological uncertainty created by postmodern historiography and the crisis of representation in my research on sporting icons from the past.

DIALECTICS

Debate over epistemology has long been a characteristic of history. For the past thirty years or more, history courses and texts have made reference to the opposing viewpoints of Carr and Elton.[6] It is the relevance of the Carr-Elton divide to present historical practice that is in question. Jenkins declares that the approaches of both men are now outdated and outmoded and that there must be new histories and new ways of writing history that are relevant to a postmodern age.[7] Although Jenkins' case is contentious, thirty to forty years is a lengthy period for any two books to remain at the center of a curriculum. Perhaps part of the reason why Carr and Elton have remained prominent for so long is the bracken-like prose of much postmodern historiography, which can be confronting and sometimes confusing for the uninitiated. On revisiting Carr's *What Is History?* after a ten-year hiatus, I found much to recommend it: lucid prose, perceptive insights, and a clear vision of the function of history as a positive social force. Similarly, Elton's *Practice of History* is thought provoking, while his more recent *Return to Essentials* is notable for its rancor toward theorists such as Dominick LaCapra, Michel Foucault, Hayden White, and Jacques Derrida.[8] Nevertheless, both Elton and Carr make astute points about the role of the historian, the use of sources, notions of objectivity, and ideas of causation.

Carr and Elton have served a necessary function. For decades they provided a key reference point and a way of thinking through historical practice for students, teachers, and practitioners. The point of departure between Carr and Elton concerns the role of evidence. Carr's "present-mindedness" is contrasted with Elton's faith in the Rankean ideal of showing "how things actually were." As Richard Evans summarizes

> He [Carr] challenges and undermines the belief that . . . history is simply a matter of objective fact. He introduces the idea that history books, like the people who write them, are products of their own times, and that their authors bring particular ideas and ideologies to bear on the past. Against Carr's relativistic approach to historical study, it is a common tactic to pit G. R. Elton's *The Practice of History*, published in 1967. Elton's book mounts a trenchant defence of the belief that history is a search for the objective truth about the past.[9]

Historians of all hues must engage with this debate, unless the aim of writing history, however partial, selective, and contested, is to show the past as it was not. This also implies that the past cannot be moulded into any shape desired from moment to moment like wet clay on a spinning wheel (more on this later). The task of history is to make sense of the past from the present and to then assess the role, power, and knowledge claims of historical interpretation in the contemporary context. Not coincidentally, this is a concern of postmodern historiography.

Intellectual work generally stands or falls on the basis of its merits, and the criteria by which judgement is made intersect with current issues and collective meanings circulating in a wider social and cultural environment. It is this context that helps to decide what "makes some accounts *count*."[10] A convincing interpretation of the past is always necessary, but to produce authoritative and resonant history, interpretation must have direct relevance to the present. Carr and Elton alone can no longer serve as adequate templates given that they wrote the majority of their books and articles while the Cold War was being fought, before the aftershocks of Vietnam were felt, when globalization was still an abstract concept, and the "new world (dis)order" of Bush Senior was only a (bad) dream.

Carr and Elton have recently moved from opposition to coalition. They stand as the figureheads of a modernist historical practice that is locked in exchange with the "new" history of postmodern practitioners. Jenkins testified to the existence of this dialectical interaction with the 1995 publication of On *"What is History?" From Carr and Elton to Rorty and White*, in which he critiques "old" ways of doing history and promotes the "new." Defenders and followers of traditional history might well view this book as a backhanded compliment. A new history can only be envisioned in relation to the key texts, methods, and ideas of the past, and a modernist model of historical practice serves this purpose. In other words, Carr and Elton are one of the poles guiding historiography and cannot be ignored.

Exchange between opposing positions and schools of thought defines, stabilizes, and motivates the practice of historians. The question of why I undertake a course of action in *this* way, as opposed to *that* way, helps me to rationalize and justify my arguments and methods. Exchange between modern and postmodern positions has increasingly been performing this function, as shown by the debates in historical journals such as *Past and Present* and *History and Theory*, and the publication of edited collections such as *The Postmodern History Reader* and *History and Theory* (and this volume you are reading).[11] Viewed in this light, the rise of postmodern historiography, in conjunction with the impressive stubbornness of masters such as Carr and Elton in leaving the stage, offers a dialectic that is more in tune with the contemporary world.

Lynn Hunt counterposes traditional and postmodern models of history when she describes a postmodern practice as a type of selection process. It is antiessentialist and recognizes that it is impossible to penetrate a somehow pure historical "reality" and/or "truth." Historians can only selectively represent *a*, as opposed to *the*, past, and are limited to *interpreting*, as opposed to recounting, what occurred in that past.[12] This conception of history is part and parcel of a "cultural turn" that has seen a movement away from the traditional aim of analysing the social *per se* and toward looking critically at meaning in culture: "To put it simply, culture is about 'shared meanings.'"[13] It is these meanings that organize and regulate the practice and understanding of history.

Table 2.1 provides an "ideal-type snapshot" of selected parallels between traditional and postmodern approaches. The table highlights how partisans have plotted, and sometimes caricatured, the traditional and postmodern positions in the literature. The difference presented is between a "fixed" analytical stance emphasizing coherency, structure, and certainty and a more "open-ended" mindset that concentrates upon shifting meanings, tensions within structure, and contending interpretations.

The most obvious problem with this snapshot is that few historians fit neatly into either column. To subscribe to one position and disregard the other is to deny the strictures and requirements of practice when investigating the past. Human behavior, be it now or then, has the frustrating habit of refusing to yield to theoretical models. Practices, ideas, theories, and

Table 2.1. Traditional and Postmodern Approaches[14]

Traditional	Postmodern
The past is a coherent totality that is understandable in terms of a chronological, linear master narrative.	The past is unknowable, questions exist over the capability of language structures to represent the past, and multiple contending interpretations and narratives exist in any understanding of events, people, and periods.
Preoccupation with presenting the past "as it happened," allows the past "to speak for itself," and attempts to divorce interpretation from contemporary concerns.	Preoccupation with the "crisis of representation" bought on in conjunction with the crises of legitimation and experience characterizing the contemporary world system. Current concerns and issues unavoidably shape historical interpretation.
A conceptualization of language as a realist and effective vehicle to represent the past and an avoidance of theory.	A radical conceptualization of language that challenges whether language, narratives, and texts can adequately represent the past. An emphasis on linguistic philosophy and theorizing.
Adherence to the principle of historical realism, the concept of 'truth,' the attainability of objectivity, and subsequently, the invisibility of the subject. History is a realist extension of a lived past that can lead to a better understanding of human experience and a superior society.	A critique of historical realism and the concepts of 'objectivity,' 'truth,' and the 'author.' The texts of history can no longer be read as a "realist" extension of a lived past. A profound scepticism toward realist, objective history as a force that can help guide us toward a superior society.
The subject is an unproblematic dimension of history. History is largely written from the perspective of white men, privilege, and cultural domination. Ignorance of or resistance to the experiences of subordinated racial, ethnic, and gendered groups.	A critique of the subject in history as witnessed by the rise of postcolonial and feminist histories. A call for new ways of doing history that account for these new images, particularly for those groups previously marginalized on the basis of race, ethnicity, and gender.
Little or no question over the legitimacy of the institutional and political structures of government, universities, funding bodies, and publishers. The influence of these structures is overridden by a commitment to the pursuit of objectivity and truth.	Concerns over the institutional and political structures in which histories are produced (e.g., publicly and privately funded universities, publishers owned by multinational corporations, government-funded histories) and the ideological effects that these structures have on interpretation.
Metanarratives of the Enlightenment project such as progress, reason, and rationality guide the writing of history. An essentialist and objective pursuit of truth is central to the functioning of a society based on consensus, freedom, and rational communicative action.	A concern for the collapse of metanarratives in history (the Enlightenment project and accompanying conceptions of progress and rationality). Antiessentialist and relativist modes of interpretation are to the fore, reflecting a distrust of reason and rationality.

concepts are sampled, read, incorporated, twisted, turned, and molded according to the requirements of the task at hand. Indeterminacy is the constant companion of history as writing about the past is an on-going and dynamic exercise that defies inflexible rules and neat categorization.

An unfortunate tendency of essays, books, and journal articles on the merits of postmodern historiography written by the new guard and the modernist old guard is that historians appear exclusively consigned to one camp or the other. Such an artificial separation denies that the theoretical expositions of Nancy Partner, John Toews, or Gabrielle Spiegel provoke as much reflection on the nature of the past and how we come to understand it as the more traditional arguments of Gertrude Himmelfarb, Bryan Palmer, or Perez Zagorin.[15] These debates are as much about staking out intellectual territory and authority as plotting an approach and providing analytical insight. In constructing both a fortified position and an opponent, combatants occasionally enlist authors whose work is neither traditional nor postmodern. Jenkins, for example, drafts White into the cause of postmodern history, despite the fact that he is better described as a structuralist whose work relates more to Ferdinand de Saussure and Roland Barthes than the postmodern stylizing of Jean Baudrillard and Jean-François Lyotard.[16] Similarly, Derrida and Foucault appear in *The Postmodern History Reader*, as well as in the crosshairs of Elton, yet both theorists are usually considered poststructuralist.[17] The term *postmodern* then, right or wrong, is applied to historians who openly use theory and acknowledge the discursive character of history. In contrast, whether they like it or not, those who maintain a faith in empiricism, avoid theoretical meanderings, and hold a firm position when faced with the vicissitudes of discourse are labeled "traditionalists." This division fails to accurately reflect the diversity of practice as the methods and approaches of most historians, given their respective situations within social life and the contending influences and fashions within the academy, are coordinated by and lie somewhere between the "ideal" traditional and postmodern models. In spite of this, some critics still claim that postmodern thought has caused irrevocable damage to shared historical understanding, an issue that is taken up in the next section.

THE "ACIDS OF POSTMODERNITY"

The carping of traditionalists such as Keith Windschuttle about the drawbacks of postmodern historiography is out of proportion to its impact.[18] Interrogating the epistemological and ontological foundations of history cannot lay waste to all that has gone before. As set out in table 2.1, many of the claims made by postmodern historians exist ideally and defy the compromises and constraints involved in writing something meaningful about the past that makes sense to others.

Cultural sociology offers some useful hints for handling the modern-postmodern conundrum. History has always been a dimension of sociological research. Karl Marx, Max Weber, C. Wright-Mills, Zygmunt Bauman, Norbert Elias and Philip Abrams are but a small selection of researchers and writers who have emphasised the role of history in the analysis of social relations.[19] For my purposes, the Durkheimian Maurice Halbwachs (1877–1945) is a chief figure. He wrote much of his work during the interwar years, coming to prominence again in 1992 with the translation and republication of many of his essays in *On Collective Memory*.[20] Interested in sources of intellectual and emotional solidarity amongst people, he examined festivals, storytelling, religion and commemorations. He was especially concerned with the way that communities recount and mythologise the past through the creation of "collective memory," which is "essentially a reconstruction of the past in light of the present":[21]

> Halbwachs argued that it was the needs, problems, and beliefs of the present that determined the memory of the past. The collective memory, then, was constantly being renewed and reshaped with each passing generation.[22]

Halbwachs' notion of collective memory recalls the position of Carr but figures most obviously in the work of David Lowenthal and his declaration that "the past is a foreign country" that can only be understood from the perspective of the current day.[23]

In a postmodern context, collective memory is a difficult idea to sustain. Signs possess multiple meanings, these meanings shift according to perspective and experience, and the notion of the collective itself is under attack from individualist ideologies and technologies in an image driven consumer society. These are interesting ideas and important developments within *selected* settings and *specific* contexts, but it is a mistake to overestimate their power. Shared meanings do exist and people act upon agreed understandings. Social life could not exist without such transactions. Commemoration of tragic events such as September 11, the celebration of admired figures like Jackie Robinson and the mourning of Diana, Princess of Wales, are experienced as real and communal despite being mediated and represented. Even allowing for the unevenness of reactions across groups and between individuals, events such as these still command collective reflection and emotional response.[24]

Building on Halbwachs' concept of "collective memory," American cultural sociologists Barry Schwartz and Michael Schudson have completed compelling studies on figures such as American Presidents Abraham Lincoln and George Washington and events such as the Watergate scandal and the construction of the Vietnam Veterans Memorial in Washington D.C.[25] These studies demonstrate how historical accounts, texts, and monuments play an undeniable role in structuring public remembering. Historical narratives—popular, contested, and mythical—filter through current meanings associated with figures such as Lincoln and Washington. Historical understanding is the result of an ongoing dialogue between historical texts and past understanding and contemporary texts and meaning.

The case outlined here is an advance on Halbwachs' argument that the concerns of the present determine the memory of the past, which implies that the past is pliant and continually manipulated. Schudson argues that the past can be "highly resistant to efforts to make it over."[26] Resistance occurs because former "construction[s] of an historical object restricts and limits the range of things subsequent generations can do with it."[27] For instance, I cannot absurdly speculate that British war hero Douglas Bader was a member of a satanic cult without inviting incredulity and outrage, as the textual traces are simply not available to sustain this conclusion. Postmodern history may undercut the notion of an uncontested truth and a linear narrative, but the contending truths and narratives that take their place must at least be credible.

The contribution of Schwartz and Schudson is to integrate the postmodern turn, contemporary experience, and the continuing role of historical meaning in social life. Schwartz summarizes this neatly, "Diminished rather than lost engagement with the past distinguishes the postmodern era."[28] In examining popular recollections of Abraham Lincoln, he states that the "acids of postmodernity" and the social change, uncertainty, and fragmentation that flows with them have lessened the collective recognition of Lincoln in the American memory.[29] However, a section of people still admire him, particularly from "the privileged strata" of society, and most people at least recognize his significance superficially. This runs against the overwhelming "corrosive logic" that postmodern thinking is supposed to represent:

> Critics of the postmodernity thesis assert that its proponents speak "on behalf of a humanity whose gods they alone have declared dead" (O'Neill 1995: 197). These critics are wrong. The decline of grand narratives and their heroes, of which the story of Abraham Lincoln is but one instance, is demonstrable. Yet if these narratives have deteriorated as fully as postmodern theorizing suggests, the minority of Americans who still revere Lincoln and other traditional heroes would not be as large as it is . . . America's metanarrative has been

greatly weakened by the postmodern turn, but it is neither "incredulous" nor bereft of "its functors, its great heroes . . . its great goal" (Lyotard [1979] 1984: xxiv).[30]

Even under the conditions of postmodernity, successive generations need collective symbols and meanings to connect with one another. An important function of history is to provide this continuity. "Islands of tradition"—grand stories, metanarratives, and heroes—may be eroding and visited in a multiplicity of ways, but they nevertheless remain.[31]

The modern and the postmodern are two sides of the same coin. Order and pluralization are intrinsically linked, and in addressing one attention must be paid to the other.[32] Schudson and Schwartz supply some useful ideas and arguments in dealing with this delicate balancing act and indicate that it is no longer possible to stand firmly on either side of the divide. The only realistic option in this climate is to apply reason and reflexivity in plotting a path on the terrain that exists between the mountains of tradition and fast-moving waters of postmodern theory.

THEORY AND PRACTICE

This section outlines my attempt to deal with the epistemological challenge of writing history in the new millennium, particularly given the crisis of representation that arrived with the postmodern turn. It is based on my research and writing on Sir Donald Bradman (1908–2001), Australia's most renowned cricketer and sports hero.[33] In line with the traditional-postmodern interplay that I have discussed throughout this chapter, my approach sought to recognize the impermanent and shifting character of meaning and representation, while still attempting to make sense of the formation of collective understanding about the past. Concepts from social theory and intellectual history were applied within a traditional narrative structure that eschewed theoretical jargon. The study attempts to come to terms with the historical representation and significance of Bradman in Australian culture and how his historical image is understood and communicated now. It involved putting the case of Schudson and Schwartz—that the past is in some respects resistant to being remade—into practice. The historical story of Bradman is widely known, displays longevity and is resistant to change; yet he has also been represented in a multiplicity of ways and for different purposes in the contemporary context. In detailing my approach, the underlying message is that the relationship between the modern and postmodern and its accompanying epistemological uncertainty resists a "one-size-fits-all" response, demanding that each project be dealt with on its own terms and in line with its specific requirements and limitations.

For those unfamiliar with the story of Bradman, he has been described as Australia's one national hero, is referred to simply as "the Don" by many, and was once described by the current prime minister as "the greatest living Australian." Biographers and commentators have alluded to Einstein, Mozart, Keats, and Shakespeare in measuring his skill. The national media outpouring at news of his death in February 2001 matched such hyperbole. Bradman's first-class playing career spanned the years 1927–1949. He continuously broke batting records, finishing with the unsurpassed and totemic test average of 99.94 runs per innings. He captained the national side, never losing a series. In retirement he received a knighthood, a Companion of the Order of Australia, and served as chairman of the Australian Cricket Board. *International Who's Who* named him as one of only two Australians among the top one hundred people who have done the most to shape the twentieth century. (The other former Australian was Rupert Murdoch. Bradman was also one of just three sportspeople selected, alongside boxer Muhammad Ali and football's Pele). He is also one of the few sportspeople in the world to have a museum, the Bradman Museum in Bowral, New South Wales, dedicated to his memory.

Facing up to the legend of Bradman involves confronting a large amount of literature that is a product of the past but that also exercises a fundamental influence on recollections of him in the present. Over fifty-five books were published on Bradman or used his name in their title between 1930 and 2001, and media reports, documentaries, museum displays, memorabilia, novels, and songs supplement these titles. An explosion of renewed interest in a mythical Bradman has occurred since the 1980s, supported by a publishing industry boom, a highly successful television miniseries, the founding of the museum, and regular attention from both the electronic and print media.[34] In a postmodern realm there are no fixed meanings: "[A]ll distinctions become fluid, boundaries dissolve, and everything can just as well appear to be its opposite."[35] Therefore, attempting to explain the various nationalist, political, economic, mythical, and gendered discourses articulated through representations of Bradman poses difficulty. Simultaneously, Bradman is a popular historical figure with an established and widely known story and a sign that has no essential meaning. In theory his representations possess infinite meanings, are intertextually rendered, and seem to have no center forcing them to maintain their shape. Crisis is an apt description as the relationship blurs between the past and the present.

In restoring vision, analyzing representation is helpful. Representation binds the relationship between shared meaning and history. Meaning is produced, transmitted, and circulated through the representation of historical reality in various forms of communication, be these words, images, objects, sounds, or impulses.[36] These words, and images, and so on—signs—do not possess meaning in and of themselves. They operate as symbols that carry meaning in relation to other symbols within particular systems of communication.[37] Bradman's story then is constructed within a representational system, which, in turn, is constituted by discourses operating within Australian culture and history. In comprehending how meaning is anchored and how shared understanding is created, Stuart Hall's concept of "articulation" is helpful in countering the theoretical possibility that a sign produces endless meanings.[38] Articulation is a process that seeks to explain how representations attain *relatively* stable meanings: "[W]ithout some arbitrary 'fixing' or what I am calling 'articulation,' there would be no signification at all. What is ideology but, precisely, this work of fixing meaning through establishing, by selection and combination, a chain of equivalences?"[39]

The meanings of representations are not permanently fixed or uncontested, but dominant or preferred readings do develop in relation to specific frameworks of history and culture.[40] In Bradman's case, there is a very well established repertoire of cultural meanings and historical stories associated with him. Collective memory of him is formed in relation to these stories. Any new representation of him unavoidably exists in the context of those already known and acknowledged. Not all the meanings elicited by Bradman mesh consistently, but despite any unevenness, they do manage to articulate a unity in the ways that he is remembered.

Representation is a practice that uses material objects and effects.[41] In the case of Bradman these are auto/biographies, histories, books, articles, and documentaries that discuss his significance and meaning. In addition, there are also those representations contained in souvenirs, advertisements, audio recordings, celebratory videos, and the commercial media that consciously re-present and re-image Bradman for various nationalist, economic, and political ends. All of these make it possible to show how the public figure of Donald Bradman is constituted by a system of representation operating within Australian culture. By investigating the major ideological sites of power in this system—nationalism, mythology, politics, economics, gender—and examining the various continuities and discontinuities, an overall case is made for how preferred or dominant historical readings of Bradman arise and are perpetuated.

In further analyzing the epistemology of historical practices and representation, LaCapra's concept of "dialogic reading" aids in explaining how dominant meanings emerge and historians construct interpretation.[42] LaCapra states that dialogism refers "in a dual fashion both to the mutually challenging or contestatory interplay of forces in language and to the comparable interaction between social agents in various specific historical contexts . . . [A] dialogic approach is based on a distinction . . . between accurate reconstruction of an object of study and exchange with that object as well as with other inquirers into it."[43] To put it another way, it is to examine the relations in and between many texts—biographies, articles, other historians, and so on. Despite LaCapra's complex explanation, this is a reasonably straightforward intertextual practice that is undertaken by most historians.

Collective memory of Bradman is not produced by or limited to one book such as his autobiography, *Farewell to Cricket*, originally released in 1950.[44] If this text had exhausted the possible knowledge and meanings of Bradman, there would have been no need for another seven in-depth biographies since, not to mention their reprints. An adequate understanding of Bradman cannot be achieved via a single text any more than it is possible to comprehend the social and political significance of The Sex Pistols from only one song or the influence of Alfred Hitchcock on cinema from one film. Meaning cannot be completely contained in its formation, expression, or consumption for, as Bennett and Woollacott argue, it "exists within a constantly mobile set of inter-textual relations."[45] Bradman is a representative figure whose meanings are constituted and stabilized via a range of available texts: books, articles, videos, documentaries, souvenirs, memorabilia, museums, songs, and advertisements. No single site can command *ultimate* control of the meaning of Bradman as each new representation is interpreted relative to the previous one, and these also interact with others already in existence. In both reflecting and constituting the meanings of the Don, these dialogic relations organize the interpretations and expectations of historians and readers.

Dialogism highlights the argument made earlier that former "construction[s] of an historical object restrict and limit the range of things subsequent generations can do with it." Schudson and Schwartz are correct in pointing out the resistance of the past to being made over, as the dialogic process of writing history constructs boundaries within which interpretation must remain if it is to be plausible. In other words, it is ridiculous to conceive of either Bradman or Bader as members of a satanic cult. Textual evidence is required to substantiate such claims. Texts and stories give a shape to the past that acts on the present and vice versa. Conversely, within textual boundaries, the notion of a single truth or a definitive "right" answer cannot be supported. Evidence can be arranged in multiple ways and read from different positions, but, nevertheless, continuities and discontinuities in the available texts do point toward some interpretations being more likely than others.

A by-product of a dialogic approach is that it avoids spurious attempts at constructing a putatively "real" Bradman—the essential "man" behind the "myth"—instead targeting the multiple social and cultural representations that construct the varied and changing understandings of the Don. The historical practice I have outlined resulted in the emergence of several Bradmans: the relentless run-machine, the boy from the bush, the brave fighter facing up to bodyline bowling, the businessman and administrator, the nation-builder, the devoted husband, the apolitical sportsman, the solitary man, the trademark, the unseen hero living in retirement, and the deceased Australian hero. All of these representations and their meanings deserve attention as they have had different effects at different times, and together they have generated the collective memory of Bradman over the best part of three-quarters of a century. All have a demonstrable relationship to the creation of historical meanings associated with the Don. None infer that Bradman was somehow an "unreal" or fictional character—anything does not go in this story. Most importantly, this approach gives an account of those representations that have elevated Bradman from cricketer to cultural icon.

WHERE TO NOW?

Despite the cries of traditionalists, the death of collective meaning and with it history is greatly exaggerated. Meanings generated from past experiences still manage to attain coherency and are shared between social groups. What the postmodern critique has provoked is a keener appreciation of the intricacies involved in this process. It has increased awareness of the slippages and tensions in accounts of the past, made us alive to the limitations of sources and methods, and when faced with the immensity of the past forces humility in constructing interpretation. Moreover, postmodern thought has created a better appreciation of the ways in which meanings can shift and change and how nothing should be taken for granted. These are useful lessons, irrespective of whether one tends to prefer a traditional or "cutting-edge" approach. By placing history as a discipline on notice and declaring former certainties no more, postmodern historiography is helping to create a more responsive historical practice. The lessons of the modernist teachers, however, have not been forgotten or surrendered. Rather, they play a fundamental role in a dialectic that is guiding how and why we study the past.

Accepting the existence and utility of a dialectical interaction between the modern and postmodern does not automatically light the path to understanding. Many historians are caught in two or more minds, ambivalent about which way to move as any topic can be approached from multiple directions. My approach to writing a cultural history of Bradman is not necessarily an answer for others. In resisting universal laws and uniform responses, contemporary historical practice requires flexibility and self-reflexivity. Each project has to be dealt with on its own merits, which also creates room for creativity and innovation. None of this means that nihilism rules and "anything goes." Such conditions only apply if, as I said earlier, the aim of writing history is to show the past as it was not. Nonetheless, historical practice must possess an overarching awareness of epistemological issues and limits. As has long been the case, this is the foundation of writing convincing and rigorous history.

The job of practicing historians is to navigate assuredly between the modern and postmodern poles by writing history that not only attempts to capture the rhythms and contours of the past but that is relevant and meaningful in the present. Sport researchers such as Phillips, Parratt, Pope, and Oriard have already shown that a *critical* engagement with postmodern thought, either explicitly or implicitly, does not destroy vibrancy or insight.[46] It is hoped that their examples will provide the impetus for evolution within sport history, resulting in the journals of the subdiscipline offering a greater diversity in content and sustained attention to debates occurring in the wider context of both intellectual and social history. If this begins to happen sport historians may claim some of the ground occupied by social theorists who are currently the authorities on the linkages between sport and the postmodern.[47]

NOTES

Thank you to Keith Jenkins, Janine Mikosza, and Warren Sproule for their helpful comments on drafts of this chapter.

1. K. Jenkins, *Re-thinking History* (London: Routledge, 1991); K. Jenkins, *On "What Is History?" From Carr and Elton to Rorty and White* (London: Routledge, 1995); K. Jenkins, "Introduction: On Being Open about Our Closures," in *The Postmodern History Reader*, ed. K. Jenkins (London: Routledge, 1997), 1–30; K. Jenkins, *Why History? Ethics and Postmodernity* (London: Routledge, 1999); A. Munslow, *Deconstructing History* (London: Routledge, 1997); R. F. Berkhofer, *Beyond the Great Story: History and Text as Discourse* (Cambridge: Harvard University Press, 1995); P. Joyce, "The Return of History: Postmodernism and the Politics of Academic History in Britain," *Past and Present* 158 (1998): 207–35; F. R. Ankersmit, "Historiography and Postmodernism," in *History and Theory: Contemporary Readings*, eds. B. Fay, P. Pomper, and R. T. Vann (Oxford: Blackwell, 1998), 175–92.

2. For examples of these two positions see G. Davison, *The Use and Abuse of Australian History* (St. Leonards, NSW: Allen and Unwin, 2000), 15–17 and Jenkins, *Re-thinking History*.

3. For example, see J. Hill, "British Sports History: A Post-Modern Future?" *Journal of Sport History* 23, no. 1 (1996): 1–19; C. M. Parratt,

"About Turns: Reflecting on Sport History in the 1990s," *Sport History Review* 29, no. 1 (1998): 4–17; M. G. Phillips, "Navigating Uncharted Waters: The Death of Sports History?" *Sporting Traditions* 16, no. 1 (1999): 51–59; S. W. Pope, "Sport History: Into the Twenty-First Century," *Journal of Sport History* 25, no. 2 (1998): i–x; S. Syndor, "A History of Synchronized Swimming," *Journal of Sport History* 25, no. 2 (1998): 252–67.

4. Jenkins, *On "What Is History?"* 1–14.

5. Z. Bauman, "The Journey Never Ends: Zygmunt Bauman Talks with Peter Beilharz," in *The Bauman Reader,* ed. P. Beilharz (Oxford: Blackwell, 2001), 340.

6. E. H. Car, *What Is History?* (Ringwood, Victoria: Penguin, 1990); G. R. Elton, *The Practice of History* (London: Fontana, 1967).

7. Jenkins, *On "What Is History?"* 1–14.

8. G. R. Elton, *Return to Essentials* (Cambridge: Cambridge University Press, 1991).

9. R. Evans, *In Defence of History* (London: Granta Books, 1997), 2.

10. A. Giddens, "Hermeneutics, Ethnomethodology, and Problems of Interpretative Analysis," in *The Uses of Controversy in Sociology,* eds. L. A. Coser and O. N. Larsen (New York: Free Press, 1979), 325.

11. *Past and Present,* 131, 133, 135, 158 (1991, 1992, 1998); *History and Theory* 33, no. 2 (1994): 34; no. 1 (1995): 38; np. 1 (1999); Jenkins, *The Postmodern History Reader*; Fay, Pomper, and Vann, *History and Theory: Contemporary Readings.*

12. L. Hunt, "Does History Need Defending?" *History Workshop Journal* 46 (1998): 242; See also L. Hunt, *The New Cultural History* (Berkeley: University of California Press, 1989); J. Appleby, L. Hunt, and M. Jacob, *Telling the Truth about History* (New York: Norton, 1994).

13. S. Hall, "Introduction," in *Representation: Cultural Representations and Signifying Practices,* ed. S. Hall (London: Sage, 1997), 1. See also W. J. Bouwsma, "Intellectual History in the 1980s: From the History of Ideas to History of Meaning," *Journal of Interdisciplinary History* 12, no. 2 (1981): 283–90.

14. Table developed from the literature listed thus far and N. K. Denzin, "Postmodern Social Theory," *Sociological Theory* 4 (Fall 1986): 194–204.

15. N. F. Partner, "Making Up for Lost Time: Writing on the Writing of History," *Speculum* 61, no. 1 (1986): 90–117; J. E. Toews, "Intellectual History After the Linguistic Turn: The Autonomy of Meaning and the Irreducibility of Experience," *American Historical Review* 92 (1987): 879–907; G. M. Spiegel, "History, Historicism, and the Social Logic of the Text in the Middle Ages," *Speculum* 65, no. 1 (1990): 59–86; G. Himmelfarb, "Telling It as You Like It: Postmodernist History and the Flight from Fact," in *The*

Postmodern History Reader, 158–74; B. D. Palmer, "Critical Theory, Historical Materialism, and the Ostensible End of Marxism: The Poverty of Theory Revisited," *International Review of Social History* 38, no. 2 (1993): 133–62; P. Zagorin, "Historiography and Postmodernism: Reconsiderations," in *History and Theory*, 193–205.

16. See Jenkins, *On "What Is History?" From Carr and Elton to Rorty and White*; H. White, "The Burden of History," *History and Theory* 5, no. 2 (1966): 111–34; H. White, *Tropics of Discourse: Essays in Cultural Criticism* (Baltimore: John Hopkins University Press, 1978); H. White, "Introduction to Metahistory," in *Literature in the Modern World*, ed. D. Walder (Oxford: Oxford University Press, 1990), 341–46; R. Barthes, "The Discourse of History," *Comparative Criticism: A Yearbook* 3 (1981): 3–20.

17. Jenkins, *The Postmodern History Reader*; Elton, *Return to Essentials*.

18. K. Windschutttle, *The Killing of History: How a Discipline is Being Murdered by Literary Critics and Social Theorists* (Sydney: Macleay, 1994).

19. K. Marx, "The Materialist Conception of History," in *Karl Marx: Selected Writings*, ed. D. McLellan (Oxford: Oxford University Press, 1977), 129–218; M. Weber, *The Methodology of the Social Sciences*, trans. and ed. E. A. Shils and H. A. Finch (New York: Free Press, 1949); C. Wright Mills, *The Sociological Imagination* (New York: Oxford University Press, 1959); Z. Bauman, *Memories of Class: The Pre-History and After-Life of Class* (London: Routledge and Kegan Paul, 1982); Z. Bauman, *Modernity and the Holocaust* (Cambridge: Polity, 1989); N. Elias, *What Is Sociology?* (London: Hutchins, 1978); P. Abrams, *Historical Sociology* (Somerset: Open Books, 1982).

20. M. Halbwachs, *On Collective Memory*, trans. and ed. L. A. Coser (Chicago: University of Chicago Press, 1992).

21. L. A. Coser, "Introduction: Maurice Halbwachs 1877–1945," in *On Collective Memory*, 34.

22. P. Smith, *Cultural Theory: An Introduction* (Oxford: Blackwell, 2001), 78.

23. D. Lowenthal, *The Past Is a Foreign Country* (Cambridge: Cambridge University Press, 1985); see also D. Lowenthal, "Nostalgia Tells It Like It Wasn't," in *The Imagined Past: History and Nostalgia*, eds. C. Shaw and M. Chase (Manchester: Manchester University Press, 1989), 18–32; D. Lowenthal, "Uses of the Past in Australia," in *Australia Towards 2000*, ed. B. Hocking (London: Macmillan, 1990), 46–54; D. Lowenthal, *The Heritage Crusade and the Spoils of History* (Melbourne: Cambridge University Press, 1998).

24. D. Dayan and E. Katz, *Media Events: The Live Broadcasting of History* (Cambridge: Harvard University Press, 1992).

25. M. Schudson, "The Present in the Past versus the Past in the Present," *Communication* 11 (1989): 105–13; M. Schudson, *Watergate in*

American Memory: How We Remember, Forget, and Reconstruct the Past (New York: Basic Books, 1992); B. Schwartz, "The Social Context of Commemoration: A Study in Collective Memory," *Social Forces* 61, no. 2 (1982): 374–97; B. Schwartz, "Social Change and Collective Memory: The Democratization of George Washington," *American Sociological Quarterly* 56 (1991): 221–36; B. Schwartz, "Introduction: The Expanding Past," *Qualitative Sociology* 19, no. 3 (1996): 275–82; B. Schwartz, "Collective Memory and History: How Abraham Lincoln Became a Symbol of Racial Equality," *The Sociological Quarterly* 38, no. 3 (1997): 469–96; B. Schwartz, "Postmodernity and Historical Reputation: Abraham Lincoln in Late Twentieth-Century American Memory," *Social Forces* 77, no. 1 (1998): 63–103; R. Wagner-Pacifici and B. Schwartz, "The Vietnam Veterans Memorial: Commemorating a Difficult Past," *American Journal of Sociology* 97, no. 2 (1991): 376–420.

26. Schudson, "The Present in the Past versus the Past in the Present," 107.

27. Schwartz, "Social Change and Collective Memory," 232.

28. Schwartz, "Postmodernity and Historical Reputation," 93.

29. Schwartz, "Postmodernity and Historical Reputation," 80.

30. Schwartz, "Postmodernity and Historical Reputation," 93; in-text references are from J. O'Neill, *The Poverty of Postmodernism* (New York: Routledge, 1995); Jean-Francois Lyotard, *The Postmodern Condition* (Minneapolis: University of Minnesota Press, 1984).

31. Schwartz, "Postmodernity and Historical Reputation," 88.

32. Z. Bauman, "A Sociological Theory of Postmodernity," in *The Bauman Reader*, ed. P. Beilharz (Oxford: Blackwell, 2001), 173–88.

33. B. Hutchins, *Don Bradman: Challenging the Myth* (Melbourne: Cambridge University Press, 2002).

34. See my study for discussion of these issues. Hutchins, *Don Bradman*.

35. Harvie Ferguson cited in Z. Bauman, *Liquid Modernity* (Cambridge: Polity, 2000), 87.

36. G. Turner, *National Fictions: Literature, Film and the Construction of Australian Narrative* (St. Leonards, NSW: Allen and Unwin, 1993), 6.

37. Hall, "Introduction," in *Representation*, 5.

38. S. Hall, "Signification, Representation, Ideology: Althusser and the Post-Structuralist Debates," *Critical Studies in Mass Communication* 2, no. 2 (1985): 93; See also J. McKay, "'Just Do It': Corporate Sports Slogans and the Political Economy of "Enlightened Racism,'" *Discourse: Studies in the Cultural Politics of Education* 16, no. 2 (1995): 191–92.

39. Hall, "Signification, Representation, Ideology," 93.

40. Hall's argument is not dissimilar to Barthe's explanation of myth and its function in relation to history and culture. R. Barthes, *Mythologies* (London: Paladin, 1973).

41. Hall, "The Work of Representation," in *Representation*, 25–26.

42. For examples of LaCapra's writing see D. LaCapra, *History and Criticism* (Ithaca: Cornell University Press, 1985); D. LaCapra, *History and Reading: Tocqueville, Foucault, French Studies* (Melbourne: Melbourne University Press, 2000).

43. D. LaCapra, "History, Language, and Reading: Waiting for Crillon," *American Historical Review* 100 (1995): 824–25.

44. D.G. Bradman, *Farewell to Cricket* (Sydney: ETT Imprint, 1994).

45. T. Bennett and J. Woollacott, *Bond and Beyond: The Political Career of a Popular Hero* (Hampshire: Macmillan Education, 1987), 6.

46. Phillips, "Navigating Uncharted Waters," 51–59; Parratt, "About Turns," 4–17; S. W. Pope, *The New American Sport History: Recent Approaches and Perspectives* (Urbana: University of Illinois Press, 1997); M. Oriard, *Reading Football: How the Popular Press Created an American Spectacle* (Chapel Hill: University of North Carolina, 1993).

47. For example, see G. Rail, ed., *Sport and Postmodern Times* (Albany: State University of New York Press, 1998) and D. L. Andrews and S. J. Jackson, eds., *Sports Stars: The Cultural Politics of Sporting Celebrity* (London: Routledge, 2001).

CHAPTER 3

A Linguistic Turn into Sport History

MICHAEL ORIARD

I came to sport history from literary studies. To be more precise, for the past fifteen years or so I have been writing about the cultural history of American football while continuing to teach American literature at my day job; and it is in the conjunction of the two disciplines that I discovered my method for reconstructing football's "cultural history."

There are many kinds of sport history, of course. The boundary between social and cultural history is particularly porous, and *culture* itself is a notoriously protean term. The culture that I explore in my own work is the web of ideas, beliefs, and meanings attached to football in the United States, as opposed to the cultural practices of participation and fandom. In locating those ideas, beliefs, and meanings in the mass media, I emphatically do not adopt the postmodern view that the mediated image—the copy, the "similacrum," the "hyperreality"—is all there is. The unique power of football depends on the actuality of what the players do in preparation and performance. Moreover, spectating, whether at home or at the stadium, is an active experience, at least for serious fans. I do not contend that football is just discourse but that the mediated narratives of football inform the public's understanding and provoke its reactions. Though discussed here in a collection titled *Deconstructing Sport History*, my method in fact grew from a respect for old-fashioned empirical historiography.

When, around 1990, I first took up the question of what football has meant in American life, I recognized two primary traditions on which I might draw: one deriving from the work of the myth-and-symbol scholars in American studies, the other from that of American sport sociologists. From the myth-and-symbol school had emerged a set of commonplaces about

American sport that had worked their way even into popular films: that baseball with its green spaces was fundamentally a pastoral sport, football a bureaucratic and violent one; basketball was urban and jazz-like, boxing urban and fatalistically Darwinian.[1] Each sport was tied to a distinctive American fantasy (or for boxing, a nightmare). My own first book, which, along with a handful of studies by other scholars, established sport literature as a distinct genre, subscribed to this fundamental idea that sport functioned as cultural myth.[2]

By 1990, the myth-and-symbol school had come under attack within American studies for a weakness that had become obvious: myth implied a timeless realm, outside of history, separate from ideology. Henry Nash Smith, whose *Virgin Land* more or less inaugurated and always represented the myth-and-symbol school at its best, generously wrote his own *mea culpa* for a collection of essays by revisionist scholars in 1986, in which he ruefully acknowledged that his book had failed to register how Western myths served ideological purposes.[3] American sport historians had little use for myth criticism, and perhaps for that reason they had shied away from cultural history altogether. Allen Guttmann's contribution to the myth-and-symbol school, *A Whole New Ball Game*, was much less influential than his application of modernization theory to modern sport in *From Ritual to Record*; but it was scholars such as Stephen Hardy and Steven Riess who established the principle mode of inquiry: seemingly a conscious rejection of myth criticism, and of grand interpretive theories more generally, in favor of detailed accounts of the rise of American sport in conjunction with the decidedly nonmythic, antipastoral forces of urbanization and industrialization.[4] I found this empirical research highly attractive, a counterweight to the anything-goes, self-referential interpretive freedom ruling my own discipline.

Over in the social sciences, American sport sociologists tended to analyze sport as either a distinct social institution or as a "microcosm" of society. An implicit cultural theory arose from these approaches: the idea that sport existed, as the title of a book by sportswriter Robert Boyle put it, as a "mirror" of American life. Racism in football, for example—stereotypes of racial performance, "stacking" at certain positions and exclusion from others, the absence of African Americans in coaching and management roles—mirrored the racism in the larger society. The relationship of the culture of sport to the institutions of American society was mimetic, unmediated. For someone coming from literary studies, such epistemological assumptions had long been discredited.

The most obvious alternative for a cultural history of football to both the myth-and-symbol and the functionalist sociological approaches lay in the still-emerging field of cultural studies, with its central concept of "hegemony." The work of the Center for Contemporary Cultural Studies at the University of Birmingham had had only a minimal impact in North American sport studies, chiefly in Richard Gruneau's *Class, Sports, and Social Development* (1983), but Frederic Jameson's "containment" model—mass cultural texts tapping into the audience's utopian longings but ultimately containing them in order to prevent their eruption into anything like revolutionary action—had not been applied to sports but was extraordinarily influential in cultural studies generally.[5] It was against this model, rather than the discredited myth-and-symbol school or simple reflection theories, that I proposed my own method for reading football as a cultural text.

My central arguments in *Reading Football*—about how the game evolved from its English roots and about the role of the popular press in transforming it within barely a decade from an extracurricular activity at a handful of elite northeastern universities into a national spectator sport—derived from the source materials I examined rather than a predetermined theory. After exploring American football's earliest development through contemporary accounts, I turned to the newspapers of the time to discover if or when the game's fundamentally narrative structure was understood and exploited. This I found and much more, reading through New York's major dailies, along with *Harper's Weekly, Outing*, and other publications, imagining the readers of those newspapers and magazines as they discovered the new college game at the breakfast table or in the parlor rather than at the ball field.

Cultural history, for me, thus began with the hard nuggets of documentary evidence, a bracing liberation from the abstractions within which both myth criticism and cultural studies floated. But having discovered a written record from which to explain how football became a "cultural text," I had to weigh carefully how best to read it. My own discipline of literary studies was rife with grand theories by which texts could mean anything and everything or nothing at all, while American cultural studies seemed trapped in a specific dichotomy: cultural expressions were either emancipatory or repressive, and "mass culture" typically bore grave responsibility for the sorry state of American society. I will not rehearse here the argument I developed in the prologue to *Reading Football* against "allegorical" or totalizing readings of cultural texts, except to say that it rejected some key premises of the British and Jamesonian schools of cultural studies. Subversion and containment seemed to me the ultimate false dichotomy: always imposed from without rather than emerging from the analysis, their application invariably both too broad and too narrow. In the Jamesonian mode, a single cultural expression (whether the film *Jaws* or the cultural text of football) was made to represent the entire culture—a sociological "mirror," however subtly refracting, in its most extravagant form. This approach also reduced "culture" to the power relations of opposed class interests. I saw no room here for diverse responses to intersecting narratives of class, gender, race, ethnicity, religion, community, and on and on, within the same cultural text.

❖ ❖ ❖

In writing *Reading Football*, then, I came to believe that the best source for discovering what football meant was to reconstruct the full range of narratives to which those within the reach of the mass media were unevenly exposed and to which they diversely responded. In arriving at a method, if not a theory, I brought to the reading of newspapers and magazines some basic assumptions from my home field of literary studies. The resistance to my *Reading Football* among some sport historians derived, I suspect, from an antagonism to the assaults on traditional assumptions about truth and knowledge—to "deconstruction," "post-structuralism," "postmodernism," and whatever other terms are loosely used to refer to a central idea that meanings are fundamentally unstable and indeterminate—which originated among philosophers, ripened in English departments, and penetrated every academic discipline in the social sciences as well as humanities. This "linguistic turn," as Jeffrey Hill noted several years ago, was resisted by those sport historians who worried that it "threatens to do away with History as we know it without putting anything substantial in its place."[6] This is not the occasion to rehearse all of the theoretical convulsions within the "human sciences" over the past thirty years, but it is important to recognize that the scholarly and curricular wars in the United States, spilling outside the academy into the culture wars of the 1990s, often set up false dichotomies of the sort I mentioned above: traditionalist versus postmodernist, rational standards versus chaos in interpretation, defense of Western civilization versus empowerment of the alienated and marginalized. The arguments usually revealed more about the politics of those making them than about the topics addressed. Yet at the heart of the linguistic turn lay some basic principles that could be detached from their off-putting theoretical grounding and might be broadly embraced.

For me, the first and most important principle in textual analysis is simply the recognition that meaning does not reside in the text alone but is produced by a collaboration of producers (that is, writers), consumers (that is, readers), and material, social, political, and economic contexts. The elusive element, of course, is the readers, the group that the cultural historian most desires to understand. In the United States, the sports we follow, as opposed to the sports we do, we experience overwhelmingly through the mass media rather than directly, which means that we constantly have them interpreted for us. But how we respond to those interpretations—the specific ones we encounter and the extent to which we agree with or reject them—cannot be surmised from the texts alone.

The ultimate elusiveness of the fan's heart and mind constitutes one of my method's two most significant potential weaknesses—the other concerns the question of cultural power, which I will address shortly—but it need not be fatal. Should we follow the logic of literary deconstructionists, with their fundamental premise that words mean whatever the reader finds in them, then we would seem compelled to abandon any hope of understanding the meaning of a sport such as American football through reading its coverage in newspapers and magazines. But as deconstruction's critics have insisted, Derrida and his followers in some ways defied common sense, because we routinely experience agreement about what writings mean. Stanley Fish's idea about communities of readers offered a way out of this impasse: readers who share certain assumptions and agreed-upon rules of reading arrive at similar understandings.[7] Readers of the sports pages can be imagined as such "interpretive communities," if we think carefully about what constitutes them as such communities and what implicit rules of reading likely prevailed.

In the essay cited above, Jeffrey Hill—himself sympathetic to a "linguistic turn" in sport history—noted "the dangers in accepting at its face value the language of the sporting press" for "understanding of what the sporting audience felt."[8] Yet strategies of analysis are possible that can at least bring us closer to the views of ordinary football fans from the past than is possible by other methods. Although we can never be certain how contemporary readers responded to their newspapers and magazines, we can attempt to imagine those readers as clearly as possible so as to read as they might have. Thus, we can imagine American readers in the 1880s encountering football in their newspapers without ever having seen a game played and thus having no competing ideas about it. We can imagine those readers as not just the college-educated but also the larger public—the circulation of Pulitzer's New York World exceeded a half-million by the 1890s by appealing to the range of classes in New York—and we can compare the visual iconography of football in the World to the engravings and lithographs in the National Police Gazette, whose readership was more thoroughly working class, and so on. Ultimately, by fully reconstructing the media world of football—with proper attention to the specific media and their relationship to their audiences, as well as to those audiences themselves—we can determine what football meant in this period with as much confidence as is possible in writing the history of ordinary people. Whatever the approach, sport history at its best can only be an art of approximation, a fact requiring no apology or defense, just careful consideration.

With the expansion of the sport and the proliferation of the media, assumptions about the media's relationships to its audiences become more problematic. For my most recent book, *King Football*, which deals with the sport from the 1920s through the 1950s, I had to consider a fully developed and semi-independent daily press throughout the country, a hugely expanded periodical press, and a thriving African American, foreign-language, and radical weekly press; as well as radio, newsreels, and feature films, the entirely new and particularly powerful media of this era. To further complicate matters, the "football culture" of this period was less dominated by what the media produced than in the 1880s and 1890s. In a recent book, Andrew Markovits and Steven Hellerman offer a useful definition of sports culture today, defining it as "what people breathe, read, discuss, analyze, compare, and historicize; what they talk about at length before and after games on sports radio; what they discuss at the office watercooler; and what comprises a significant quantity of barroom (or pub) talk; in short, what people *follow* as opposed to what people *do*."[9] One of the striking aspects of this definition is its implicit claim that what people *read* contributes relatively little to American sports culture today. Sports-talk radio represents a new use of an old medium to give ordinary citizens an unprecedented voice, and disagreement rather than consensus is its characteristic feature. By accident rather than intention, I am sure, Markovits and Hellerman fail to mention what people *watch*, yet surely they intended to include television, which with its dozens of games each week and twenty-four–hour sports networks has overwhelmed all other media in the United States. What they emphasize are the informal and unmediated sources of sports culture, the watercooler and barroom arguments and personal conversations. These crucial aspects of sports culture are the most difficult to study in our own time and are wholly unavailable to historians. But what is discussed by the water cooler or vilified on talk radio is likely something seen or heard on television or read in the morning newspaper. The position I adopted in *King Football* is the one I would advocate for understanding sports cultures today: I assume that the power of the mass media resides in determining which issues and meanings are most broadly and prominently circulated and in framing these issues in particular ways to which a diverse audience responds in varied and conflicting ways.

❖ ❖ ❖

To reconsider my own methods for this cross-cultural volume, I surveyed football studies from the 1990s, predominantly from the United Kingdom, whose scholarship was largely unfamiliar. From this work one particular alternative to my textual approach stands out, but before discussing it I want to call attention to key differences in the sporting landscapes of the United Kingdom and the United States that can generate different scholarly methods and agendas. Having abandoned the traditional emphasis on social class as the primary or even solitary frame of reference, recent football scholarship in the United Kingdom seems preoccupied with questions of identity: with national identities on the one hand, typically explored in collections of essays on football as played in various countries; and with local identities on the other hand, as embodied in the supporters of particular football clubs.[10] Although Americans might feel nationalistic for the two weeks of the Olympic games every four years, our greater tendency is to take American teams and *American* sports—baseball, basketball, and *real* football—to be the only ones that matter. Genuinely oppositional local football cultures, I suspect, are nearly absent as well (more on this shortly).

British scholars also express a nearly uniform uneasiness about the commercialization and globalization of professional football (soccer to Americans) in the 1990s, a development so thoroughly completed in the United States that Americans can hardly imagine another form. The primary version of American football, from its beginnings after the Civil War into the 1960s, was the intercollegiate game: that anomaly among the world's sports, a highly commercialized popular spectacle staged by institutions of higher learning. The structure of American professional football resembled the English version into the 1930s—clubs in small industrial towns with exclusively working-class fans (the players, however, mostly college-educated)—but the organization of the National Football League in 1933 into ten teams located only in major metropolitan areas (with Green Bay, Wisconsin, the sole exception) fundamentally reoriented the game. Interest remained limited to those cities with franchises until the arrival of TV in the 1950s, through which the NFL marketed itself as a league, not as separate teams, each with its own partisan fans. Television created a national (broadly middle-class) audience for the first time and elevated pro football to the pinnacle of American spectator sports by the 1970s. After 1933, professional football continued to exist in several minor leagues as well as club teams—including a handful of African American clubs (the New York Brown Bombers and the Chicago Panthers, for example)—but these always existed in the shadows of commercialized big-time football. Immigrant athletic clubs—playing the "football" they brought from Europe rather than the kind they found in the United States—were important institutions in the 1920s and 1930s, but their role in immigrant life was relatively short-lived and diminished with assimilation. If "sandlot football" generated rich neighborhood cultures altogether outside the scrutiny of the media, that story has not yet been told. Strangely enough, highschool football in some parts of the country comes closest to the English club sport in providing a focus for community identity and pride (while the consequences of children playing this role for adults make interscholastic football anything but an ideal for organic community sport). Even here, media coverage—by the local press—has always been a primary link between the community and its teams.

The British scholarship I surveyed seems to share a fundamental principle: mass-mediated sport is inherently bad; local or subcultural sport is at least potentially good. The World Cup provides the chief occasion for examining international football's importance for national identity, but what most interests British scholars appears to be local subcultures of football fans. The football *mainstream*, about which I write, is apparently as unattractive to most sport scholars in the United Kingdom as it is in the United States. Because the serious study of sport (and other forms of popular culture) has taken place for only thirty years or so, during a period when oppositional scholarship of myriad kinds became dominant in the academy, we sometimes find ourselves in the peculiar position of knowing more about the cultural margins than about the center. The cultural mainstream is too easily set up as a monolith against which marginalized groups register their resistance and assert their "authentic" alternatives. A more complex and critical understanding of the mainstream can offer much that is valuable (including a better understanding of the ways that subcultures and marginalized groups relate to it). The commercialism that seems to have overwhelmed British football in the 1990s is uniformly denounced by the scholars I read, on behalf of the people and the loss of "their" game. Yet this commercialized football is apparently not only more "civilized," as the government and ruling bodies want it, but also antiracist—addressing in a positive way one of the other issues many of these scholars raise. (When the official, or mainstream, culture is antiracist—as is true in the United States as well—the "subversiveness" or "authenticity" of persistent racism is hard to celebrate.)

I see in the United Kingdom scholarship responses to a belated experience such as American football went through decades ago, well before professional football became our favorite spectator sport, and the American experience illustrates the complexities at the heart of the mainstream. Commercialized, professionalized college football in the United States has surely violated American universities' educational mission, yet it also provided educational opportunities for the despised sons of eastern and southern European immigrants in the 1920s and 1930s and for the descendants of African slaves over the following decades. The win-at-all-costs attitude rightly criticized in big-time American football was also the primary force in opening up the elite college game to these outsiders. Observers remarked as early as the 1920s that the sons of the poor were more likely to endure the rigors of football training than the privileged sons of the elite; and the desire to win games, not a moral commitment to racial justice, was the driving force in integrating football. American football's cultural mainstream has not been a simple consensus or a uniform set of coherent ideas but all the variety, the conflicts, and the dialectical tensions that characterize the nation.

Significant differences in American and British sport notwithstanding, methods of studying sporting cultures can cross the Atlantic. Recent British scholarship includes readings of football "texts" such as the ones that I have explored—newspaper, TV, and radio coverage—as well as soccer chants, a call-in radio program in Cameroon, and most conspicuously, football fanzines.[11] When the goal is to imagine the audience for such texts, a simple but consequential principle governs my preferred method for reading them, whether individual texts on a specific topic or the full range of media discourses such as I have attempted to take up in my two books on football: to look for competing narratives, so as to acknowledge, if only implicitly, the differences within the audience. If readers can only be imagined, a dialogic text points to these imagined readers more persuasively than would a monologic one. In a study of football fanzines, the British sociologist Richard Giulianotti has coined the term *post-fan* to describe today's self-aware, highly ironical football supporter, a rejoinder to those who have characterized fans in general as either thugs or dupes. Such ironic self-awareness regarding football is not new, however, nor absent from the football mainstream in the United States. It is evident, for example, in *Life* and *Judge*, two of the American "smart" humor magazines of the 1920s and 1930s that were filled with cartoons, jokes, and satirical illustrations and sketches that lampooned every aspect of the big-time American college game. Cartoons in the *Saturday Evening Post* and *Collier's*, with their huge middle-class audiences, were similarly self-aware and irreverent, as were the college-football film comedies of the 1930s with their oafish athletes and conniving boosters. The football mainstream reveals a range of fan consciousness, from naïve to "post-," throughout its history.

Among recent readings of football's media texts, I would cluster those that can loosely be termed "cultural studies" or "popular cultural studies" or "postmodern" (ignoring, that is, the internecine warfare over what critical practices can properly claim to be "cultural studies").[12] The absence of football from three recent American collections on sport from explicitly cultural studies and postmodernist perspectives—including essays on aerobics and bodybuilding, for example, but not on football—highlights the apparent unattractiveness of mainstream sports among self-consciously cutting-edge scholars, except for basketball with its pronounced racial coding.[13] (Although Nolan Ryan serves as cultural text for one book-length study, Major League baseball is also largely ignored, while there has emerged a scholarly mini-industry on Michael Jordan alone.)[14]

The totalizing theories that dominated similar work in the 1970s and 1980s have largely given way to a more nuanced model: culture viewed as semiautonomous rather than determined by economics and class positions, cultural expressions as neither wholly repressive nor subversive, but "contested." Whether the concept of "hegemony," or questions of power conceived differently should remain central to this work seems to me a key question. Hegemony can be quite persuasive in explaining how a dominant culture, particularly in liberal democracies, is embraced by the citizens rather than imposed by a manipulative power elite, but it is far less useful in explaining the power of specific cultural expressions. For sport studies, the operations of hegemony are considerably more apparent in general sporting *practices* and institutional arrangements—in the dominance of males in the major spectator sports, of whites in management positions, of certain commodified forms rather than others, and so on—than in what sports *mean* to their vast public. The introduction to one recent collection of essays on American sport illustrates the problem when the writer states, "All of the contributors to this collection share a common view of culture as a site of ideological conflict between dominant and subaltern groups over the construction of social identities."[15] "Dominant" and "subaltern" assert a fundamental judgment before analysis even begins. Males are presumably "dominant" in American sport, yet black males are dominant in some respects and not in others; while Latino males, gay males, short males, slow males, skinny males, any number of other kinds of males may not feel "dominant" at all. Whites are presumably "dominant" in relation to all other races, but a litany of comparable qualifiers apply here as well. "Dominant" and "subaltern" are contingent and fluid categories, at least in an American context, with little theoretical power in exploring specific sporting cultures. The quality of the individual chapters in this collection depend not on their theoretical predisposition but on their specific analyses.

My (uncritical?) cultural studies approach to football abandons any attempt to argue the degree to which the representations of football actually determine beliefs (let alone actions) relating to gender, race, personal and group identities, and so on, in favor of maintaining as rich a sense as possible of the variety and complexity of football's meanings for its huge American audience. The power of the media is everywhere implicit in my two books on football, but nowhere particularized; likewise, the power of the media is always understood to be limited by individual and group interests, but again, to a degree never specified. In effect, I simply set aside direct engagement with questions of power that, for those who insist that their scholarship is a form of politics, are the only questions that truly matter. I assume that for such scholars my approach is fatally flawed on this count.

To my mind, the most promising body of new work in the scholarship I surveyed—and the clearest alternative to my textual approach—is the ethnographic fieldwork of British sociologists and anthropologists such as Richard Giulianotti and Gary Armstrong, who have studied specific fan groups, particularly so-called soccer hooligans, in order to rescue them from reductive class analysis from both the Left and the Right.[16] While the actual fans whom I attempt to understand remain dimly in the background, this fieldwork-based research puts them at center stage: real people (overwhelmingly male) doing and saying specific things about football in general and their favorite clubs in particular. This new ethnography of sport also introduces useful concepts such as "neo-tribes" (from the work of Michel Maffesoli) to explain the forms of loose, intermittent affiliation and collective identity formed through support of a favorite football club, that are very different from traditional forms of community.

While the value of ethnographic studies for specific cultural practices is obvious, as access to the desires, beliefs, and values of the individuals within the group, ethnography faces its own well-known obstacles. As every cultural anthropologist knows—and as Giulianotti himself points out in one of his studies—the presence of the researcher can alter the behavior being studied.[17] Likewise, the ethnographer cannot assume common values and motives throughout the target group; the question of motives has become particularly vexed in our psychoanalytic times. Even with their real human subjects, ethnographic studies of sporting subcultures have no firmer hold on questions of cultural power than do other approaches. Whether or not soccer hooligans in the United Kingdom are genuinely resisting or subverting the dominant sporting culture cannot be determined simply by talking to them and watching how they act.

A comment by Gary Armstrong and Malcolm Young in an essay on the chants of British football fans illustrates the problem:

> Football is thus about social differentiation. It is about us against them, and their defeat. It denies egalitarian ideals, and revels in our superiority, which it sings and dances on its way to success. It denies the Christian ethic that would turn the other cheek, and rather reemphasizes danger, victory and domination in battles against some clearly differentiated "other."

That statement could set up an analysis of football-as-false-consciousness: fans not only distracted by the mere game from the serious social inequalities that affect their lives, but also replicating in the arena of spectator sport the very ideology of competitive individualism that dooms them to marginal economic and social status. It also could lead to an analysis of football-as-containment, rooted in a more nuanced argument, in the Jamesonian mode, that the game releases the fans' genuine longings for freedom only to contain them, ultimately, through its reinscription of competitive-individualist ideology. What in fact Armstrong and Young claim is that the ritualized chanting of British football fans constitutes "a self-empowering social process, for it becomes self-justifying, self-perpetuating and then succeeds, as it does, simply deploying a ritualized control over the idea of interpreting what is true."[18] Perhaps. Like beauty, all such claims are in the eyes of the beholders.

My point is not to denigrate the work of Armstrong and Young—it is very good—but to point out that ethnographic research does not lead to self-evident conclusions. If ethnography cannot provide transparent access to football fans, however, ethnographic accounts of sporting subcultures can be extremely valuable for understanding the cultural role of sport today (the past, of course, falls outside the domain of ethnography). In the United States, the exploration of local football cultures has been done not by scholars but by journalists such as H. G. Bissinger (on highschool football in west Texas) and Susan Faludi (on the Dawg Pound supporters of the Cleveland Browns).[19] Should scholars enter this field, I would foresee ethnographic research as complementing rather than supplanting my own approach, which would remain useful not only for developing a sense of the larger national football culture but also for establishing the contexts within which specific football subcultures are meaningful.

Contrary to the claims of extreme postmodernists, although American football may come in postmodern packaging today, it retains a core of modern (and premodern or antimodern) narratives. Narrative was supposed to have disappeared from American fiction sometime back in the 1970s, but of course it returned (and never actually went away). Postmodern self-reflexiveness seems to be a transition from a discredited, overly narrow older modernism toward a reconstructed new modernism yet to fully emerge. The need to tell stories about ourselves seems to be a deeply human impulse, and football remains a potent source of cultural storytelling. The packaging could eventually prove to be itself the story, but we have not yet arrived at that point. Among the most powerful storytellers in the United States today are the folks at NFL Films who orchestrate, choreograph, and dramatize the many narratives of football for television and the video market. Identifying the "storyline" is one of the routine roles of football broadcasters. American cultural narratives of football are highly specific, dealing not just with class conflict and group or national identities, but also with heroism and failure, physicality and intellect, violence and beauty, risk and caution, self-assertion and selflessness, gender, race, ethnicity, region, religion, and so on. The decline of print, the saturation by network and cable television, the advent of talk radio, and the expansion of informal sites of cultural exchange have made the cultural historian's challenge more difficult and the resulting claims more tentative. But in contrast to the cultural critic's own reading of football, or even the ethnographer's eyewitness account, the textual approach to football attends to the full range of often conflicting narratives that are attached to the game.

❖ ❖ ❖

This chapter, in effect, is the methodological chapter omitted from *King Football*, and a word about that omission might usefully conclude it. As scholars, with varying degrees of self-consciousness no doubt, we position ourselves in relation to particular audiences and with certain intentions. For *Reading Football*, I imagined myself addressing three disparate groups—sport historians, scholars in American studies, and that mythical "general public"—thinking that I offered something to each. For sport historians, I hoped that the book as a whole would illuminate the early years of American football and the role played by the popular press in its development. For scholars in American studies, through a methodological prologue I hoped to articulate some shortcomings in the reigning model of cultural studies, while persuading them to incorporate sport more fully into their own explorations of American culture. For the general public, through the substantive chapters exclusive of this prologue, I hoped to recreate an earlier period in the history of football in engaging and informative ways.

My methodological prologue, instead, not only had no discernible impact in American studies, but it also proved an obstacle to general readers and an irritation to at least some sport historians, who misconstrued my intent as not a plea for inclusion of sport in mainstream American studies but an arrogant attempt to impose cultural studies on traditional sport history (an ironic confirmation of my basic principle that readers do not all agree on what a text means).

For *King Football*, I wrote only for sport scholars and those ever-elusive lay readers, but with a single objective: a book about football, not about current scholarship in sport history and sport studies. I fully recognize the value of a different book based on the same material but addressed specifically to the disciplinary issues in sport scholarship. That is simply not my book, and for reasons that are important to me. As an undergraduate English major in the late 1960s, I found everything in my college library to have been written as if for me. As an English professor three decades later, I find little in the library published over my professional lifetime to have been written for my students. I certainly do not wish to see sport history follow literary studies along a path of inaccessible theory-driven discourses. This is an old complaint but perhaps timely again on this occasion of disciplinary self-scrutiny.

In literary studies, the ascendance of theory coincided with a factor not often noted: the basic work of explication on the supposed "major" American writers had been done in the 1940s, 1950s, and 1960s. Distinct from the politics of canon-revision, a simple need to find unexplored topics led to excavations of obscure corners of the canonical tradition—and to obscurantist analysis of what was found—in addition to the recovery of noncanonical writers. Put simply, literary scholars needed new subjects about which to write. In sport studies, our fields not even having existed before the 1970s, we still have an enormous amount of basic work to do; there is no compelling disciplinary imperative to lapse into the esoteric unless the results truly justify that move. As I see it, our challenge in doing that work is to absorb the key insights of the most compelling theorists and render them intelligible to nonspecialist as well as specialist readers. In my own case, *King Football* is assuredly a "scholarly" book—a long one, abundantly footnoted, with few anecdotes or vivid personalities—no rival to the best sports journalism. But whether I succeeded or not, I wrote and revised it with the hope that no serious nonspecialist reader would give up on it.

I suspect that the issues I describe here are ones that all of us who write about sport consider at some point. In my own experience, defensiveness over writing about "mere" sport was endemic in the generation of the 1970s and early 1980s. Today, sports scholars find themselves in the odd position of being courted by marketing-minded editors of university presses, who recognize in sports books the potential for sales beyond a shrinking number of research libraries. As sport becomes increasingly conspicuous in the global marketplace, scholarly books on sport are published even by major commercial publishers. Who we write for and to what purpose determines what and how we write. Building our disciplines from within is crucially important, but there are limits on the value of speaking only to each other. Major literary critics used to be public intellectuals. Today, no one reads academic literary criticism except for other academics. As sports scholars, if we are to have any influence beyond the shaping of our disciplines, we need to share what we learn with the larger public, and we can do that only by speaking the public's language.

NOTES

1. The magnum opus of this school was Michael Novak's *Joy of Sports: End Zones, Bases, Baskets, Balls, and the Consecration of the American Spirit* (New York: Basic Books, 1976). It may have begun with Murray Ross, "Foot-

ball Red and Baseball Green: The Heroics and Bucolics of American Sport," *Chicago Review* 22 (January–February 1971): 30–40.

2. See Wiley T. Umphlett, *The Sporting Myth and the American Experience* (Lewisburg, PA: Bucknell University Press, 1975); Robert J. Higgs, *Laurel and Thorn: The Athlete in American Literature* (Knoxville: University of Tennessee Press, 1981); Christian K. Messenger, *Sport and the Spirit of Play: Hawthorne to Faulkner* (New York: Columbia University Press, 1981); Michael Oriard, *Dreaming of Heroes: American Sports Fiction, 1868–1980* (Chicago: Nelson-Hall, 1982).

3. Henry Nash Smith, "Symbol and Idea in *Virgin Land*," in *Ideology and Classic American Literature*, eds. Sacvan Bercovitch and Myra Jehlen (New York: Cambridge University Press, 1986), 21–35.

4. Allen Guttmann, *From Ritual to Record: The Nature of Modern Sports* (New York: Columbia University Press, 1978) and *A Whole New Ball Game: An Interpretation of American Sports* (Chapel Hill: University of North Carolina Press, 1988); Stephen Hardy, *How Boston Played: Sport, Recreation, and Community, 1865–1915* (Boston: Northeastern University Press, 1982); Steven A. Riess, *City Games: The Evolution of American Urban Society and the Rise of Sports* (Urbana: University of Illinois Press, 1989).

5. Fredric Jameson, "Reification and Utopia in Mass Culture," *Social Text* 1 (Winter 1979): 130–48.

6. Jeffrey Hill, "British Sports History: A Post-Modern Future?" *Journal of Sport History* 23 (Spring 1996): 15.

7. See Stanley Fish, *Is There a Text in This Class? The Authority of Interpretive Communities* (Cambridge, MA: Harvard University Press, 1980).

8. Hill, "British Sports History," 18.

9. Andrew S. Markovits and Steven L. Hellerman, *Offside: Soccer and American Exceptionalism* (Princeton, NJ: Princeton University Press, 2001), 9.

10. In addition to the references that follow, see Rogan Taylor, *Football and Its Fans: Supporters and Their Relations with the Game, 1885–1985* (Leicester and London: Leicester University Press, 1992); John Sugden and Alan Bairner, *Sport, Sectarianism and Society in a Divided Ireland* (Leicester: Leicester University Press, 1993); Steve Redhead, ed., *The Passion and the Fashion: Football Fandom in the New Europe* (Aldershot: Avebury, 1993); Gary Armstrong and Richard Giulianotti, eds., *Football Cultures and Identities* (London: Macmillan, 1999); Alan Bairner, *Sport, Nationalism, and Globalization: European and North American Perspectives* (Albany: State University of New York Press, 2001).

11. On fanzines, see David Jary, John Horne, and Tom Bucke, "Football 'Fanzines' and Football Culture: A Case of Successful 'Cultural Contestation,'" *Sociological Review* 39 (1991): 581–97; Richard Haynes, *The Football*

Imagination: The Rise of Football Fanzine Culture (Aldershot: Arena, 1995);
H. F. Moorhouse, "From Zines Like These? Fanzines, Tradition and Identity
in Scottish Football," in *Scottish Sport in the Making of the Nation: Ninety
Minute Patriots?* eds. Grant Jarvie and Graham Walker (Leicester and
London: Leicester University Press, 1994), 173–94; Richard Giuilianotti,
"Enlightening the North: Aberdeen Fanzines and Local Football Identity,"
in *Entering the Field: New Perspectives on World Football,* eds. Gary Armstrong
and Richard Giuilianotti (Oxford: Berg, 1997), 211–27; Richard Giulian-
otti, *Football: A Sociology of the Global Game* (Cambridge: Polity, 1999). On
football songs, see Joseph M. Bradley, "'We Shall Not Be Moved!' Mere
Sport, Mere Songs?" in *Fanatics! Power, Identity and Fandom in Football,* ed.
Adam Brown (London: Routledge, 1998), 203–18; Gary Armstrong and
Malcolm Young, "Fanatical Football Chants: Creating and Controlling the
Carnival," in *Football Culture: Local Contests, Global Visions* (London: Cass,
2000), 173–211. On TV, radio, and the press, see Neil Blain and Raymond
Boyle, "Battling along the Boundaries: The Marking of Scottish Identity in
Sports Journalism," in *Scottish Sport in the Making of the Nation,* 125–41; Paul
Nchoji and Bea Vidacs, "Football: Politics and Power in Cameroon," in
Entering the Field, 123–39; Les Back, Tim Crabbe, and John Solomos,
"Racism in Football: Patterns of Continuity and Change," in *Fanatics!,*
71–87; Paul Dimeo and Gerry P.T. Finn, "Scottish Racism, Scottish Identi-
ties: The Case of Partick Thistle," in *Fanatics!* 124–38; Liz Crolley, David
Hand, and Rolf Jeutter, "National Obsessions and Identities in Football
Match Reports," in *Fanatics!* 173–85; Stephen Wagg, "Playing the Past: The
Media and the England Football Team," in *British Football and Social Change:
Getting into Europe,* eds. John Williams and Stephen Wagg (Leicester and
London: Leicester University Press, 1991), 220–38; Tony Mason, *Passion of
the People? Football in South America* (London: Verso, 1995); Eric Dunning,
"The Social Roots of Football Hooliganism: A Reply to the Critics of the
'Leicester School,'" in *Football, Violence and Social Identity,* eds. Richard Giu-
lianotti, Norman Bonney, and Mike Hepworth (London: Routledge, 1994),
128–57; Jeff Hill, "Rite of Spring: Cup Finals and Community in the North
of England," in *Sport and Identity in the North of England,* eds. Jeff Hill and
Jack Williams (Keele: Keele University Press, 1996), 85–111; Richard Holt,
"Heroes of the North: Sport and the Shaping of Regional Identity," in *Sport
and Identity in the North of England,* ed. Hill and Williams, 137–64.

    12. See, for example, Neil Blain, Raymond Boyle, and Hugh O'Don-
nell, *Sport and National Identity in the European Media* (Leicester and Lond:
Leicester University Press, 1993); Steve Redhead, *Post-Fandom and the Mil-
lennial Blues: The Transformation of Soccer Culture* (London: Routledge,
1997). On the right to profess "cultural studies," see John Storey, ed., *What
Is Cultural Studies? A Reader* (London: Arnold, 1996).

13. See Aaron Baker and Todd Boyd, eds., *Out of Bounds: Sports, Media, and the Politics of Identity* (Bloomington and Indianapolis: Indiana University Press, 1997); Genevieve Rail, *Sport and Postmodern Times* (Albany: State University of New York Press, 1998); Randy Martin and Toby Miller, eds., *SportCult* (Minneapolis: University of Minnesota Press, 1999).

14. See Nick Trujillo, *The Meaning of Nolan Ryan* (College Station: Texas A&M University Press, 1994) and the special issue of the *Sociology of Sport Journal* in 1996, "Deconstructing Michael Jordan."

15. Baker, *Out of Bounds*, xiv.

16. See Gary Armstrong, *Football Hooligans: Knowing the Score* (Oxford: Berg, 1998); Giulianotti, *Football*, and "'Keep It in the Family': An Outline of Hibs' Football Hooligans' Social Ontology," in *Game without Frontiers: Football, Identity and Modernity*, eds. Giulianotti and John Williams (Aldershot: Arena, 1994), 327–37; Raymond Boyle, "'We Are Celtic Supporters . . .': Questions of Football and Identity in Modern Scotland," in *Game without Frontiers*, 73–101; and Eduardo Archetti, "'And Give Joy to My Heart': Ideology and Emotions in the Argentinian Cult of Maradona," in *Entering the Field*, 31–51.

17. See Giulianotti, *Football*.

18. Armstrong and Young, "Fanatical Football Chants," 179.

19. See H. G. Bissinger, *Friday Night Lights: A Town, a Team, and a Dream* (Reading, MA: Addison-Wesley, 1990) and Susan Faludi, *Stiffed: The Betrayal of the American Man* (New York: Morrow, 1999).

PART TWO

On Practice

CHAPTER 4

Partial Knowledge

Photographic Mystifications and Constructions of "The African Athlete"

JOHN BALE

This chapter deconstructs a single photograph that has been disseminated during the past century in a range of publications, many of which have been related to the world of sports. My objective is to reveal the instability of visual images and the considerable slippage in the ways in which a photograph may be used and read during its existence. Additionally, it is often felt that the photograph provides the world of sport with a degree of realism that is missing from the words on a page. One of the aims of this chapter is to deny the realist argument. Indeed, it is widely recognized today that there is no one meaning in a photograph.

Photography has been, and still is, a central agent in the representation of sports and sports participants. Photography features prominently in sports magazines, technical handbooks on sports training, and (auto)biographies of sports people. Works on sports history sometimes include photographs although usually they are dependent on the written text. From an academic perspective, the photograph has acted as a historical record from which content analysis may unearth useful information about historical aspects of sport. Classic photographs help to memorialize specific sporting acts. Photography has also served the technical function of determining winners and losers via the use of the photo-finish camera. Additionally, it has assisted in the scientific analysis of the sportized body, following, for example, the pioneering work of Etienne Jules Marey and Eadweard Muybridge.[1] A photograph is obviously different from a written text in that it is an iconic representation, but problems of representation remain. Today, there is as much a crisis of representation in photography as there is in writing. A photograph can be read in many ways. There are no right or wrong answers to questions about what a photograph says about, for example, power, race, gender, and identity, and images are both denotative and connotative.[2] My approach in this chapter is loosely based on the work of the visual anthropologist Elizabeth Edwards.[3] I want to highlight the ambiguity of a photograph (figure 4.1) that is often read as representing the fantastic sporting achievement of an African native from the period of early twentieth-century colonization. However, knowledge of the context of the image leads me to conclude that it is far from innocent. It may appear to be an image of an athletic achievement, but it also carries a large number of connotations. It cannot even be said to be representing a sporting event although it could easily be constructed as one.

The image under consideration is, in many ways, typical of a sports photograph. Central to sports photography is the striking image of the human body in action. It can, however, be connected to wider issues and identities. As David Rowe observes, "the body in sports photography is always invested with a wider representational role, as sexualized, gendered, racialized, and so on."[4] Another quality of sports photography is its ability to "capture" (an appropriate metaphor in the context of colonial photography) the "action shot," or to be "caught in the act." The action shot serves to record extraordinary performances such as Roger Bannister breaking the tape at Oxford in the first four-minute mile or the clenched fist of the athletes making the black power salute at the 1968 Mexico City Olympics. The sports photograph usually represents a triumphant body that is motivated to do something supremely athletic with itself.[5] In colonial photography, action shots (sometimes posed) were common in the depiction of a variety of indigenous body-cultural practices. These included dancing, wrestling, throwing, rowing, running, and jumping.

The photograph shown as figure 4.1 satisfies the criteria that Rowe recognizes as characterizing the sports photograph. It is indeed a striking image that captures and freezes the crucial moment when the athlete clears the rope; it is a triumphant, black body. However, like the sports photographic image, frozen in time and space, the image of the colonized body "is never entirely 'still'; it is always subject to revision and reformulation according to prevailing social ideologies and the circulation of cultural 'data.'"[6] In this chapter I will first seek to set the event photographed in some kind of context, including possible intentions at the moment of "photographic inscription."[7] I will then deconstruct some spatial aspects of the photograph and finally examine "acts" undertaken on it and suggest how the photograph was used. In doing so, I hope to illustrate how, despite "the promise held out by

Figure 4.1

the seductive realism of photographs one still faces the ultimate unknowability of the past."[8]

THE EMERGENCE OF THE EVENT

Colonial attempts to represent colonized people faced the problem of how one could describe the other. By this I refer to something (or some body) against which we compare ourselves, that is, something that we have to construct. It is understood, not on its own terms, but is given qualities believed to be the opposite of those that define it. It is often the different and distant negative against which authority is defined, against which home is defined, the antithesis of civilization. "Othering" often involves the use of binary dualisms such as North-South, cultural-natural, modern-premodern, and present-past. Problems of representation arose when the body-cultural performance of the other clashed with that of Europeans' expectations.

During the late nineteenth century the first European explorers set foot in the small, central African nation of Rwanda. One feature of the country that early visitors recorded was the apparent three-fold division of the population into peoples known as Hutu, Tutsi, and Twa. The Tutsi were read as the ruling group though making up only about 17 percent of the population. The early European incursions did not engage in detailed anthropological studies, and it was not until 1907, when the Duke of Mecklenburg's party traversed the region, that the first in-depth study of the country was made. The Duke had studied anthropology at the University of Dresden and was already a sportsman in the nineteenth-century use of the term. He was later to become a major figure in the modern German sports movement and was a member of the International Olympic Committee from 1926 to 1956 and of the German Olympic committee from 1949 to 1969. At the time of Mecklenburg's visit, both the academic study of anthropology and the global sports system were developing rapidly. The first modern Olympics had been held in Athens in 1896, and the year before the first of the expedition's reports was published, the 1908 Olympics had been held in London and achieved considerable international attention. Members of the expedition carried images of the emergent world of achievement sport as part of their mental maps.

In 1907 Mecklenburg represented the German imperial realm of which, at the time, Rwanda was part. Traversing much of central Africa, his party was made up of ten scientists and five hundred African bearers. Among the scientists was the anthropologist Jan Czekanowski, who was responsible for the detailed anthropological and ethnographic report of the expedition.[9] The reports of Mecklenburg and Czekanowski each alluded to a Rwandan form of body culture, described by them as the "high jump" (*hochsprung*). To my knowledge, the first known photographs of it were taken in 1907 by a member of the Mecklenburg party. Two of these photographs (one of which is figure 4.1) were first published in 1909 in the German edition of Mecklenburg's popular travel book, *Ins innerste Afrika.*[10] An English edition was published a year later and titled *In the Heart of Africa.*[11] A third, much less well-known, photograph of the same event appeared in Czekanowski's multivolume scientific treatise in 1911.[12] Subsequently, many more representations of this body-cultural practice were published in the decades up to 1960.[13] Mecklenburg explicated that the form of jumping that he had photographed was native to the Tutsi and that they must always have been excellent jumpers ("der sport hochsprungens sei bei den Watussi bodenständig ist richtig. Die Watussi solien von jeher ausgezeichnete Springer gewesen sein")[14] This is supported (which does not quite mean confirmed) in other sources.[15] The Rwandan term for this body-cultural activity is *gusimbuka-urukiramende*, but this was not used by Mecklenburg nor by virtually any subsequent writers who alluded to it.

The photograph shows the jumper taking off from a raised mound or stone. He landed feet first but with no landing area to soften his fall. Several subsequent written, photographed, and filmed images of such jumping show athletes following each other in a line as they approach take-off. It was more like a team performance than an individual effort. *Gusimbuka* was practiced at celebrations of various kinds, and in Rwandan and in European sources it was almost always projected—as in Mecklenburg's statement above—as being associated with Tutsi.[16]

But the event depicted in the photograph was far from being a Rwandan construction. Of course, the photograph itself makes the event a European production. It also appears that it was the German explorers who organized the jumping as well as the photography. In 1928, Mecklenburg recalled his travels in Rwanda and observed: "since we perceived with them the pleasure they [Tutsi] take from this sport we [that is, Mecklenburg and his adjutant, von Weise] organized the high jump event" ("Die Watussi sollen von jeher ausgezeichnete Springer gewesen sein, und da wir ihnen die Beliebtheit dieses Sportes wahrnahmen, veranstalteten wir [. . .] das Hochspringen").[17] While superficially appearing to resemble the Western sportized high jump (note Mecklenburg's naming of it as a sport), it possessed none of the characteristics associated with what is often termed "modern sport."[18]

The fact that the first known photograph of *gusimbuka-urukiramende* appears to be a European construction of something that Europeans had (as far as is known) not previously witnessed, raises the question of whether it was a vision of "authentic primitiveness" or one of a "hybrid reality."[19] The photograph illustrates the power of the European to orchestrate or negotiate the reenactment of an indigenous performance genre. It illustrates less an act of "discovery" and more a sign of German beneficence—organizing (better?) for the African what he was already practicing.[20] And the photograph contains so much evidence of the photographer's culture that it is arguably the least typical photograph of *gusimbuka* ever taken and can hardly be regarded as a valid image of Rwandan body culture. The bags of sand at each end of the rope are reminiscent of the apparatus used in German *schulturner* jumping. The roughly hewn branches comprising the uprights with their crude calibrations (or notches in which to rest the rope) are also atypical of the conventional equipment shown in other early photographs of *gusimbuka* in which long, rigid reeds formed both the upright and the crossbar.[21] In the more authentic Rwandan jumping, a thin reed was placed on top of two upright reeds facing away from the oncoming jumper.[22] I will consider later the question of how much of the photograph's content is, in fact, Rwandan.

Mecklenberg's anthropological and sporting interests intersected in his description of the jumping. He described it in both idealized and scientific terms. In the text accompanying the photograph he described the jumping as "noteworthy," "remarkable," and "wonderful." The athletes had "slender, splendid figures." The jumping was "incredible." He paralleled his lyrical descriptions with the rhetorical mode of quantification. He claimed the height of the athlete's leap was 2.50 meters. He also took care to note that this was a substantial improvement on the "world's record" of 1.94 meters.[23] Czekanowski stated that that the jump was 2.35 meters, but Mecklenburg's more popular work meant that the 2.50 figure was recognized by more readers and was repeated as received wisdom and "truth" in subsequent publications.[24] The figure of 2.50 meters became the defining reality of Rwandan athleticism. Whatever the height was, the Europeans appropriated *gusimbuka* for the world of modernity by naming it "high jumping" and also by comparing it, by means of the universal sporting currency of the quantified result, with the European-American form of jumping.

The photograph also reveals the presence of the colonial culture within the reenactment, an example of what Taussig termed "copy *and* contact"—a case of an "image *and* bodily involvement of the receiver of the image, a complexity we too easily elide as nonmysterious."[25] Mecklenburg and his adjutant were not unfortunate "traces" in the photograph, which would spoil an otherwise anthropological record, but a central presence in its construction. However, it also reminds us of the inadequacy of the word *representation* in the sense that usually it simultaneously depends upon and erases "the networks of associations conjoined by the notion of the mimetic."[26] In this case the photograph not only recorded—or reconstructed—an indigenous custom and live objects of display, but also it revealed all too clearly a European power that, at the same time, it reinforced. Yet, as noted earlier, this is widely thought to be the first photograph of *gusimbuka*. If this is the case, no first instance of anything approaching authenticity seems to exist. Mecklenburg's photograph looks secondhand, impure, and artificial. There appears to be no "referent lodged in an allegedly pristine real."[27] But could there ever have been? Once the Europeans had encountered *gusimbuka*, whatever their involvement, it could never remain "pure."

For Nicholas Thomas, an emphasis on *European* power would be much too obvious a way of reading this and other such images. To read such a photograph solely like this could be interpreted as being

> complicit in the result of the photographic process and to pass over the fact that this enactment [of *gusimbuka*] must have been the outcome of some sort of deal or negotiation. Even if the capacities of the European photographer and the [Rwandan] actors to shape the terms of the arrangement are unequal, the [Rwandan] were possessed of a kind of agency and willed involvement which the photograph effaces, and [in the years to come] they may well have been familiar with the kind of image that [the Europeans] sought to produce. In other words, what is true of the representation that reached a public in . . . Europe is not true of the colonial encounter from which it derived.[28]

This quotation, used by Thomas to describe a posed photograph of Fijian stereotypes, is an important reminder of the possibility of Rwandan complicity in, or subtle resistance to, the European photographic venture. The authenticity of the photograph is fundamentally unsettled by the conditions of its production. Did the Mecklenburg party offer gifts or payment to those who were photographed, hence further destroying any notion of the authentic? Stephen Greenblatt stresses that representational modes may give themselves over to whomever embraces them, to be assimilated for their own ends.[29]

"Travel scripting"[30] often required specific objects (in this case *gusimbuka*) to be seen in specific ways, that is, the athlete making a successful clearance. To be seen knocking the bar off—as one of the other photographs from the Mecklenburg expedition did—or falling onto a person standing underneath would be antithetical to the mode of idealization and to the perceived Tutsi ideal. Therefore, the photograph in figure 4.1 cannot in any way be said to "conform to preconceived ideas of the racial inferiority of Africans and then presented as evidence of such ideas."[31] Far from it; instead it typifies the problematical reconstruction of "the African" as an athlete in the Olympian mold. The recognition of the African as Olympic went against the grain of prevailing, early-twentieth-century colonial rhetoric. Mirzoeff's view,[32] that photography "was a key tool in visualizing colonial possessions and demonstrating Western superiority over the colonized" can hardly be sustained by an image that was presented and read as an African breaking the world's record of the emerging global sports system.

THE SPACE OF THE PHOTOGRAPH

The Mecklenburg photograph can be read in many ways. Two spatial dimensions of it are relevant to my deconstruction. One is at the international (macro) scale, the other at the local (micro) scale. The photograph was rapidly diffused through both geographical and disciplinary space. The initial discourse in which it appeared was that of German travel writing. This was, I suspect, the immediate market for which Mecklenburg had the photograph taken. It appeared in the German and English editions of his book. It soon entered the North American market, via two issues of the *National Geographic*, within a seven-year period. Both issues included the photograph, which now became part of the overlapping discourses of travel and sport via an article titled "The Geography of Games" in the second of these two *National Geographic* inclusions.[33] It became a "sports photograph" and subsequently appeared in—among other places—a track and field training manual published in the United Kingdom, in Carl Diem's well-known sports history, *Weltgeschichte des Sports und der Leibeserziehung* in 1960, in an East German athletic manual, in a German text on sport and colonialism, in the *National Geographic* for a third time, and in the magazine of the International Athletic Federation.[34] In addition to travel writing and sports history it also featured on the cover of a political history of German colonization in Rwanda and, somewhat gratuitously, in the text *Church and Revolution in Rwanda*.[35] So it was clearly not initially, nor ever solely, a "sports photograph."

However, it is at the micro scale—at the level of the spatial organization of the photograph's contents—that I would like to focus the most attention. First, why should the Germans have placed themselves in the photograph? After all, if the aim of the expedition was to record an accurate image of the "real Africa," the photographer's role was "to preserve the purity of the cultural other that he represents."[36] To include a European, as an unfortunate trace in an otherwise "accurate" image, would "disturb the effectiveness of the photograph as a reproduction rather than a production."[37] The traditions of realism dictated that, from a scientific anthropological perspective, the European should be behind the camera.

One obvious reason for featuring Mecklenburg and von Weise in the image would have been to provide a scale by which to gauge the height of the jumps. Another might have been to demonstrate to the reader that the traveler involved in writing the text really was there—a means of authenticating the expedition. The images might have provided personal mementos of the African visit. However, a number of other interpretations can be adduced, based on an exploration of more symbolic meanings of the European presence.

As noted earlier, it seems certain that the event photographed by the Duke of Mecklenburg's expedition was actually organized by the members of the expedition themselves. But the setting up and the *taking* of the photograph—itself a demonstration of surveillance and appropriation—was not always enough, and I would argue that the physical presence of the European was thought necessary to reveal and make explicit the colonial power. Central to popular European imagination in the early twentieth century was the notion of occidental superiority. To be included in a photograph of native lands and/or people suggested asymmetric power relations. Whether it was the African's athletic power or the European political and cultural power that was being shown to the European audience, the African was still being photographed frequently for purposes he did not define.[38]

But what of the relation between African and European, as revealed in this stunning image? The photograph shows the Duke and his adjutant, standing between the two high jump uprights with a high jumper passing over their heads. The presence of two kinds of image (i.e., African/European) side by side may create meanings not produced by either image on its own.[39] Bringing Rwandan and European together, the photograph connotes feelings of power (or, possibly, reciprocity) that would be absent in two individual representations. The African objects of the gaze are captured, but the overdressed Duke of Mecklenburg and his militarily uniformed adjutant are also shown, standing somewhat stiffly and self-importantly under the seminaked athlete as he clears the rope between the two uprights. As the Germans distance themselves from local life by their attitude and posture (these are insistently not men about to "go native"[40]) they also demonstrate European power, contained centrally within the image. The positioning of the camera enables the jumper to be outlined against the sky, hence (literally) heightening the dramatic effects of his performance (and a technique replicated in other photographs of "Tutsi high jumping"). Yet it cannot be said unequivocally that he is given "visual primacy" over the German visitors. Although the *gusimbuka* performance is regarded as the object of the photograph in most of its captions (see below), the Europeans' centrality, upright posture, and military uniform carry messages of power and control—as the condition of European dominance over Africa. However, it is not known whether the pose of the Europeans reflected an awareness of the symbolism of the photograph's spatial organization. Hence, it is unclear who the photographer wished to privilege.

The scene was perfect for reproduction in *The National Geographic*, which was fond of showing not only the juxtaposition of the binary opposites of "black" and "white" and "civilized" and "primitive" but also the control which white domination bestowed on the tropics.[41] The Europeans command the center even if they are not the objects of the photograph. The man next to the upright (seemingly questioning the entire episode) is present in each of the three photographs known to have been taken of this event.[42] In none of them is his gaze directed at the athlete. He appears to be some kind of "assistant" (to the Germans or the jumper is not clear). He is certainly not in charge: he knows his place. But this "assistant" could be read as being part of a cultural—even "racial"—hierarchy. Whatever his role, for me he produces a kind of "sensitive point"[43] that disturbs the symmetry of the rectangular *urukiramende* (the high jump apparatus) and the vertical Europeans topped by the more horizontal Tutsi athlete. He appears to me as a rather poignant figure. He is all the more poignant if the jumper is read as representing a stereotypical, dominant, and powerful Tutsi, and he is the passive attendant, an imperfect body compared with the perfection of the Tutsi, and located at the margins of the action. Could he be a representation of a stereotypical Hutu or Twa?

The arrangement of the photograph recalls V. Y. Mudimbe's reading of a photograph of the Belgian artist Pierre Romain-Desfossés surrounded by his African students. In the composition and space of the photograph, there is an "overly well-organized balance" with "subtle arrangement," "geometric positioning," and the "exploitation of nature." There is a "regression of sensibilities" from the "master," through the young athletes toward the "symbolic unconquered forest." The only white figure is in the center. Mudimbe reads this as "a gradual progression from nature to culture . . . Following Freud one might refer to a will to master a psychic topography."[44] The centrality of the European in colonial photographs was clearly a common form of spatial arrangement. In this case they were framed by the edge of the picture and also by the rectangle of the high jump equipment (seemingly emerging from the portals of Africa) with clear evidence of the African other (spectators) in the background. There is again a visual hierarchy in which the Europeans are at the center with the Africans occupying various degrees of peripherality, symbolizing a map of the colonial world system.

The microgeography, as shown in the photograph, also reveals *gusimbuka* as a site of power orchestration. It is an image of order; African corporeality is confined to a cleared space. There is ample room for the event, and it takes place in an atmosphere of structure, and possibly rehearsal. The audience is orderly and well controlled. Their seminudity and their exotic activity identify the Africans, but the photographic capture and the European-imposed order domesticate them.[45] But power and oppression are not the sole properties of this image, and I cannot deny that the photograph also idealizes—even promotes—"the African." It projects corporeal achievement. Not for this athlete is the camera's gaze one of "blunt frontals" of the head and shoulders variety used for the anthropomorphic surveillance of native "types."[46]

In addition, the photograph connects with the question of representation. The athlete is performing or "representing" with his body the characteristics of one form of Rwandan body culture and his own athleticism. But these characteristics are also being re-presented to the Western world in the very different language of sport, a language that appropriates Rwandan body culture in Western terms. Mecklenburg's two other photographs of the high jump event did not contain any Europeans. This may be one of the reasons why they have not been reproduced so frequently, despite being somewhat more pure (but very far from accurate) anthropological records.

The representation of the Tutsi high jumper, as captured in this classic image, may be read at several levels. It is typical of representations that "were, by themselves, often too ambiguous to convey a simple, single message. Indeed, the very abundance of information in photographs, invariably well in excess of that intended by the photographer, opens them to a multitude of uses and meanings."[47] It certainly *denotes* an African clearing a rope above the heads of two Europeans. But what does it *connote*? Is it a sign of an African or a European triumph—or both? There is no one meaning, and many acceptable meanings could be taken from it. Certainly, the objects of the camera's gaze can often be substituted for the objects of supervision, if not "discipline."[48] Simon Ryan notes that a "dissociation of the see/being seen dyad . . . represents the visual desire of the explorer to reduce the threatening complexity of interactive observation by distancing the observer from the observed, and to construct observing moments as a 'small theatre' and the indigene as an 'object of information,' never a subject of communication."[49] The super vision of the camera could assume the role of supervision. However, this super vision recorded a body, not an identifiable person. It illustrates the Europeans not only (through the accompanying text) as named people but also through the clarity of their faces, identifiable as such. In contrast, the face of the athletic object is reduced to almost a blank surface, little more than a silhouette. Although this may have resulted from an inadequacy in the photographic technology, it classically symbolizes the athlete's objectification. But his face is unimportant; it is the body that is valorized and provides the necessary message.[50]

More significant, I think, is the way the photograph seems to illustrate a landscape of discipline. The clear demarcation of the Africans and the Europeans suggests an emphasis on "difference"; the photograph stresses the binary opposites of white and black, European and African, dressed and seminaked. The juxtaposition of nakedness and clothed bodies reinforced the view that while nakedness signified "uncivilized," clothing was an obvious accessory of "civilization." The attraction (for the viewer and subject) of the European photographed *with* the Rwandan may have lain in these contrasts or the simple "co-presence of two discontinuous elements, heterogeneous in that they did not belong to the same world."[51] At the same time it can also be suggested that while the image was, to be sure, one showing the indigene as different, he was also shown to be similar. After all, he was undertaking an activity with which the Europeans felt they could identify. Not only could they identify with it, viewing it as a sport, but the record(ing), using the universal currency of the measuring tape, showed them to be superior at a body-cultural activity that the Europeans had thought to be their own.

ACTS ON THE PHOTOGRAPH

The accompaniments to the photograph included captions and other juxtaposed written text. Colonial photographs were also frequently reorganized through the practice of montage that provided readers with what the photographer wanted them to see.[52] Additionally, retouching was common, "an absolutely routine procedure in publishing at this time."[53] Edwards terms these strategies as "acts upon photographs," which result in shifting their meaning and performance, over time and space, producing an image that has culturally specific meanings that are classified and reclassified into culturally constructed categories.[54]

In claiming impressive performances for the Rwandan high jumpers, it was recognized by some observers that the Duke of Mecklenburg could have been mistaken. However, the visual image was said to provide "undeniable photographic proof" that the athlete had cleared the incredible height of 2.50 meters.[55] Even so, Mecklenburg's claim—and his photograph—clearly proved too much for some European critics. After all, at the time the world's record for the high jump was only 1.97 meters. So, when viewing the photograph in figure 4.1, some people believe it to be a forgery, an "*ungeprüfen foto*."[56] However, the Mecklenburg image seems to me to be more the result of retouching than montage, but with partial knowledge of the circumstances I cannot be certain. But the speculation of forgery (i.e., montage) is not central to this chapter. What is important is that the photograph follows the trope of colonialism and was set up for the camera; it is a metaphorical montage if not a literal one.

Among the most potent forms of writing surrounding photographs are their captions. These serve to guide the reader or suggest one of several possible meanings of the photograph. As Walter Benjamin put it, captions are "signposts" having a quite different function from the title of a painting.[57] Consequently, the caption can sometimes assume supremacy over the image and can divert the audience's attention away from what might, at first sight, appear to be the central object of the photograph. In such cases, "the image no longer *illustrates* the words; it is now the words which, structurally, are parasitic on the image."[58] In the context of the Mecklenburg photograph it can be argued that the main way in which captions assumed supremacy over the image was when they informed the reader that the athlete was Tutsi. This was something that the reader could not possibly have established with any certainty by simply looking at the photograph. And in the great majority of cases there was no doubt in the minds of those who wrote later captions for this photograph that the jumper was Tutsi. Yet one cannot be certain that this was the case. At least one observer of colonial Rwanda has recorded that Hutu and Twa also took part in *gusimbuka*.[59]

Over time, a photograph can be accompanied by different captions in a variety of publications. Such recaptioning provides insights into changes in the interpretation of other societies and into the caption's general message.[60] In its original German source, the photograph was simply captioned "Hochsprung eines Mtussi (2.50 m.). Niansa." Here, the caption appropriates "the Tutsi" and *gusimbuka* by using the European term *Hochsprung* and by applying metric measurements. But what was unclear in the photograph alone now becomes apparent: the image is centrally about "the African" ("the Tutsi") and not the European. When reproduced three years later in the *National Geographic* its caption was amplified as "The Champion High Jumper of Africa." Here the caption applies the contemporary occidental idea of a champion of Africa, a further form of rhetorical appropriation. In Guttmann's *Games and Empires*, however, it is captioned as a "Wattussi Tribesman Leaping over the Head of Herzong (sic) Adolf Friedrich von Mecklenburg, Leader of an Ethnographic Expedition to German East Africa."[61] Here the African body is othered by only naming the European; additionally, Tutsi are mistakenly named as a "tribe." In the year of the Atlanta Olympics (1996) the photograph appeared yet again in the *National Geographic*, which carried a section on the Olympics. Its theme was the old and the new in sports. The Mecklenburg image was used to illustrate a sort of prototype of the modern high jump and was compared with an image of the "Fosbury Flop." The caption again described the athlete as "a champion high jumper" but proceeded to state that "innovative jumping styles" (e.g. the Fosbury Flop) have raised the Olympic record 22.25 inches since 1896, suggesting that the Rwandan performance was inferior to that of Fosbury.[62] This negates the African by not explicating that the recorded height in 1907 was actually read as being better than the current world's record (at the time

Fig. 127. 15-year-old Canadian negro SAM RICHARDSON, Empire Long Jump Champion, 23 ft. 6¼ in.

Fig. 128. JESSE OWENS, U.S.A., World's Long Jump Record Holder. 26 ft. 8¼ in. Olympic Champion 1936

Fig. 129. C. JOHNSON, U.S.A., Joint Holder of World's Record, 6 ft. 9¼ in. Olympic Champion 1936

Fig. 130. A Watufessi, Central African warrior, was credited with 8 ft. 2½ in. jumping from a small mound

Figure 4.2

of writing). Additionally, the author is unable to appreciate that the Rwandan jumping was unrelated to that of "the West"—an inability to acknowledge difference.

Two rather more specific acts on the photograph reveal further ways in which it was used. First, consider the inclusion of the Mecklenburg photograph as part of a photographic compilation of "Negro Jumpers" in one of the many coaching manuals written in the 1920s and 1930s by the British track and field coach F. A. M. Webster (figure 4.2).[63] As already noted, photographs including Rwandans and Europeans or Americans was a common model during colonial times. However, Webster's compilation is different because each of the Americans who is included is an African American sportized jumper. This provides representational space for an essentialist view of the black athlete. The compilation fills a single page and starts at the top, with two long jumpers—the "Canadian negro" Sam Richardson, champion of the British Empire, and Jesse Owens. Below these are photographs of Cornelius Johnson, the world high jump record holder and Olympic champion and next to it the much-reproduced Mecklenburg photograph of "a Watufessi" (sic) high jumper. Each of the four photographs has a brief caption. The juxtaposition of the four photographs, plus their collective caption, seems to establish two significant messages. One is that sportized jumping is a cultural universal. By dissolving cultural context, *gusimbuka* and Western high jumping are fantasized as being essentially equivalent. As illustrated and annotated, the Rwandan is performing (literally and metaphorically) *alongside* the Olympic champion from the United States. Second, this compilation of black jumpers essentializes "the Negro." Irrespective of the cultural background (Canada, the United States, Rwanda) of the four athletes shown, it suggests that black athletes per se are in some way privileged as long *and* high jumpers. Here, explicated by the caption, a "Tutsi body" becomes part of a crudely defined "racial" representation.

A second act on the photograph was undertaken by the sports scientist Ernst Jokl, who claimed to have visited Rwanda in the 1930s to carry out research into the kinesthetic elements of *gusimbuka-urukiramende*. In two publications on this subject,[64] he used the Mecklenburg photograph (taken about thirty years before his alleged visit) as a typical representation of the jumping genre, rather than use a contemporary image—one that he might have been expected to have taken himself. Jokl stated: "The Watusi do not use our delicately balanced rigid bar, but a hemp rope which is suspended between tree forks and which is difficult to dislodge."[65] This description almost certainly refers to the arrangement shown in the Mecklenburg photograph, which, I have stressed, was not a Rwandan-organized event. As far as I am aware, Jokl's description fails to fit any photographs of Rwandan jumping, except those taken by the Mecklenburg expedition. What all photographs of *gusimbuka* from the 1910s and 1920s that I have seen show exactly what Jokl denies, that is, a "delicately balanced rigid bar" composed of a reed resting on two uprights arranged at an angle of about fifty degrees away from the oncoming jumper.[66] "Tree forks" or "hemp rope" are never shown. Jokl, then, used a totally untypical image, created by Europeans, in order to define the characteristics of an indigenous body culture.

PARTIAL KNOWLEDGE AND THE "AFRICAN ATHLETE"

The way that the Rwandan athlete was represented in Mecklenburg's semi-nal misrepresentation has three important implications for both the sports histories and the political histories of Rwanda. The first is that, through its image and adjacent text, the photograph communicated "the Tutsi" athlete as a high jumper in the European mold. The photograph first appeared in the discourse of travel writing. It was to enter the written world of sport ten years after it was first published, but Mecklenburg used sporting language and quantitative measures to describe its contents. The power of the newly emergent twentieth-century world of sport had already conditioned many—like Mecklenburg—to a particular way of seeing. The application of quan-tification, the use of the English term *high jumping* rather than the native term *gusimbuka-urukiramende*, the comparison of the performance with the world's record, and the use of the term *champion* all serve to construct an African sportsman as a mirror of the western Olympian. This may have led to expectations of "the African" out-performing the European in a body-cultural practice in which the European was, at the time, considered supreme. There seemed to be no way in which the European could see it as anything but a version of modern sport. The surface appearance of it being a "sport" reflected the poverty of the European's ability to see it as some-thing fundamentally different. The reification ("thingification") of the word *sport* is a problem with which sports history continues to grapple. This chapter has shown that its use with reference to precolonial body cultures is far from helpful.

Second, the image of the Tutsi as athlete helped in the construction of the "black superman"—one of "Darwin's athletes."[67] This is best exempli-fied in Webster's compilation of images as described above. It was not, how-ever, the only way of reading "the Tutsi," and they were often differentiated from other blacks and instead identified as Hamites. Even so, Webster's willingness to read them as "Negroes," alongside Jesse Owens and other champions, fueled the view that "black athletes" were somehow naturally endowed with athletic superiority. Such a view reflects the desire to catego-rize and essentialize.

Third, the visual image of the alleged Tutsi high jumper served to stereotype Tutsi per se. The high jumpers were overwhelmingly recorded as Tutsi. The widely published photograph supported, in its own small way, the trajectory along which Rwandan history was being recorded from the nineteenth century. The Tutsi, the definite article describing a definite category, were, in 1907, already being represented as the superior group in Rwanda, intellectually and physically. In the first known photograph of *gusimbuka*, the already prevalent positive stereotype was enhanced by Meckelnburg's extravagant image and its associated written text. Here the separation of sports history and political history becomes an illusion.

Although Mecklenburg's expedition to Rwanda was apparently the first to record the physical and cultural nature of the region in any detail, he both obtained, and subsequently communicated, highly partial knowledge about the so-called Tutsi high jump. There is a tendency in written work, both popular and academic, to infer a degree of certainty and transparency about what one is writing. However, "we cannot know the whole of it."[68] In this chapter I have tried to heed Edwards's words: "If we do not explore the interrogatory potential of the medium itself and the intellectual possibilities of photographs, entangled as they are in their multiple histories and trajectories, we will surely, through privileging surface over depth, be blind to what photographs have to tell us."[69]

NOTES

1. On the work of Marey and Muybridge see, for example, John Pultz, *Photography and the Body* (London: Weidenfeld and Nicholson, 1995).

2. Stuart Hall, "The Spectacle of the 'Other,'" in *Representation: Cultural Representations and Signifying Practices*, ed. Stuart Hall (London: Sage, 1997), 223–90.

3. Elizabeth Edwards, *Raw Histories: Photographs, Anthropology and Museums* (Oxford: Berg, 2001).

4. David Rowe, *Sport, Culture and the Media* (Buckingham: Open University Press, 2000), 121.

5. Rowe, *Sport, Culture and the Media*, 125.

6. Rowe, *Sport, Culture and the Media*, 137.

7. Edwards, *Raw Histories*.

8. Edwards, *Raw Histories*, 121.

9. Jan Czekanowski, *Forschungen im Nil-Congo-Zwischengebeit*, vol. 3 (Leipzig: Klinkhardt and Biermann, 1911).

10. Duke of Mecklenburg, *Ins innerste Afrika* (Leipzig: Klinkhardt and Bierman, 1909).

11. Duke of Mecklenburg, *In the Heart of Africa* (London: Cassell, 1910).

12. Mecklenburg, *In the Heart of Africa*.

13. John Bale, *Imagined Olympians: Body-Culture and Colonial Representation in Rwanda* (Minneapolis: University of Minnesota Press, 2002), 31–32.

14. Quoted in H. Kna, "Die Watussi als springkunstler," *Erdball* 12: 459–62.

15. See Bale, *Imagined Olympians*, 31–32.

16. I do not use the designation "*the* Tutsi" since the definite article implies a definite category. On the problem of distinguishing Tutsi from Hutu and Twa see Bale, *Imagined Olympians*.

17. Quoted in Aimable Ndejuru, "Studien zur Rolle der Leibesübungen in der traditionellen Gesselschaft Ruanda," doctoral dissertation, University of Cologne, 1983.

18. Allen Guttmann, *From Ritual to Record: The Nature of Modern Sports* (New York: Columbia University Press, 1978).

19. These terms are taken from Christopher Pinney, *Camera Indica* (London: Reaktion Books, 1997), 46.

20. The gendered pronoun is deliberate; women did not participate in *gusimbuka*.

21. Marcel Pauwels, "Jeux et divertessements au Rwanda," *Annali Lateranensi* 24 (1960).

22. See Bale, *Imagined Olympians*.

23. Mecklenburg, *In the Heart of Africa*. Strictly speaking, there were no world's records as we know them in 1907, the IAAF not being founded until 1910.

24. On the question of the height jumped see Bale, *Imagined Olympians*, 71.

25. Michael Taussig, *Mimesis and Alterity: A Particular History of the Senses* (New York: Routledge, 1991), 21.

26. Taussig, *Mimesis and Alterity*.

27. Anne-Marie Willis, "Photography and Film: Figures in/of History," in *Fields of Vision*, eds. Leslie Devereaux and Roger Hillman (Berkeley: University of California Press, 1995), 77.

28. Nicholas Thomas, *Colonialism's Culture: Anthropology, Travel and Government* (Cambridge: Polity), 36.

29. Stephen Greenblatt, *Marvelous Possessions: The Wonder of the New World* (Oxford: Clarendon), 4.

30. Derek Gregory, "Scripting Egypt: Orientalism and the Cultures of Travel," in *Writes of Passage: Reading Travel Writing*, eds. James Duncan and Derek Gregory (London: Routledge, 1999), 114–50.

31. Nicholas Mirzoeff, *Bodyscape: Art, Modernity and the Ideal Figure* (London: Routledge, 1995), 139.

32. Nicholas Mirzoeff, *Introduction to Visual Culture* (London: Routledge, 1999), 139.

33. Duke of Mecklenburg, "A Land of Giants and Pygmies," *National Geographic* 23 (1912): 366–88; J. Hilderbrand, "The Geography of Games," *National Geographic* 36 (1919): 139–50.

34. F. A. M Webster, *Why? The Science of Athletics* (London: Shaw, c1937); Carl Diem, *Weltgeschichte des Sports und der Leibeserziehung* (Stuttgart: Cotta, 1960); Deuchen Hochschule für Körperkultur, *Körperkultur und Sport* (Leipzig: Verlag Enzyklopädie, 1960); Peter Rummelt, *Sport im Kolonialismus—Kolonialismus im Sport* (Cologne: Pahl-Rugenstein, 1986); Phil Minshull, "First in Flight," *IAAF Magazine* 11 (1996): 62–65.

35. Gudrun Honke, *Au plus profound de l'Afrique: Le Rwanda et la colonization allemande 1885–1919* (Wuppertal: Hammer, 1990); Ian Linden, *Church and Revolution in Rwanda* (Manchester: Manchester University Press, 1977). The above citations, in this and the previous note, represent a highly partial listing of publications in which the photograph was reproduced.

36. Christopher Pinney, "The Parallel Histories of Anthropology and Photography," in *Anthropology and Photography 1860–1920*, ed. Elizabeth Edwards (New Haven: Yale University Press, 1992), 74–96.

37. Pinney, "The Parallel Histories of Anthropology and Photography," 76.

38. Pultz, *Photography and the Body*, 24.

39. Victor Burgin, "Art, Common Sense and Photography," in *The Camera Essays*, ed. Jessica Evans (London: Rivers Oram), 74–85.

40. These words are based on James Clifford's comments on the appearance of the anthropologist Bronislaw Malinowski, photographed with some of his objects of study: James Clifford, *Routes* (Cambridge: Harvard University Press, 1997), 74.

41. Catherine Lutz and Jane Collins, *Reading National Geographic* (Chicago: University of Chicago Press, 1993); Tamar Rothenburg, "Voyeurs of Imperialism: *The National Geographic Magazine* before World War II," in *Geography and Empire*, eds. Anne Godlewska and Neil Smith (Oxford: Blackwell, 1994), 155–72.

42. Two other photographs of the jumping event, taken by the Mecklenburg expedition, are reproduced respectively in John Bale and Joe Sang, *Kenyan Running* (London: Cass, 1996), 60; Bale, *Imagined Olympians*, 112.

43. Barthes describes such a point as a "photograph's *punctum* . . . that accident which pricks me (but also bruises me, is poignant to me)," Roland Barthes, *Camera Lucida* (London: Vintage, 1993), 27.

44. V. Y. Mudimbe, *The Idea of Africa* (Bloomington: Indiana University Press, 1994), 157–58.

45. James Faris, "Photography, Power and the Nuba," in *Anthropology and Photography*, in ed. Elizabeth Edwards (New Haven: Yale University Press, 1992), 214.

46. Suren Lalvani, *Photography, Vision and the Production of Modern Bodies* (Albany: State University of New York Press, 1996), 87–137.

47. James Ryan, *Picturing Empire* (London: Reaktion Books, 1997), 220.

48. Pinney, "The Parallel Histories of Anthropology and Photography."

49. Simon Ryan, *The Cartographic Eye: How Explorers Saw Australia* (Cambridge: Cambridge University Press, 1996).

50. Fatimah Tobing Rony, *The Third Eye: Race, Cinema and Etnographic Spectacle* (Durham: Duke University Press, 1991), 58.

51. Barthes, *Camera Lucida*, 23.

52. See, for example, Virginia-Lee Webb, "Manipulated Images: European Photographs of Pacific People," in *Prehistories of the Future*, eds. E. Baran and R. Bush (Stanford: Stanford University Press, 1995), 175–201.

53. Christopher Pinney, "Classification and Fantasy in the Photographic Construction of Caste and Tribe," *Visual Anthropology* 3 (1990): 281.

54. Edwards, *Raw Histories*, 14.

55. H. Kna, "Die Watussi also Springkunstler," *Erdball* 12 (1929): 460.

56. Rummelt, *Sport im Kolonialismus—Kolonialismus im Sport*, 88. To my knowledge, no evidence of any alternative arrangements of the contents of the photograph exists. Hence, assertions of it being a montage can be, at best, speculations.

57. Walter Benjamin, "The Work of Art in the Age of Mechanical Reproduction" 1935, http://www.student.math.waterloo.ca/ l cs492/Benjamin.html (accessed 29/1/02).

58. Roland Barthes, *Image Music Text* (London: Fontana, 1977), 26.

59. Robert Borgerhoff, *Le Ruanda-Urundi* (Brussels: Dewitt, 1928), 36.

60. Lutz and Collins, *Reading National Geographic*, 79.

61. See respectively Mecklenburg, *Ins Innerste Afrika*, 114; Mecklenburg, "A Land of Giants and Pygmies," 388; Allen Guttmann, *Games and Empires* (New York: Columbia University Press, 1994), 54.

62. Frank Debord, "Let the Games Begin," *National Geographic* 190, no. 1 (1996): 54.

63. F. A. M. Webster, *Why? The Science of Athletics* (London: Shaw, c1937), facing 376.

64. Ernst Jokl, "High Jump Technique of the Central African Watussis," *Physical Education and School Hygiene* 33 (1941): 145–49; Ernst Jokl, *Physiology of Exercise* (Springfield, IL.: Thomas), 124–27.

65. See Bale, *Imagined Olympians*. From the 1930s onward, many representations of Rwandan high jumping show the use of Western equipment.

66. Jokl, *Physiology of Exercise*.

67. John Hoberman, *Darwin's Athletes* (Boston: Houghton Mifflin, 1997).

68. Edwards, *Raw Histories*, 121.

69. Edwards, *Raw Histories*, 126.

CHAPTER 5

Anecdotal Evidence

Sport, the Newspaper Press, and History

JEFFREY HILL

In a recent review of Terry Eagleton's *The Gatekeeper*, the literary theorist Terence Hawkes remarked of autobiography that it is "one of the sublest forms of fiction."[1] If we can agree with Hawkes that within the genre of life history there lurks a great deal of invention, how true might this also be of newspapers. Examples abound. The extent to which the "good story" has influenced the writing of newspaper people has long been recognized, but do we also recognize that the compulsion to put things in narrative form might actually shape our perceptions of the world? Anyone who used the press to piece together the complexities of the foot-and-mouth epidemic in Britain during the spring and summer of 2001 will recognize this problem. In attempting to convey to their readers what was going on, press reporters were not consciously inventing, but they were operating according to a very definite "way of telling." It involved stories of funeral pyres, slaughtermen, the illicit movement of cattle, and government indecision. The facts of the case were presented in a particular narrative form, which colored "the truth" and positioned the reading public to understand the epidemic from a specific point of view. A similar approach to the presentation of facts as story is to be found in the vogue for "reconstructions" in the contemporary media; fragmentary evidence, in itself likely to make for rather boring reading or viewing, is dramatized with fictionalized embellishments. It is presumably felt to produce a more interesting form of communication. Recent examples have included the story of British intelligence services in Northern Ireland infiltrating terror gangs in order to eliminate Republican

117

activists, and the reporting of crimes in programs such as the BBC's popular and long-running *Crimewatch*.[2] There is even a suggestion that some reporters are themselves beginning to recognize the influence exercised by the narrative structures within which they work and think. John Lloyd, for example, discussing the arrangements for the Queen Mother's funeral in April 2002 and the attack on the prime minister that the occasion provoked in sections of the popular press, has claimed that narratives imprison both media and politicians. Journalists, with "their ability to create vast narratives composed of selected facts, woven into realms of speculation and embroidered with distortion" compete in invention with the politicians whose "spin" is manufactured to match them.[3] A nineteenth-century editor of the *Times* might famously have claimed that "the business of the press is disclosure," but the process of disclosing has never been a straightforward one. It is tempting to recall once more the old adage of the editor who urged his reporters never to "let the facts get in the way of a good story."

Indeed, this complements another popular saying—part of the subterranean discourse of common sense unearthed many years ago by Richard Hoggart, that "you shouldn't believe everything you read in the papers."[4] Whatever the validity of this saying, and popular sayings have a tendency toward at least a degree of veracity, it is one that has not deterred historians. Newspapers have figured high on their list of sources. In spite of skepticism among the public about some aspects of the press, newspapers have been regarded by historians as an almost unblemished source of plain fact. Historians of sport in particular have resorted to the press. The files of the provincial press have been rigorously excavated, particularly for the nineteenth and twentieth centuries, the period most sport historians have studied. Press reports have become a staple—perhaps *the* staple—source in the task of reconstructing the history of sport and games.

Few would doubt that, used judiciously, press sources can produce an excellent foundation for history. They are, depending on one's choice of metaphor, the straw that makes the bricks, the raw material of the subject, the evidence of past activity, and so on. In that sense the press is perhaps responsible for there being something called "sports history" at all, at least in the academy. Without a work such as Tony Mason's outstanding *Association Football and English Society 1863–1915*,[5] copiously constructed from primary evidence in which press accounts of various kinds occupy a principal place, there might never have been an academic history of sport. However, when reliance on the press becomes excessive there are objections that can be made. For example, in his work on the international relations of football Peter Beck has observed an inclination on the part of sport historians to use the press to the exclusion of other sources, and therefore to the detriment of the history they produce.[6] In a distinctive metaphor Beck has pleaded for his colleagues to add Kew and Cambridge to a research itinerary that has seemed fixated with the destination of Colindale.[7] Similarly Matthew Taylor has expressed some sympathy with this view in noting the absence of "extensive archival research" in many histories of association football, though he sensitively acknowledges that a shortage of primary sources in this area has led *faute de mieux* back to the press: "for the historian of football, there often seems to be nowhere to look except the press."[8] Be that as it may, and many of us (not only historians of football) have cause to share Taylor's despairing view, the regular surveys of archival deposits produced for the British Society of Sports History by Richard Cox and the wealth of primary material on display in a book like Mike Huggins's prize-winning *Flat Racing and British Society*[9] show there is ample material outside the newspaper libraries for historians of sport to consult. Perhaps Beck is right, then, to remind his colleagues to look farther afield and at least to explore the riches that lie beyond the newspaper archive.

It might appear surprising therefore that this chapter seeks to prolong the gaze on the press. This is not out of a wish to disagree with Beck. His exhortation for us to broaden our archival repertoire is admirable. But it is made in the expectation that we wish to practice and perpetuate a certain kind of history. There are assumptions about methodology being made here. Above all there is an implication in Beck's strictures that, in effect, more means better; in other words, by encompassing a wider range of sources our comprehension of the past will be better informed and better balanced, and that this being so we will go on to produce better history. Such a sentiment, it seems to me, makes a fundamentally conservative assumption about the practice of history; and while it posits a practice from which many (perhaps most) historians would probably not demur, the assumption nevertheless ought not to pass without remark.

In making the remark, a brief excursion into theory is needed. A broadening of the archival repertoire would intensify the empirical base of our discipline, to be sure. But in itself this simply reaffirms conventional beliefs about the nature of sources. Historians who have used the press have generally done so in much the same way that they have used other kinds of evidence, that is to say by employing what is often referred to in epistemological circles as the "correspondence theory of truth." The source—press report, cabinet minute, personal letter, whatever—is seen as a point of access to a knowable past. It is reflective of a reality held to exist outside the source itself. On this simple assumption a whole edifice of professional history has been built for over a hundred years. It has of course been periodically questioned, but the questionings have often exercised little effect on what is a powerful corporate empire within the academy. Partly this is because the questionings have failed to satisfy intellectual doubts, but equally as often it has been because of the self-sealing devices that close around the empire when its credo is threatened. These devices are oiled by a good deal of intellectual common sense together with deep reserves of innuendo and personal invective. Because of this, challenging the truths of History (with a capital H) is not an enterprise for the faint-hearted.

Postmodernism is the term usually associated with such questionings. Among many British historians the term has, unfortunately, become a code-word for fashionable nonsense. Many no doubt dismiss it without understanding what the term involves, though they are all too aware of what it implies.[10] Of course, "postmodernism" conceals as much as it reveals, and "postmodernists" have often unnecessarily alienated their fellow historians by the sin of talking for too long at too abstract a level and not getting on with the "history." This is a feature evident in Alun Munslow's otherwise excellent book *Deconstructing History*.[11] For all its elegant explication of difficult theory, there is scarcely any engagement with empirical cases and very little indication of how postmodernism might help in the actual doing of history. Indeed, the reader is rather left to assume that theory renders history redundant as an empirical practice; and nothing is calculated to get historians' backs up more than the suggestion that they themselves are about to be consigned to the dustbin of history. Nonetheless, Munslow raises some important issues, notably the important but frequently overlooked fact that doing history is a fictive art.[12] This is something that all historians surely know, though many seek to conceal it by emphasizing the discipline's positivist/scientific credentials. But in the last analysis, whether we systematize history's narrative content in the formal manner of Hayden White, with his categorizing of the rhetorical means employed by historians to reconstruct the story of the past,[13] or simply remind ourselves that in many languages the word for "history" is the same as the word for "story," we cannot deny that it is concerned with the act of narrating—both the narrating contained in the sources themselves, and the narrative imposed by the historian on them.

Using newspapers—particularly using newspapers—brings these points well to the fore. They were brought to my attention when, a few years ago, I did some work on the subject of sport and identity that involved my looking at association football rituals in northern English towns in the late nineteenth and early twentieth centuries. I examined in particular the ways in which a town's involvement in the final of the national knock-out competition—the FA Cup Final—was celebrated.[14] The main source for this was the local press, which reported these rituals in great detail. The period—roughly from the 1880s to the 1950s—represented what was probably the heyday of the provincial press, before its titles began to be amalgamated into chains and before it had to compete with the claims of radio and television for its readers' attention. This was the era when newspapers, national and local, daily and weekly, were the great instrument of popular communication. By the late nineteenth century provincial newspapers had largely left behind the immense political controversies that had characterized the causes of Reform and Chartism and had settled into a less partisan form. Titles were still readily identifiable with political positions—usually Liberal or Tory/Unionist/Conservative, only rarely Labor—but often their politics were muted, submerged into a greater appeal to community. This was especially so in smaller towns, which sustained only one main title. But even in the bigger regional centers such as Manchester, Birmingham, and Leeds, competing papers challenged each other as much over their ability to voice the interests of the whole community as in the superiority of the political principles they espoused. Themes of community, locality, "our town" provided the main tropes of local newspaper reportage. The voice assumed by the press was the voice of "us," the locality; the local paper spoke, or was felt to speak, for the people of the community it served.[15]

This press had been vitally important in the creation and dissemination of new sport in the late nineteenth century. In spite of this, the role of the press represents a surprising gap in British sports historiography. There is no serious study to compare with, for example, Whannel's work of the presentation of sport on television or Michael Oriard's work on the role of the press in American sport.[16] Oriard's magisterial synthesis of the mediating function of the press—and its accompanying media forms of radio, magazines, newsreels, films, and latterly television—in creating an understanding of football in American society leaves us in no doubt that the "experience" of sport derived essentially from the meanings communicated by the written and spoken word and from the everpresent and carefully chosen images of the photographer and cameraman.[17] In Britain until the 1960s, when television began to take over its function, the newspaper was the principal means by which people "knew" sport: how to understand, interpret, make sense of it. Far more people read about sport than ever watched a sporting spectacle. Local newspapers fulfilled this function in an especially important way. They devoted space to local clubs of various degrees of skill and in particular gave prominence to the clubs that bore the town's name—in association football, rugby, cricket, speedway, and so on. A mutuality of interest developed between newspapers and these clubs. Editors appeared to believe that, in a well-worn phrase, "sport sells papers"; and for their part the clubs valued the publicity that press coverage gave them, especially if they were clubs that sought spectators. The relationship between the reporter and the club was frequently an intimate one, with the club providing privileged information for the reporter's copy and the reporter writing it up in a form that gave prominence to the club's activities. It was almost an advertizing service for the sports concerned.[18]

The coverage of sport took many forms. Reports of matches were the most common, but detailed summaries of annual general meetings, interviews with players and managers, "pen portraits" of popular sportspeople, especially newcomers to a club, and (as sensationalism grew in the interwar years) dressing room gossip, all featured as part of the general representation of the world of sport. All of this presents the historian with a variety of sources. All, even the dullest report of an annual general meeting, are aspects of storytelling, and therefore contain particular voices, narrative styles, and forms of emplotment. None is without its "fictive" elements. But some sources are more fictive than others, and to emphasize this we might at this point begin to replace the term *source* with that of *text*.

As texts, the local press accounts of association football celebrations that I used in my work presented an intriguing mixture of the factual and the inventive. Two different levels of press writing are interesting here. In one sense, it was possible to use the press texts in the historian's customary way as "neutral" or "objective" observations on what was happening. In this sense they possessed a "mirror" effect. I was able to draw inferences from the text that suggested some interesting patterns of urban culture. For example, there seemed to have been a gradual transformation of Cup Final celebrations from a spontaneous commemoration of club to an official and orchestrated civic ceremonial. This proved valuable in thinking not only about sport but also about local power and how sport was appropriated in an attempt to sustain civic authority and forge local identity. It was tempting to think of the texts as sources again, even as more objective data, which unproblematically mediated this process to me as the historian. But of course the press was not really neutral in its observations. It was complicit in the whole process of civic identity as both reporter and accomplice: by telling what was happening it also became the chief agency for communicating the ideology. Athough the text might have been innocent, the medium itself occupied a very precise role in a knowledge/power situation.

At a second level, I noted the extent of the coverage of the events celebrating the appearance of local clubs in Cup Finals. It was singularly detailed. We should remember the peculiar tension between the national and the local that has always been at the heart of British association football and that accounts for the continuing popularity of the cup competition. Association football thrived on the pitting of one local identity against another local identity in a national framework. During the period in question (and in marked contrast with the early-twenty-first century), it was still possible for relatively small provincial towns to be a force in national football and to express this by featuring in and winning the FA Cup. The appearance in the final of clubs from towns such as Preston, Huddersfield, Blackburn, Barnsley, Brighton, West Bromwich (whether or not the team won was usually immaterial) was an occasion for asserting local pride on a national scale. The reporting of this assertion involved a multiplicity of stories, but there are persistent structural features in the telling of the stories. One was the narrative form in which the entire event was told. It was one that historians of tourism would recognize as the narrative of pilgrimage, with three distinct components to the plot: journeying, arrival, and return.[19] Journeying and arrival, which concerned the movement of people to London and their experiences there, were characterized by "liminality"—of experiences that were out of the ordinary, involving a suspension of normal rules and behavior, where "excess" was accepted (in eating, drinking, staying up late). They also presented opportunities for the introduction into the discourse of notions of the other—usually London and Londoners (the metropolis) representing different and alien mentalities, by contrast with which "our" (provincial) way of life was reaffirmed as being the "right" way. Finally was the return, which reported the arrival back into the town of the team, whether successful or not. This was the scene for massed crowds, cheering, speeches, celebration, and time off work. But in spite of the obvious abnormality of the event the large crowds that gathered to witness the team's return were represented as a symbol of the unity of the town itself, all its thoughts and energies focused for a short time on the heroes of the day. It provides a clear illustration of Benedict Anderson's concept of the "imagined community,"[20] for once integrated, its everyday antagonisms set aside.

A further feature of this aspect of reporting was its durability. The story was told in the same way for at least half a century, until the narrative form began to change with the arrival of the more visual medium of television. In other words, press reporters told the story in the manner they had come to expect the story to be told. Within this mode of storytelling there was a profusion of stories and reminiscences with a local flavor, a human interest, and therefore a readerly appeal: stories of people loading barrels of beer into trains, sleeping in railway stations, men attempting to walk some two hundred miles to London, visiting the Cenotaph to honor "the Fallen" of the Great War, getting lost in the big city, bringing small-town mentalities into play when searching for the pub called the "Old Lady" in Threadneedle Street, or asking the way to the circus at Piccadilly. These little narratives teased me as a historian. What were they—fact or fiction? They often seemed to exist on a borderline between the two categories. They certainly defied "scientific" treatment and I suspect might have been dismissed by historians of a positivist persuasion as being irrelevant, or at best anecdotes, representing what is offensive to the historian because lacking in evidence—merely "anecdotal," "no-account items" as Catherine Gallagher and Stephen Greenblatt (who have sought to rescue them) have characterized their status in the eyes of "mainstream" historians.[21] How were they read, and what did they mean to readers of the time? What was I, a historian arriving on the scene more than a century, in some cases, later to make of them? Presented with this conundrum of "thick description" I put away my historian's tools for a while and following Clifford Geertz, took to the methods of my colleagues in literary studies.[22]

One such piece of press reportage (if that is the correct term) will suffice here to illustrate the point. In the last Cup Final to be played at the Crystal Palace ground, in 1914, Liverpool played Burnley. The location, a commercial pleasure garden in leafy Sydenham, south London, had staged the final since 1895. Besides being the venue for the Cup Final, the Crystal Palace was beloved by visitors as a place of popular recreation. Its musical events, brass band competitions in particular, were especially renowned.[23] In such a place, the Cup Final had acquired, over its relatively short history there, a holiday atmosphere. The match of 1914 was no exception, and like others before it had the additional feature of bringing the North to London. It was suffused with celebration of the local; for the competing clubs both came from Lancashire, the birthplace of the Industrial Revolution and, many claimed, of modern football itself. The local press treated its readers to columns of detail about the antics of the local supporters who had made the journey to London and who were making the visit a holiday, an occasion for enjoyment and excess. The narrative worked upon the theme of the "invasion" of the metropolis by the North and employed oppositions of "north" and "south"—with all the cultural contrasts these categories implied—to represent "our" folks back to themselves. The setting's potential for drawing comedy out of the small-town visitor making her or (usually) his way in the big city connected with other cultural forms that had used the same ingredients. The seaside postcard was the most familiar. Both worked to create local identity.[24]

One press story, as much as anything else, summed all this up. A man from Burnley, it was reported, took the opportunity to visit, before the start of the match, the famous glass edifice of the Crystal Palace, the centerpiece of the entire location. Since its creation by Joseph Paxton for the Great Exhibition of 1851 in Hyde Park, the structure had been dismantled and removed to the pleasure gardens in Sydenham, where it was reerected and, until its demolition by fire in 1936, became one of the great landmarks of the metropolitan landscape, a place of pilgrimage on the tourist's itinerary. There was, of course, nothing to compare with it in Burnley, and it was therefore a "must." The visitor, careful (as northerners are) with his money, had initially demurred at paying an additional entrance fee to the Crystal Palace over and above the price of his match ticket. But he was later forced to acknowledge that the price had been worthwhile; the glass structure was certainly an impressive experience. He added, though, as a summation of the whole experience: "By gum, aw wouldn't like to go and mend a brokken pane up theer."[25]

The remark could be passed off as incidental, anecdotal, and to the modern reader not remotely funny. It is, though, important in several ways and condenses into a single statement so much of what the local press was all about at this time. Here is an attempt to suggest the various levels at which the remark might be taken.

- The author of the joke, if so it can be described, is undoubtedly impressed by what is a national monument: no rebuke is being directed at an edifice that represents in many ways the pride of the nation; (its provenance was, after all, the Great Exhibition; there could be no greater symbol of the country's achievement).
- But note that the remark is delivered in a dialect form (or at least an attenuated dialect form). It thus introduces the local into the national and reminds us that the nation is composed of a variety of people, with different habits, cultures, and speech patterns.
- The remark is about the potential for broken window panes. It thus brings practical considerations into the reckoning. The Crystal Palace is indeed a grand building, but its very grandness involves many repair jobs. We must not, therefore, allow ourselves to be carried away by the grandiose. There is always the practical and everyday to be considered.
- Through this implication the author is refusing to be overimpressed, counterbalancing his "awe" with a recognition of the "practical."
- Local readers back in Burnley would have recognized the irony contained in these sentiments and marked it down as capturing their own mentality: down to earth, a proper perspective on life, not being carried away. The author of the remark thus becomes an "everyman" figure, and the situation represents in microcosm the relationship between provinces and metropolis.
- This brings us to an interesting speculation. Who was the author of the remark? Though reported in the press as one incident among many hundreds of similar situations that took place on that day, we should doubt its literal truth. In all probability the remark was never made; it was certainly not attributed to any particular individual; it is (probably) a mere anecdote, a story, a fiction, part of the myth of the North.

- But, the newspaper reporter who composed that section of the paper no doubt felt that the remark had a ring of truth. His readers would undoubtedly have expected someone to have said something like this, in this particular situation. The pleasure experienced by the reader in the story derived from the way it both presented and confirmed a vision of the self.

This chapter has taken a rather narrow—anecdotal—focus on its evidence, and it might therefore be worth concluding by considering some of the broader implications of the foregoing discussion. We began by noting criticisms of sports historians' overuse of newspaper sources. We have ended by suggesting that, for all their recourse to the newspaper press, sports historians have barely scratched its surface as text. It would be unfair to claim that sports historians have assumed a rigidly "positivist" approach to the press; there have been many instances of the use of the press to probe those aspects of sport that lie beyond the events that immediately surround the sporting spectacle. Matthew Taylor, for example, has recently explored the very interesting subject of association footballers' diaries presented as weekly columns in the local and national press, a subject that raises important questions about the construction of the hero.[26] Even so, there has been little recognition of the "literariness" of the newspaper as source and of the techniques and codes by which its content is communicated to the reader. The absence of reference by sports historians, either implicitly or explicitly, to terms such as *discourse, narrative, voice,* even *text,* is not to be explained simply by their wish to be jargon-free and to write in plain language. It is much more to do with the extensively held belief that such tools are not those of the historian. Perhaps it is this adhesion to what are felt to be the proper tools of the trade that has caused historians to eschew those sections of the press that appear to be literary and to confine themselves to those sections where the content is thought transparently to be historical.

What this perspective often produces is a neglect of how the newspaper was *read* and of what, historically, was important in the text for the reader. If we are to suggest, as this chapter does and as Michael Oriard's weighty body of work demands, that sport is understood, not in any essentialist way but through the various forms through which an idea of sport is mediated to and its meanings negotiated by those interested in it, we must not lose sight of the reader's ability to influence this process. But, of course, the issue of what the reader actually takes from the text is a mighty tricky one, probably never fully resolvable. Controlled experiments of reader responses, in the manner for example of David Morley's celebrated research on British television programs[27] are but one very limited way of grappling with this issue and a way unavailable to historians whose readers are usually dead. To a limited extent the issue can be confronted for the past by using reviews, trade surveys, and ethnographic archives such as Mass-Observation, but if such evidence exists it is a stroke of good fortune. Mostly it does not, and the historian interested in reader response has to engage in a spot of imaginative reconstruction, to be blunt, intelligent guesswork. Oriard attempts to square the circle by a neat if not entirely convincing assertion that by employing a range of popular texts, incorporating a variety of narratives, the possible extent of readers' negotiations and interpretations is at least approximated. It is a methodology that relies rather too much for comfort on an assumption (which pressmen themselves have been only too willing to advance) that newspapers give the readers what they want. But, for all its shortcomings, it is probably the best we can do.[28]

The newspaper text emerges from all this as a curious artefact the content of which, varied as it is, certainly cannot be taken for granted. Interrogating such a source brings to the fore many problems about the nature of the historian, her/his relationship to the source, and the nature of historical investigation itself. It is beyond question that the events that formed the focus of my research took place. They are "real" events in that sense, although a fictional fringe might have been tacked on to them, as in the case of the remark about the Crystal Palace. In general though what happened was not the product of the imagination. And yet my knowledge of them derived from fragments of highly selective accounts, often constructed in a narrative form the purpose of which was linked to the expectations of another reader, reading for a different purpose. In this sense the source is not a passive text; it works on the reader just as much as the reader attempts to control and contain it. Thus, the conventional desire to "read through" the source to a reality that it is assumed existed beyond it, of which the source is a "reflection," demands too straightforward a mediation; this problem is pointed up more emphatically with the kind of source I have analyzed here, which is clearly fictive in its form and purpose. But lest it is assumed that there are other aspects of newspaper reportage that present less problematical epistemological issues, we should remember that the layers of interpretation and the conventions of storytelling apply to all sections of the newspaper and indeed to all aspects of historical reconstruction. Some sources are more fictive than others, but all, in their way, have fictive elements.

This being so, in answer to the conventional question posed by historians about sources—What does this tell us about the society that existed at the time?—it is tempting to respond with a hint of the opaqueness of the source itself and to say that it tells us only that it was a society capable of creating such a source.

NOTES

1. Terence Hawkes, *London Review of Books*, 7 February 2002, 25–26.

2. See, for example, *BBC Panorama*, 17 and 23 June 2002.

3. John Lloyd, "The Royals' Revenge," *New Statesman*, 24 June 2002.

4. See Richard Hoggart, *The Uses of Literacy: Aspects of Working-class Life, with Special Reference to Publications and Entertainments* (London: Chatto and Windus, 1957), especially chapters 2 and 3.

5. Tony Mason, *Association Football and English Society 1863–1915* (Brighton: Harvester, 1980).

6. Peter J. Beck, *Scoring for Britain: International Football and International Politics 1900–1939* (London: Cass, 1999), vii; Peter J. Beck, "Political Football: The British Government and Anglo-Soviet Footballing Relations 1945–54," paper presented at the conference of the British Society of Sports History, Liverpool, 29–30 April 2000.

7. For those not acquainted with British archives: Kew in west London is the location of the National Archives; Cambridge refers to various archives in both the University Library and individual colleges in Cambridge; and Colindale in north London is where the British Library's newspaper collection is housed.

8. Matthew Taylor, "Football Archives and the Historian," *Business Archives* 78 (1999): 1.

9. See, for example, Richard William Cox, "Index to Sports History Journals, Conference Proceedings and Anthologies published in 2000," *Sports Historian* 21, no. 2 (2001): 68–90; and *Sport in Britain: A Bibliography of Historical Publications 1800–1988* (Manchester: Manchester University Press, 1991). A new three-volume edition of this source is to be published soon. Mike Huggins, *Flat Racing and British Society 1750–1914: A Social and Economic History* (London: Cass, 2000).

10. The mentality was cleverly encapsulated in a cartoon in the *Times Higher* 21 January 2000, which had an obviously "feminist" type accusing an equally obviously "reactionary" male academic that he "just can't come to terms with Postmodernism"; to which the reply was "no—but I trod in some once." There are some fairly uncomplimentary comments in a similar vein in Arthur Marwick's *New Nature of History: Knowledge, Evidence, Language* (Basingstoke: Palgrave, 2001), especially 253–60.

11. Alun Munslow, *Deconstructing History* (London: Routledge, 1997).

12. See an interesting exchange between Munslow and Richard J. Evans in *The Guardian*, 6 February 2001, and Evans's own *In Defence of History* (London: Granta Books, 1997).

13. See, for example, Hayden White, *Tropics of Discourse: Essays in Cultural Criticism* (Baltimore: Johns Hopkins University Press, 1978).

14. Jeff Hill, "Rite of Spring: Cup Finals and Community in the North of England," in *Sport and Identity in the North of England*, eds. J. Hill and J. Williams (Keele: Keele University Press, 1996), 85–112; "Sport and 'Local Knowledge': the Cup Final and Multiple Identity in Northern England, c.1880–1960" *Memoria y Civilizacion* 3 (2000): 311–29.

15. Royal Commission on the Press 1947–1949, *Report* (London: HMSO, 1949), 10–12, 89, 122. Also Ian Jackson, *The Provincial Press and the Community* (Manchester: Manchester University Press, 1971).

16. See Gary Whannel, *Fields in Vision: Television Sport and Cultural Transformation* (London: Routledge, 1992); Michael Oriard, *Reading Football: How the Popular Press Created an American Spectacle* (Chapel Hill: University of North Carolina Press, 1993); and *King Football: Sport and Spectacle in the Golden Age of Radio and Newsreels, Movies and Magazines, the Weekly and the Daily Press* (Chapel Hill: University of North Carolina Press, 2001).

17. Oriard, *King Football*.

18. See T. Mason, "All the Winners and the Half Times," *Sports Historian* 13 (1993): 3–13.

19. See, for example, V. Turner and E. Turner, *Image and Pilgrimage in Christian Culture: Anthropological Perspectives* (Oxford: Blackwell, 1978).

20. Benedict Anderson, *Imagined Communities: Reflections on the Origins and Spread of Nationalism*, rev. ed. (London: Verso, 1991).

21. Catherine Gallagher and Stephen Greenblatt, *Practicing New Historicism* (Chicago: University of Chicago Press, 2000), 49.

22. See Clifford Geertz, "Thick Description: Towards an Interpretive Theory of Culture", *The Interpretation of Cultures* (New York: Basic Books, 1973), 3–32.

23. Michael Musgrave, *The Musical Life of the Crystal Palace* (Cambridge: Cambridge University Press, 1995); see also Hill, "Rite of Spring."

24. Musgrave, *The Musical Life of the Crystal Palace*; see also Hill, "Rite of Spring."

25. *Burnley Express*, 27 April 1914.

26. Matthew Taylor, "The Diary of Willie Cook, Professional Footballer," paper presented to the annual conference of the British Society of Sports History, Leicester, April 2002.

27. David Morley, *The Nationwide Audience: Structure and Decoding* (London: British Film Institute, 1980).

28. Oriard, *Reading Football*, especially 8–19.

CHAPTER 6

Wasn't It Ironic?

The Haxey Hood and the Great War

CATRIONA M. PARRATT

THE "APPROPRIATE INTERPRETATIVE MEANS"

The Great War of 1914–1918 gave many British people from diverse walks of life occasion for a reappraisal of the most fundamental order. As more and more began to understand, to represent, and to experience the conflict as an enormous, scandalous tragedy, the greater the gulf that seemed to separate the prewar world from that which came after.[1] The impact on people's lives was devastating. The war struck the prosperous, comfortably middle-class Vera Brittain as an "explosion which . . . reverberate[d] through my personal life to the end of my days." Brittain's *Testament of Youth* was an attempt to "rescue something that might be of value, some element of truth and hope and usefulness, from the smashing up" of her "youth by the War." It was an unflinching, bitter portrayal of the "stark agonies" that the Great War generation, when still only in its twenties, faced, an unapologetic "indictment of a civilisation."[2] Brittain was far from alone in the impulse to wrest some meaning from her trauma through writing about it, and her youthful cohort's war-inspired prose and poetry stand as a masterful and moving body of literature.

Much of this work, Paul Fussell observes, takes "a terrible irony" as the "appropriate interpretative means" for apprehending the war and its aftermath, and it is from it, to a considerable extent, that present-day memories

I am indebted to Norma and Eric Neill for their kindness and invaluable help with the research for this project.

131

of these things derive. For some of the generation of English youth that came to adulthood in the 1960s and 1970s, myself included, the poetry of Wilfred Owen and T. S. Eliot offered a textual access to World War I and a judgment of it that in the Vietnam War era had a powerful resonance. When the United States was dispatching thousands of its young men to suffer and die and kill in Southeast Asia, the antiheroic, accusatory verse of a soldier-poet such as Owen told never-to-be-forgotten "truths."[3]

Recently I have been reflecting on those truths in light of my work in sport history and bringing them together with research on the Twelfth Night custom of the "Haxey Hood."[4] At some point in this process the Great War started, as Chris Ward expresses it so evocatively, to "present itself" to my imagination, "to loom out of the fog of that half-explored landscape of [my] own culture. . . ." "That war's susurration," Ward continues, "for decades internalized and dismissed, yet heard almost everywhere in England, like the sound of distant traffic becomes distinct, louder, more insistent. You begin to notice the monuments on every side: in railway stations, in town centers and villages, by parish halls or in churches . . . in the old universities, even in department stores."[5] It may well be that in the course of my frequent recent journeys to the Isle of Axholme and wanderings around its villages, the ubiquitous memorials to local men who fought and fell began to register in a way they had not before.[6] Or that previous research on the Victorian and Edwardian periods brought me sequentially to an event in history that has been seen as bringing those eras to a crashing close. Or that in sources on and local tellings of the history of the Haxey Hood the war is momentous because of the threat it was deemed to pose to the custom's survival.[7] Whatever the precise origins of my impetus, as I thought about and imagined how a history of the Hood and the Great War might be read, represented, and interpreted, it did indeed seem that irony was a most appropriate way to approach the task.

At the deepest, affective levels I know why this should be so. For as long as I can remember I have lived in wretched anticipation of the "cruel twist of fate," that bitter "wormwood" in "the wonder . . . of the whole."[8] This was a philosophy I learned early in life from my mother. Around the time I was born, quite possibly on the day I was born, a brother-in-law of whom she was very fond died. He was in the full vigor of his youth, a handsome, strapping farmworker, a gifted cricketer and football player. He was it seemed far too healthy and vital for his death to have been anything other than horribly shocking to family and friends. It was also wickedly ironic. He had been having symptoms of a urinary or renal disorder and was afraid that he had cancer. Convinced he was doomed, but unable to confront the disease directly by going to the doctor and having it diagnosed, he resigned himself to his fate. He did nothing and told no one until there could be no doubt that something was terribly wrong, until what was in reality a fairly benign and treatable condition was far beyond treatment.

For my mother the coincidence of Uncle Bill's death with my birth meant that she could never celebrate with me or for me without sorrow, without being overwhelmed with despair that we live our lives in the shadow of mortality, "the one ultimate Satire of Circumstance."[9] And so every year, and especially toward the end when she was in a pretty much perpetual clinical depression, my birthday would end with a mournful litany that began: "If only your Uncle Bill had lived, he would be [however many years' old]. If only he'd gone to the doctor when it all started . . ."

There was no stopping this train of sorrow and tears once it got going. From Uncle Bill and my birthday, Mum moved on to other family members, friends, and workmates, laying out for me the details of their sufferings at the hands of an ironical fate. And figuring prominently among them was *her* uncle, a young man of the Vera Brittain generation, who went off to fight that optimistically misnamed "war that will end war."[10]

My great-uncle was one of hundreds from villages in the Isle of Axholme who served in the First World War, one of the thousands throughout the nation who not only went off and never came back but whose bodies disappeared without trace in the blood and mire of the Western Front. There are now only the most meager signs that they were ever there: a name inscribed on a monument, a singed fragment of a service record, a pair of regimental shoulder flashes uncovered by a souvenir hunter.[11] But many families continue to tell stories about the boys and men who did not come home, and in this way they are remembered: sons, fathers, husbands, brothers, and uncles. In my family, the story of the great-uncle who the Great War swallowed up was never told but as one in a series of lessons to live by and worry about, a series for which the only apt title would be that of a collection by Thomas Hardy, master ironist of English literature—*Life's Little Ironies*.[12]

In coming to the Haxey Hood and the Great War along these emotional avenues I am keenly aware of making that initial ordering of the textual traces of the past that Hayden White denotes prefiguration, the preliminary, and most basic level of interpretation in which the historian engages. Drawing on Northrop Frye, White suggests that in the process of prefiguration, we resort to and deploy the literary mechanisms such as narrative plots and tropes that are our only means of inscribing patterns of meaning on the histories we write. Necessarily, in order for these histories to appeal, to be plausible, they must accord with "well-known . . . literary conventions, conventions which the historian, like the poet, begins to assimilate from the first moment he is told a story as a child."[13] And so it is that, well versed in one such convention, I arrive at my history of the Haxey Hood and the Great War, ready to see it in exactly the way that Fussell sees

the latter, as a tragic satire consisting of "its own smaller constituent . . .
ironic actions" and circumstances.[14]

THE ISLE'S GREAT WAR: A SERIES OF SAD IRONIES

With the benefit of almost ninety years of historical hindsight and a sensibility that family lore and individual psyche have finely tuned to the ironic,
I read *The Epworth Bells,* the local newspaper for the Isle of Axholme, for the
years 1914–1919. Among the notices of upcoming social events, accounts of
wrongdoers appearing before the local magistrate, and reports of agricultural
fortunes and prices, signs that the war is coming to the Isle soon begin to
accumulate. It is not long before, in even this most "middlebrow" publication, running alongside the appeals to and affirmations of heroic struggle and
sacrifice, of patriotic devotion to duty, are darker threads and themes and figures.[15] I read of innocence and idealism betrayed, of hopes abridged, of
savage reversals of fortune. I find numerous examples of ironic negation and
contrast and of the veiling and masking and instability of meaning. I feel
that I am sharing in a "sadder wisdom" of the Great War, one that many of
those who lived through even some of it must have come to know.[16]

"Irony is the attendant of hope, and the fuel of hope is innocence." For
Fussell, Britain's Great War was more ironic than any other because it began
in such innocence and with such high hopes of a speedy, righteous victory.[17]
In the first flush of the conflict during the gloriously sunny weeks of 1914,
fragmentary tales of military action and naval engagements filtered back to
pique Islonians' excitement and nationalistic enthusiasm. Just days after the
war began *The Bells* brought news of the sinking of British and German ships
and recycled hazy rumors of "fierce battles" being fought in Belgium (rumors
because the government had imposed tight censorship, banished press corre-
spondents from the theatres of action, and even interned some). Within the
first month, Isle men had begun to step forward to fill the ranks of Secretary
of War Lord Kitchener's New Army. Recruiting notices in the press (six
shillings a day "all found" for motor drivers joining the Army Service Corps)
and recruiting sergeants in residence in community centers (the Temperance
Hall in Epworth) encouraged and eased the flow of volunteers.[18]

Philip Larkin's poem, "MCMXIV," gazing back over a half century to
images of men who queued up to answer Kitchener's call, captures the early
mood of buoyancy that prevailed in a sun-bleached and sun-drenched world
the title's Roman numerals direct us to read as universal, timeless, or archaic.
But Larkin's evocation of this bountiful, agrarian landscape outside of time

and place also rings true as a description of the real Isle of Axholme at the height of its summer:

The place names all hazed over
With flowering grasses, and fields
Shadowing Domesday lines
Under wheat's restless silence (Ll. 18–21)

In the final stanza, in possession of his own "sadder wisdom," Larkin overlays the optimism of the summer moment of "MXMCIV"[19] with the lost innocence that gives the poem its poignancy:

Never such innocence,
Never before or since,
As changed itself to past
Without a word (Ll. 25–28)

And so to the descendants of those cheerful volunteers from the Isle of Axholme, a place that—as Larkin said of Hull, his adopted home just over the Humber estuary to the north[20]—"is in the world, yet sufficiently on the edge of it to have a different resonance," the poet gifts his sense of the "historical moment" of August 1914, "poised between peace and war, arrested and held for an inspection that is solemn with afterknowledge."[21]

As the war drifted on through the autumn and into the winter and a new year, The Bells relayed the movements back and forth between home and "over there" of those caught up in it—soldiers, auxiliaries, and civilians—and registered its growing toll on life, its mounting destruction. Soldiers wrote letters home, some describing the horrors of trench warfare, others adopting the cheery, humerous front and tone that were meant to mask those horrors and buffer loved ones from them.[22] J. W. Taylor, who had served as an eight-year veteran with the sixty-sixth Battery Royal Field Artillery in India glossed over the bleak conditions that the British Expeditionary Force found itself enduring in France and Belgium in January 1915. "I had a good Christmas," he wrote to a friend, "plenty to eat, etc. The weather is very cold and wet, but we have to stick to it; we are fighting for our country. I had a fine present from Princess Mary to-day. Every soldier fighting out here received one. I hope there are plenty of young men at home enlisting, just to keep up the name of our old home. You must excuse my dirty paper, but I have just left my hotel, 'The de la Barn.'" Frank Brett, training with the King's Royal Rifles in Farnborough, Hampshire, was equally upbeat. "I was going to be married this Christmas, but the war stepped in and prevented me. I have got on well since I joined the Army in August. I am with the machine gun section. Tell all my old pals I am doing my bit for King and country, and hope they are doing the same." (Frank Brett died on Sunday, 28 May, 1916 near Ypres.)[23]

All the while the casualties of the war multiplied. The Isle took in its first group of Belgian refugees and its men began to appear in the lists of fatalities, wounded, and missing.[24] Lance Corporal John Webster of the First Battalion, Lincolnshire Regiment was the first Crowle man to be killed in action. Also among the first of the fifty-four thousand officers and men who would die fighting in and around the infamous Ypres Salient and "whose graves are not known," Webster is commemorated on the Menin Gate Memorial, Ieper.[25] Other Isle men came home on leave or to heal before going back for another tour of duty. Some, too damaged for further service, came back to endure months of recuperation in military hospitals in nearby Lincoln and Doncaster, or a terribly drawn out death. Arthur Wroot of Crowle was one of the last of the Isle soldiers to succumb, fifteen months after the November 1918 Armistice, in February 1920; he had received the shrapnel wounds that eventually killed him in April 1915.[26] Some, like Sapper Thomas Preston, son of the headmaster of the Haxey Church of England School, simply came home to be buried.[27]

The terrifying machinery of the war also came to the east coast further north in December when the German fleet bombarded Scarborough and Whitby, killing a reported 106 and wounding 617, and "many times" to the Isle itself in the form of Zeppelin bombs that caused no physical damage or injury but whose shockwaves rattled nerves as well as windows.[28]

Yet some contributors to the *Bells* could still persist in the complacency that many have judged an essentially prewar, prelapsarian state. One item in particular may be cast in these terms. In February 1915, the author of a brief piece on the pristine beauty of the Isle in winter, employing the language of rural idyll and rustic homeliness that other writers would increasingly use to impart their horror and disgust at trench warfare noted blithely that there were "no signs of the War" to be seen.[29] Perhaps this was an example of the "irony of benign ignorance" or a resolute, self-defensive denial that the Isle's cultural, emotional landscape was being deeply scarred by the war.[30] But it brings to mind the poetry of Edmund Blunden whose work Fussell has described as delicately deploying "the properties of traditional English literary pastoral in the service of the gentlest . . . kind of irony." The menacing, threatening "residue" of Blunden's war experiences lurks in his 1925 *The Midnight Skaters*, a poem that, like Larkin's "MCMXIV," might have been a description of the Isle of Axholme—this time in the depths of winter, with the awful figure of death watching and waiting.[31]

The Midnight Skaters

The hop-poles stand in cones,
The icy pond lurks under,
The pole-tops steeple to the thrones
Of stars, sound gulfs of wonder;
But not the tallest there, 'tis said,
Could fathom to this pond's black bed.
Then is not death at watch
Within those secret waters?
What wants he but to catch
Earth's heedless sons and daughters?
With but a crystal parapet
Between, he has his engines set.
Then on, blood shouts, on, on,
Twirl, wheel and whip above him,
Dance on this ball-floor thin and wan,
Use him as though you love him;
Court him, elude him, reel and pass,
And let him hate you through the glass.[32]

By the spring of 1915 Islonians must have been hard pressed to maintain either blithe optimism or benign ignorance in the face of the war's depredations—and on no one did the brunt of those depredations bear more heavily than their young men. It is heart wrenching to scan the lengthening lists of those killed or missing in action in the *Bells'* pages for 1915–1918, to see the tiny photographic portraits of the khaki-clad soldiers, and to read their letters to families and friends, letters shared through the newspaper with the larger community. Two such letters, to the parents of Private Harry Sissons of Epworth, epitomize the savage ironies of circumstance that constituted the Isle's Great War. The first was from Sissons himself, who had been wounded on December 17 while on a nighttime wiring patrol on the front near Ypres; a piece of shrapnel penetrated just below his hip bone "making a hole as big as a half crown." On Christmas Day Sissons wrote a "cheery epistle" to his parents from a casualty clearing station, to let them know that his condition was improving: "I am having a fine time of it to-day. I'm a little stronger in myself to-day."[33] Two days later he died. The second letter was from the sister in charge of the casualty clearing station, informing Mr. and Mrs. Sissons of their son's death. They had received both letters on the same day; they had opened and read that from Harry first. Could fate have devised a crueler way—such a "small" wound—for Sissons to perish or a more twisted way to deliver the news of his death to his parents?[34]

THE HAXEY HOOD AND THE GREAT WAR:
AN IRONIC SURVIVAL

The Haxey Hood fell victim to the war in that first winter of 1915. Marking the break in the customary calendar with sober understatement the *Bells*, in a brief notice, both acknowledged the "play up and play the game" convention of war as sport and referenced the incongruity of the latter form of agon during such dark times. "Wednesday last was Haxey Hood Day, but there was no celebration this year. A sterner game now engages the attention of the men of the parish, a good proportion of whom have responded loyally to the call of duty with the colours."[35] It would be 1920 before the Hood was next held and on that occasion it seemed that the toll that the conflict had taken on the Isle's youthful soldiers had dealt a deadly blow to the custom, too. The church bells rang out on Hood Eve and on the day of the game, as they had through the "long past ages," the "Lord" and the "Fool" performed their customary roles, and "a good company" attended. But the "Boggans," among whom typically were numbered the most athletic and vigorous of the parish's young men, its manhood in their prime, "were much fewer in number than heretofore."[36]

The loss of the Isle's Great War generation of young men became central to the lore of the game, synonymous with its evidently declining fortunes. By the mid-1930s, local people had crafted a historical narrative of the Hood in which the war had brought it to the verge of destruction. This rendered in local terms, on a local scale the main themes of that "Myth of the War" Samuel Hynes indicates was beginning to be written in the trenches of the Somme in the summer of 1916 and was firmly fixed in Britain's cultural imagination by the end of the 1920s. The key elements of that myth—the sacrifice of a cohort of young, idealistic men in the name of "Honour, Glory, and England," the huge chasm cutting off the "remote, peaceable" past, the jarring dislocation of cultural traditions—were all writ small in the history of the Hood.[37]

A very different kind of hero than the muddied and bloodied soldier of the Western front is accorded the distinction of intervening in that history and rescuing the game when it was on the brink of "Oblivion." Philip D. Taylor, headmaster of the Haxey Senior School in the 1930s and 1940s appears to have been the first to have identified the Reverend James William Franck Sheppard, the vicar of Haxey from 1914, as the Hood's savior. In an article written for the *Lincolnshire Magazine* in 1934, Taylor states that Sheppard "rescued" the "famous game" and gave it "a new lease of life."[38] Tom Major, who attended the school in the interwar period, is well versed on Sheppard's role. In a 1996 interview, Major responded to a question on whether there had been attempts to suppress the Hood: "No, no, it wasn't banned, it was during the First World War when a certain Cannon Sheppard was here, he kept it alive because everybody was at war, and he kept it alive with having the schoolboys, you know, playing the game, that's only the nearest thing it's ever gotten to being banned."[39] Eric and Norma Neill—respectively, president and secretary of the Haxey and Westwoodside Heritage Society—concur with this. Eric, who was the headmaster of the Haxey Primary School in the 1970s, also affirms that he gave his pupils a holiday if Twelfth Night fell during the week so that the local children could participate in the Hood and thus learn to value and perpetuate the custom. Jeremy Cooper's official history of the game recognizes Sheppard as the Hood's early twentieth-century hero, too, noting that the vicar offered "support" for it in 1924; in which year the Bishop of Lincoln was present, presumably at Sheppard's invitation or encouragement.[40]

The idea that the war was the destroyer of "civilization," of social stability, of a cherished cultural heritage and national traditions was broadly current in the tense period before formal hostilities began, and it continued to be an important theme once peace returned. The Reverend Sheppard had articulated this fear in his parochial message of January 1915. "The ordinary greeting and the usual wishes seem out of place in the face of the great—this terrible war," he began. "Unless all we hold dear must go under, and righteousness and peace cease to kiss each other . . . we need victory." In company with numbers of other religious leaders and commentators, Sheppard cast the conflagration as an opportunity for a renewal of faith—in more than the religious sense of that term—that would come as the nation met its severest test and emerged triumphant. "God . . . alone can give us such victory and can save by many or by few so that when the end comes we may be truer, nobler, more Christian, for the fiery trial through which we are passing."[41]

After the war, affirming that the ordeal had purified and tempered those who had come through it, and reassuring everyone that the loss of those who had *not* come through had been worthwhile, became part of the nation's complex grieving and mourning process. In the grandest, most public rituals of remembrance and memorial architecture and in the most modest and private, the state and the people strove to express gratitude, to find comfort, and to try to move on by looking back and reflecting on what it had all meant. It is the spirit of this process that I believe imbues the Haxey Hood's Great War history. For the sacrifice of Haxey and the Isle of Axholme's soldiers to have meant something, there had to have been something worth fighting for and, once the war was over, something worth rescuing out of the bloody business of sacrifice. The Hood was such a thing, a "curious annual custom" that connected "the present with the long past ages, and which . . . from time immemorial" was observed in Haxey. The war had severed the cultural links of Haxey's past and present, destroying the young men through whose Twelfth Night ritual the chain of heritage and history was annually remade. The Reverend Sheppard repaired the break, and the Hood endured.[42]

But I do not think that the crisis of 1914–1918 suddenly pushed the Haxey Hood to the edge of existence. And although the Reverend Sheppard very likely gave the custom a valuable infusion of life at this point in its history, I suspect that it was not from the Great War that he rescued it, but from a far more prosaic fate, a slow, piecemeal petering out that may have been underway from the early to mid 1800s. Tom Major's self-editing when he spoke about the wartime game hints at as much: "It was the only time when it ever—I won't say it went out of fashion."[43]

Newspaper and eyewitness accounts of the game through the nineteenth century every now and then intimate that it did indeed suffer the vagaries of fashion. The *Stamford Mercury* for January 1836, for example, reports that "this coarse amusement is losing much of its celebrity, and the attendance was not so nearly numerous as in years gone by."[44] In the 1890s, when middle-class cultural producers were in high gear "rescuing" English "folk" customs left and right, folklorist Mabel Peacock reported that "an interested observer" from the Isle of Axholme had informed her that the Hood "seem[ed] to be losing its popularity" and would "soon have to be numbered among the bygone amusements of English country life." The time seemed opportune for publishing Peacock's collected notes on the game, supplemented by the observations of a Mr. C. C. Bell. According to Bell the numbers of "boggans," key members of the "Lord" of the Hood's retinue, had dwindled from the traditional twelve to "four or five." "I believe Monday's game was rather unusually well attended for these days," Bell wrote to Peacock of the 1896 Hood, but there were only six or seven boggans. Also in decline, in Bell's judgment, was the quality of the performance of some of the principals. The Fool's speech, formerly "a great feature, being made the occasion of a good deal of topical wit and satire," was "a very tame affair, lasting only a couple of minutes, and consisting of a few traditiony phrases."[45] The pall of decline was an essential element of legitimating the folkloric revival or "making of the folk" in which the likes of Bell and Peacock were engaged, of course, but that fact does not make any less credible the idea that the war per se did not threaten the end of the Haxey Hood, far from it.

The widespread and deeply held fears about cultural destruction that the war provoked and the need to recover from and sanctify the savage loss of life once the war was over made the renewal of older ways of being and doing a compelling idea in the 1920s and 1930s.[46] In the Isle of Axholme that renewal most appropriately included the Haxey Hood, a custom that generations since have learned to see as an enduring link with the past and with the heritage of the place. So this is my final irony: that the Great War was exactly the right event at the right moment in history for keeping the Hood safe and ensuring its longer term survival.

NOTES

I began thinking of this chapter as an exercise in teasing out the interpretive and epistemological threads of the Haxey Hood by examining how and when the game's "founding myths" first appeared as part of its historical record and exploring those who played a central role in constructing these myths. This was an overambitious idea that would have required ranging through ancient to modern historiography, fields of study such as folklore, popular culture, the politics and poetics of place and space, Arthurian romance, and gender and class relations. My reading on the possibilities presented by the "literary turn" in history (especially on Hayden White's theories of metahistory and narrativity), together with my more recent research on the Hood and reading of the scholarly literature on the First World War era have brought me to my present narrower and more manageable—but nonetheless worthwhile, I think—focus.

1. Samuel Hynes, *A War Imagined: The First World War and English Culture* (London: Bodley Head, 1990).

2. Vera Brittain, *Testament of Youth: An Autobiographical Study of the Years 1900–1925* (London: Gollancz, 1933; reprint, London: Penguin Books, 1989), 22.

3. Paul Fussell, *The Great War and Modern Memory* (Oxford: Clarendon, 1975). Robert Darby notes that the "plain-speaking" work of poets such

as Owens did not come to be widely accepted as "the characteristic voice of the war . . . [and] a permanent contribution to culture" until the 1960s. "An undoubtedly futile and unjust war in Asia . . . also provoked reassessments of the century's first conflagration in musicals such as *Oh What a Lovely War!* and books such as *The Great War and Modern Memory* itself." Robert Darby, "Oscillations on the Hotspur-Falstaff Spectrum: Paul Fussell and the Ironies of War," *War in History* 9 (2002): 307–31, 308, 320.

4. The Hood is a folk football game, said to date from the Middle Ages, that takes place each year on Twelfth Night in Haxey, a village in the Isle of Axholme, North Lincolnshire. For details on and interpretations of the custom see Catriona M. Parratt, "Of Place and Men and Women: Gender and Topophilia in the 'Haxey Hood,'" *Journal of Sport History* 27 (2000): 229–45; Venetia Newall, "Throwing the Hood at Haxey: A Lincolnshire Twelfth Night Custom," *Folk Life* 18 (1980): 7–23; Jeremy Cooper, *A Fool's Game: The Ancient Tradition of Haxey Hood* (Haxey, Lincolnshire: Lord and Boggins of the Haxey Hood, 1993).

5. Chris Ward, "Impressions of the Somme: An Experiment," *Rethinking History* 1 (1997): 279. There is a growing and fascinating literature on the ways in which the First World War has been and is remembered, memorialized, and reexperienced. See, for example, David Lloyd, *Battlefield Tourism: Pilgrimage and the Commemoration of the Great War in Britain, Australia, and Canada, 1919–1939* (New York: Berg, 1998); Alex King, *Memorials of the Great War in Britain: The Symbolism and Politics of Remembrance* (New York: Berg, 1998); Ken Inglis "World War One Memorial in Australia," *Guerres Mondiales* 42 (1992): 51–58; Nicholas J. Saunders, "Excavating Memories: Archaeology and the Great War, 1914–2001," *Antiquity* 76 (2002): 101–08; J. Barlett and K. M. Ellis, "Remembering the Dead in Northrop: First World War Memorials in a Welsh Parish," *Journal of Contemporary History* 34 (1999): 231–42.

6. Village war memorials are certainly features in the landscape of memories I have of growing up in the Isle of Axholme in the 1960s.

7. Interview with Tom Major, Haxey, January 1996.

8. Fussell, *The Great War and Modern Memory*, 6.

9. Fussell, *The Great War and Modern Memory*, 6.

10. "The War That Will End War" was the title of a collection of articles that H. G. Wells published in the first year of the conflict. The phrase, Samuel Hynes writes, "became first the war's greatest cliché and then its bitterest irony." Hynes, *A War Imagined*, 20; H. G. Wells, *The War That Will End War* (London: Palmer, 1914).

11. Stephen Badsey observes that there has been a growing public as well as scholarly interest in the Great War in the late twentieth to early twenty-first centuries. He suggests that television dramas, recent documen-

taries, and increasing "academic respectability" are part of the explanation for this. The periodic discovery of soldiers' remains and previously unidentified battlefield graves must also play a part, in some cases suddenly pitching people dramatically, emotionally into the conflict. In June 2001, for example, archaeologists excavated a grave containing the bodies of twenty-three men who had died in the Battle of the Somme. The Ministry of Defence positively identified one body as that of a soldier in the First Battalion, Lincolnshire Regiment, and traced and contacted his blood relatives; one of them had not even known that he had had a great uncle, let alone his wartime fate. *The Times*, 20 June 2001; 22 June, 2001; *Lincolnshire Echo*, 26 July 2002; 20 September 2002; 21 September 2002; 11 November 2002; *Grimsby Telegraph*, 9 November 2002.

12. Thomas Hardy, *Life's Little Ironies: A Set of Tales* (London: Osgood and McIlvaine, 1894).

13. Hayden White, *Tropics of Discourse: Essays in Cultural Criticism* (Baltimore: Johns Hopkins University Press, 1978), 59. For White's analysis of the literary structure of works of history, see also *Metahistory: The Historical Imagination in Nineteenth-Century Europe* (Baltimore: Johns Hopkins University Press, 1973). On White's theories of history, see, for example, Nancy S. Streuver, "Irony and Experimentation in Hayden White's Metahistory," *Storia della Storiografia* 24 (1993): 45–57; J. L. Gorman, "Reality and Irony in History," *Storia della Storiografia* 24 (1993): 59–69; Eugen O. Golob, "The Irony of Nihilism," *History and Theory* 19 (1980): 55–65. I have also found two books by Keith Jenkins very helpful: *Re-Thinking History* (London: Routledge, 1991) and *On "What Is History?" From Carr and Elton to Rorty and White* (London: Routledge, 1995).

14. Fussell, *The Great War and Modern Memory*, 6.

15. Rosa M. Bracco, *Merchants of Hope: British Middlebrow Writers and the First World War, 1919–1939* (Providence: Berg, 1993).

16. White writes of the historian Jacob Burckhardt that his voice was that "of the Ironist, the possessor of a higher, sadder wisdom than the audience itself possessed." But the ironist's sadder wisdom is surely not necessarily a higher one. *Metahistory*, 250.

17. Fussell, *The Great War and Modern Memory*, 6, 18.

18. Peter Simkins, *Kitchener's Army: The Raising of the New Armies, 1914–1916* (Manchester: Manchester University Press, 1988); James Norman Hall, *Kitchener's Mob: The Adventures of an American in the British Army* (New York: Houghton Mifflin, 1916.)

Former members of the regular army reenlisted, too: George Thompson Ogman, previously a corporal in the Yorkshire and Lancaster Regiment who took the "King's shilling," once again, from Colour-Sergeant Hancock at the Epworth recruiting station early in January 1915. Isle men joined a wide variety of regiments, but a significant number served in the region's "local" units: the Lincolnshire Regiment, the York and Lancaster Regiment, the King's Own Yorkshire Light Infantry, the Sherwood Foresters (the Nottinghamshire Regiment), and the East Yorkshire Regiment. Two Owston Ferry men enlisted in the "Grimsby Chums," one of the ill-fated "pals" battalions that suffered so badly in the 1916 Battle of the Somme. *The Epworth Bells*, 8 August 1914; 15 August 1914; 12 September 1914; 2 January 1915; 9 January 1915; 23 January 1915.

19. White, *Metahistory*, 250; Philip Larkin, "MCMXIV," *The Poetry Review* 52 (1962): 201. For commentaries on "MCMXIV" see, for example, Steve Clark, "'The Lost Displays': Larkin and Empire," in *New Larkins for Old: Critical Essays*, ed. James Booth (New York: St. Martin's, 2000), 166–81; Lolette Kuby, *An Uncommon Poet for the Common Man: A Study of Philip Larkin's Poetry* (The Hague: Mouton, 1974), 124–26; David Lodge, "Philip Larkin: The Metonymic Muse," in *Philip Larkin: The Man and His Work*, ed. Dale Salwak (Iowa City: University of Iowa Press, 1989), 120.

20. Larkin was born in Coventry in the West Midlands in 1922 and studied at Oxford. By 1955 he was the head of the library at the university in Kingston-upon-Hull, just over the Humber estuary that is at the northern geographical boundary of the Isle of Axholme. *New Perspectives on World Football*. See Andrew Motion, *Philip Larkin: A Writer's Life* (London: Faber and Faber, 1993).

21. Philip Larkin, foreword in *Rumoured City: New Poets from Hull*, ed. Douglas Dunn (Newcastle-upon-Tyne: Bloodaxe Books, 1982); Lodge, "Philip Larkin," 120.

22. *Epworth Bells*, 3 October 1914; 17 October 1914; 28 November 1915; 12 December 1914; 19 December 1914; 2 January 1915.

23. *Epworth Bells*, 9 January 1915. "Debt of Honour Register in Memory of F. Brett, 10th Battalion, King's Royal Rifle Corps," Commonwealth War Graves Commission, http://www.hostu24.co.uk/cwgcsearch/detailed.asp?casualty=157748.

24. *Epworth Bells*, 12 December 1914.

25. *Epworth Bells*, 28 November 1914; "Debt of Honour Register in Memory of John Taylor Webster, 1st Battalion, Lincolnshire Regiment," Commonwealth War Graves Commission, http://www.hostu24.co.uk/cwgc-search/detailed.asp?casualty=913406.

26. Private Tom Wilson of the Lincolnshire Regiment, who had been shot in the hand and sustained internal injuries at Armentiere, visited his parents' home in Westwoodside for the first Christmas of the war before entering the military hospital in Doncaster. *Epworth Bells*, 2 January 1915; 9 January 1915; 17 April 1915; "Debt of Honour Register in Memory of Arthur Wroot, 1st Battalion York and Lancaster Regiment," Commonwealth War

Graves Commission, http://www.host24.co.uk/cwgcsearch/detailed.asp? casualty=380192.

27. *Epworth Bells*, 27 February 1915; "Debt of Honour Register in Memory of Thomas Eustace Preston, 15th Signal Company, Royal Engineers," Commonwealth War Graves Commission, http://www.hostu24. co.uk/cwgcsearch/detailed.asp?casualty=380196.

28. *Epworth Bells*, 19 December 1914; account book of the Haxey overseer of the poor, handwritten note of the Reverend James W. ff. Sheppard, cited in *Nine Hundred Years of Haxey Parish Church*, eds. Norma and Eric Neill (Haxey, Lincolnshire: Haxey and Westwoodside Heritage Society, 1991), 96.

29. *Epworth Bells*, 20 February 1915.

30. Fussell, *The Great War and Modern Memory*, 255.

31. Fussell, *The Great War and Modern Memory*, 254–69, 256.

32. Edmund Blunden, *The Midnight Skaters* (London: Bodley Head, 1968).

33. *Epworth Bells*, 6 January 1917.

34. "Debt of Honour Register in Memory of H. Sissons, 2nd Battalion, Royal Irish Regiment," Commonwealth War Graves Commission, http:// www.hostu24.co.uk/cwgcsearch/detailed.asp?casualty=201570.

35. *Epworth Bells*, 9 January 1915. The Hood is held on Twelfth Night, January 6 unless that happens to fall on a Sunday, in which case the game is played on the preceding Saturday. Newall, "Throwing the Hood at Haxey," 7. On the various ways in which sporting communities and organizations responded to the Great War, and especially on the complex cultural and gender resonances, see, Colin Veitch, "'Play Up! Play Up! And Win the War': Football, the Nation and the First World War 1914–15," *Journal of Contemporary History* 20 (1985): 363–78; Murray G. Phillips, "The Unsporting German and the Athletic Anzac: Sport, Propaganda, and the First World War," *Sport History Review* 27 (1996): 14–29; Murray G. Phillips, "Sport, War and Gender Images: The Australian Sportsmen's Battalions and the First World War," *International Journal of the History of Sport* 14 (1997): 78–96; Daryl Adair, Murray Phillips, and John Nauright, "Sporting Manhood in Australia: Test Cricket, Rugby Football, and the Imperial Connection, 1878–1918," *Sport History Review* 28 (1997): 46–60.

36. *Epworth Bells*, 20 December 1919; 3 January 1920; 10 January 1920.

37. Hynes, *A War Imagined*, ix–xi, passim.

38. Philip D. Taylor, "'Haxey Hood' Game," *Lincolnshire Magazine*, July 1934, p. 61.

39. Tom Major, interview, Haxey, 1996.

40. Norma Neill and Eric Neill, personal communications with the author; Cooper, *A Fool's Game*, 43–47.

41. Reverend James William Sheppard, "Haxey Parish Magazine," January 1915, quoted in *Epworth Bells*, 9 January 1915.

42. *Epworth Bells*, 10 January 1920.

43. Tome Major, interview, Haxey 1896.

44. *Stamford Mercury*, 11 January 1836, Haxey Folder, Local Studies Library, Lincoln.

45. Mabel Peacock, "The Hood-Game at Haxey," *Folk-Lore* 7 (1896): 330–49, 330–31, 340–41.

46. Hynes, *A War Imagined*, 353.

CHAPTER 7

Decentering "Race" and (Re)presenting "Black" Performance in Sport History

Basketball and Jazz in American Culture, 1920–1950

S. W. POPE

> Nothing handed down from the past could keep race alive if we did not
> constantly reinvent and re-ritualize it to fit our own terrain.
> —Barbara Fields, "Slavery, Race, and Ideology
> in the United States of America"

Whereas today basketball style is firmly ensconced within hip hop culture, an earlier innovative, pre–World War II style was connected to jazz. Cultural studies scholar Todd Boyd notes that "the steamy poetry of the bandstand and dance floor has long found exquisite parallels in the intensity and fancy footwork of the African American sportsman." It should be no surprise that musicians and athletes "linked in the public mind as white social symbols and black role models, have always felt a kinship. They share celebrity status across racial lines, competence, in highly pleasurable and competitive activities." Boyd avers that "basketball is the modern-day aesthetic embodiment of Black culture, similar to jazz in its prime" because they share similar "ways of doing things, although the specific qualities of the something that is done varies with time and place and is also influenced by a number of elements outside the tradition."[1]

The key link between black athletic and musical styles is improvisation. The process of musical improvising shares analogies to sport, as jazz historian James Collier observes—both "the improvising jazz musician and the athlete must train intensely to build up sets of conditioned reflexes that enable them to respond without thinking of events that are unfolding around them in fractions of seconds."[2] Philosopher Michael Novak explicated the relation-ship between basketball and jazz in his 1976 book, *The Joy of Sports*. "Teams move in patterns, in rhythms, at high velocity," Novak observed. "They have a score, a melody; each team has its own appropriate tempo." "Basketball is jazz," he postulated: "improvisatory, free, individualistic, corporate, sweaty, fast, exulting, screeching, torrid, explosive, exquisitely designed for letting first the trumpet, then the sax, then the drummer, then the trombonist soar in virtuoso excellence."[3]

Basketball and jazz are animated by the stylized nuances of African American culture. This style derives from the musical, dance, and perform-ance traditions associated with slavery and commercialized minstrelsy and incubated during the long history of oppression and legalized discrimination. Both emerged prominently within major cities during the 1920s when tour-ing black teams were formed, and musicians converged in New York and Chicago. Just as white basketball players encountered a quicker game of fast breaks, explosive speed, innovative ballhandling, and varied shot selection when playing against black teams, so, too, did white musicians learn about rhythmic improvisation and a hip, cool attitude from the early generation of black jazz pioneers. Basketball is an example of how blacks, Gerald Early explains, "transformed an *American* ludic endeavor into an *African American* cultural expression thereby redefining the meaning of being American in their own terms though the game." In so doing, "they took a larger cultural trait, not an inherently racial one, and adapted it as a ritualized style, as a performance . . . [so as] to distinguish themselves from whites."[4]

Few scholars have examined the historical development of a distinct African American aesthetic in music, dance, and basketball styles—particu-larly the ways in which these cultural forms that comprised a key element of 1920s to mid-1940s social life.[5] Body styles and practices are prominent topics within the study of sport, cultural studies, and African American cul-ture.[6] Stylized physical and musical performances are widely admired but rarely analyzed because they are primarily nonverbal, and thus, their descrip-tion and analysis remain elusive matters for most scholars. This is ironic given that performance is the essence of both sport and contemporary popu-lar culture. "Styles of sport," Stephen Hardy observes, taking his conceptual cues from the late French sociologist Pierre Bourdieu, "take us into the heart of body culture, with its battles to convert physical capital into cultural, social, or economic capital." Sport historians should consider the conceptual framework articulated by Bourdieu who argued that all social groups strive and strategically seek to accumulate *capital* (the end product of accumulated labor and a form of power in that it determines the possession and distribu-tion of values, assets, resources, and rewards).[7] According to Bourdieu, strug-gles for material and symbolic resources (capital) take place in social arenas or "fields"; as such, he argues, sport is "part of the larger field of struggles over the definition of the *legitimate body* and the *legitimate use of the body*."[8] "The body and its specific behavior," cultural studies scholar John Fiske maintains "is where the power system stops being abstract and becomes material. The body is where it succeeds or fails, where it is acceded to or struggled against." In their analysis of Bourdieu's work, Douglas Booth and John Loy emphasize how the body not only is key to understanding prestige and distinction, but it also constitutes "the material core of sporting activity." Bourdieu developed two eminently useful concepts for theorizing sport and embodied practices—*habitus* ("a system of lasting unconscious dispositions and acquired schemes of thought and action, perception and appreciation, based on individuals' integrated social experiences under specific sets of objective social conditions") and *hexis* (the "embodied nature of the habitus," signifying "deportment, manner and style in which actors carry themselves": stance, gait, gesture, etc.).[9]

Heretofore, explorations of black athleticism have been indiscriminately lumped under the "race and sport" umbrella by sport historians, whereby it has been either implicitly or explicitly assumed that distinctive African American performance styles derive from "racial" peculiarities. I seek to interrogate and thereby challenge this well-worn conceptual (and historiographical) orientation by suggesting that we can theorize such embodied cultural practices without resorting to the essentializing concept of "race." Moreover, I argue that the dominant "black" style of play is historically and culturally distinctive rather than genetically derivative.[10]

The development of a distinctive, embodied cultural style in basketball and jazz provides a suitable case study for reconsidering the nature of "race," "black culture," and cultural diffusion within a segregated social order. I argue that we can study what appears from my research to be the contested, melding, merging, converging, borrowing processes constituting the creation of a culturally distinctive style without linking it to race. White fascination with the artistic accomplishments of black expressive culture is one way in which *otherhood* is reified and whiteness is normalized—making race a common part of everyday life—perpetuated, unwittingly by ordinary people and conscientious scholars. People use the term to interpret and explain differences in daily life. Thus, the notion that white basketball players pick and roll and blacks fake and slam dunk, or that black musicians have a more primal, natural sense of rhythm, need to be deconstructed as racialized constructs rather than as evidence of biological, genetic tendencies. Moreover, such easy, convenient conclusions are not nearly as interesting and revealing as the historical creation of such styles and how their meanings and influences are diffused within the broader cultural fabric. Such a project requires that we rethink our approach to *race, sport, and cultural history*.

RACE IN THE STUDY OF SPORT

Despite the formidable body of scholarship on sport and "race" (especially that produced by sport historians) scholars have paid insufficient attention to how race as a classificatory system operates. "Race" is equated simplistically with black athletes and "people of color" (a tendency perpetuated by white and black sport historians alike) thereby excluding the racialized nature of "whiteness." In their splendid essay on "race," sport and British society, Ben Carrington and Ian McDonald lament the way in which race and sport have been theorized in the sport studies literature by calling for new approaches to "sports racism and its relationship in specific historical periods and particular social contexts." For example, how do "the types of practices, representations and discourses that sport produces in terms of its physically competitive, symbolic, and public displays of meritocratic competition, help to sustain (and occasionally challenge) our understanding of 'race' and racism outside sport?"[11]

A decade ago, sociologist Susan Birrell critiqued the way in which sport studies scholars examine race and racial relations. By focusing on black male athletes, sport sociologists simplistically equate "'race' . . . with *Black*, obscuring other racial identities."[12] There have been, however, a few noteworthy exceptions to this stock approach to race in sport history. Patricia Vertinsky and Gwendolyn Captain show that it is meaningless to talk about "fixed racial boundaries," yet they observe how the concept of race "continues to inform people's actions, acting as a cultural construct regardless of whether there is any biological reality." They have explored how the making of race has become part of ordinary events of everyday life—perpetuated, often unwittingly, by ordinary people (most of whom would not consider themselves racist).[13] Evelyn Higginbotham states the case more directly. By continually expressing overt and analogic relationships, "race impregnates the simplest meanings we take for granted, and allows it to function as a metalanguage, an umbrella, which obscures class and gender differences. . . . It is 'real' in the sense that it has real, though changing effects in the world and a real impact upon an individual's sense of self, experiences, and life chances."[14]

We should move beyond documenting how sport has been central to black communities and identities through the lives and achievements of prominent black athletes toward seeing blacks and their bodies in new ways that, as Gilroy suggests "do not endorse the racialization of action, conflict, skill, and emodiment." In moving beyond such essentialist categories, we might, as Patrick Miller suggests, "start erasing 'racial' boundaries altogether."[15] Such a revisionist project mandates that we rethink our conceptualization of 'sport' as an essential, foundational (functionalist) concept (with limited independence or autonomy) toward an awareness that sport can only be understood by the way it is articulated within, according to David Andrews, "a particular set of complex social, economic, political, and technological relationships that compose the social context." Such an approach mandates that the dynamics of race and sport be informed by an understanding of the "power, prominence and deep structural significance of race in America (i.e. the context of racialized culture)."[16]

RACE: A MORE CRITICAL PERSPECTIVE

Sport historians must move beyond a functionalist conceptualization of race toward a more critical engagement with the recent, theoretically informed writing on race within cultural studies and cultural anthropology (much of which has been heretofore ignored by sport historians). *Race* did not originate as a neutral taxonomic term in science; rather, it prevailed long before modern science tried to explain it in biological terms. Race was, as Audrey Smedley demonstrates, a "folk idea created to reflect and to rationalize separate, distinct, and exclusive divisions" in an inegalitarian society. It was designed to make social, political, and economic inequality a God-given part of nature.[17] In colonial North America, race was a set of social prescriptions invented by gentry planters to exploit and constrain people classified as black so as to rationally resolve the labor shortage in the seventeenth-century Virginia colony. Thereafter, racism was developed into a law and an ideology.[18] Myths and justifications emerged in popular discourse to explain and rationalize the differences among Africans, Indians, and Europeans that prevailed until well after the American Civil War officially ended legalized slavery. Slavery and racism went together because they bolstered the same oppressive class relationships and thereby fortified the very unequal social relations within American society. According to historian Barbara Fields, "race explained why some people could rightly be denied what others took for granted. . . . Euro-Americans resolved the contradiction between slavery and liberty by defining Afro Americans as a race."[19]

Although rarely acknowledged by sport historians, race as an objective, viable concept has been a problematical construct among North American and British social scientists since the early 1940s when Ashley Montagu called it "man's most dangerous myth." Historian Jacques Barzun, one of Montague's contemporaries writing during the heyday of fascism, declared that "a satisfactory definition of race is not to be had," and, thus, the "quasi-universal habit of race-thinking which lumped together individuals on unverified grounds of similarity is a superstition." Central to Barzun's argument is a belief that no matter how race is defined, it falls apart at the level of physical characteristic, gene pool, nation, language, common experience, and history—a point recognized by a host of scholars that has yet trickled into either public or scholarly awareness.[20]

Race is more an ideology than an objective classificatory term.[21] According to Fields, it has been accorded "a transhistorical, almost metaphysical status that removes it from all possibility of analysis and understanding." In a similar vein, Evelyn Brooks Higginbotham presents race as a "global sign," a "metalanguage . . . shaping outlook, defining reality, and ascribing value in terms of the colors black and white, which stand in binary opposition while delineating the gulf between." As the ultimate trope of difference, race is (and has been) used to "describe and *inscribe* differences of language, belief system, artistic tradition, 'gene pool,' and all sort of supposedly 'natural' attributes such as rhythm, athletic ability, cerebration, usury, and fidelity." We must recognize, Stuart Hall advises that *as a discursive category*, race operates much more "like a language than (biological or physiological) science; as such, it's only when differences are organized within systems of [linguistic] meaning that the differences can become a factor in conduct."[22] Early anthropologists constructed evolutionist paradigms (e.g., the infamous "stages of civilization" exhibit at the 1893 World's Columbian Exposition in Chicago) to legitimize notions of race. Most contemporary anthropologists consider such pseudoscientific formulations as more akin to (rhetorical) figures of thought—arbitrary, linguistic constructs rather than reports of cultural reality.[23]

A SUGGESTIVE CASE STUDY: THE DEVELOPMENT OF "BLACK" STYLES IN JAZZ AND BASKETBALL

Historian Patrick Miller reminds us of the problems inherent in evaluating genetic, "scientific" explanations "without bothering to address the long legacy of segregation and racial prejudice that largely contributed to the development of distinctive social customs and expressive cultural practices" thereby discounting "the hard work and discipline, as well as the creativity, that distinguishes artistic innovations irrespective of the color of the artist."[24] Historical investigations necessitate that we decenter racialized baggage. Musical and physical performances were shaped by the particular historical contexts within which they developed.[25] Jazz is a musical style whose roots reach back to the involuntary migration of West Africans to North America between the seventeenth and the nineteenth centuries. It was originally a cultural phenomenon associated with the southeastern corner of the United States that linked European harmony with the "blues," a powerful music that grew out of the field hollers, work songs, and church hymns of slaves (after Emancipation) and working-class blacks. "In the sweat- and ache-laden work song," Stanley Crouch explains schematically, "the demanding duties of hard labor were met with rhythm, and that rhythm, which never failed to flex its pulse in the church, was the underlying factor that brought together the listeners, that allowed for physical responses in the dance halls and the juke joints where blues emerged." The "miracle" of this improvisational art form, according to him, is that the "techniques with which Africans arrived evolved into a particular cultural taste that reinvented every kind of American music they came in contact with, from folk to religious music to dance tunes, and finally achieved the order that is jazz, where all those aspects of American musical expression were brought together for a fresh synthesis."[26]

Slaves in the American South created a performance style that incorporated rhythmic complexity, persistent improvisation, and athletic bodily movements that Shane and Graham White characterize as an "impression of aliveness, vibrancy, unpredictable rhythm and tensions of the performer evoking a sense of constant surprise."[27] A sense of cultural difference "pervades whites' descriptions of African-American dance. Even if the steps black dancers [used] were familiar to whites, those steps were [performed] at different speeds, combined in different ways, and executed with different movements of the torso and limbs," and one might say the same about contemporary discussions about basketball and sport in general. Central to this style were the practices of "breaking" (away from the group) and "cutting" (strutting one's stuff and playful competition), both of which have shaped American popular culture from the minstrel show to Soul Train (and beyond).[28] Nineteenth-century funerals, church services, Saturday night dances, holiday frolics, and athletic contests were key venues for slaves in the plantation South to develop the groundwork for the dancing, musical, and athletic styles of the twentieth century.[29] Roger Abrahams contends that we have yet to "describe effectively the dynamic, expressive interrelations of [black and white] cultures living side by side" in antebellum America. His detailed study of corn-shucking rituals provides a model for understanding how a great deal of Southern culture developed not only in the slave quarters of the Big House, but "in the yard between . . . in contested areas betwixt and between the two worlds."[30]

In spite of considerable opposition from religious fundamentalists, prohibitionists, and white supremacists, jazz spread northward through the migration of southern black workers and musicians in search of wartime industrial jobs, but it ultimately became acceptable to whites attracted to the exotic, sensual environs of jazz haunts. In this world of brothels, phonograph parlors, vaudeville halls, nickelodeons, amusement parks, dance halls, ballparks, and movie palaces, "going out" meant enjoying commercialized amusements with strangers in large, urban crowds. Although persons of color were excluded or segregated from such venues as *spectators,* they were conspicuously overrepresented on stage as *performers.* Neither African Americans' segregated status in audiences nor their overrepresentation in parodic form was coincidential. As cultural historian David Nasaw argues, "to the extent that racial distinctions were exaggerated on stage, social distinctions among 'whites' in the audience could be muted." To act "blackface" African American performers had to look at "darkies through whites' eyes—in effect, they had to play whites." Yet, these masks, what Ralph Ellison termed "the darky act," became the reality of black existence for most whites who, as historian Grace Hale notes, "missed the performance by mistaking the masks for selves."[31]

Jazz as a new musical form developed in New Orleans in the late nineteenth century. New Orleans had an amazingly diverse population of freed slaves who had assimilated with French descendants whose lifestyle was indebted to a French and especially Catholic heritage and lifestyle of carnival, public festivals, and parades, all of which placed a high priority on pleasures, sociability, food, drink, and the sensuality of music. This culturally specific context merged and synthesized varying strands of rural blues, honkytonk, piano, and small wind instrument bands—developed earlier in carving contests and perfected within the improvisational venues of saloons, sporting houses, dance halls, and brothels that New Orleans provided. Jazz developed within this fertile New Orleans incubatory context and spread to northern and midwestern venues after the red-light Storyville section of town was hastily closed in 1917 by the U.S. Navy due to fears of rampant vice among enlisted men awaiting tours of duty on the World War I European front.[32] The military closing of Storyville interrupted the thriving jazz community and, thus, forced many musicians to scatter throughout the country in search of work, many of whom migrated to Harlem (in New York city), which became the most prominent postwar site for jazz clubs and ballrooms.

Although it was an urban idiom, jazz remained a primarily *regional* cultural form, but as musicians converged in northern and midwestern cities and blended regional styles, it became a recognized *national* phenomenon and focal point around which a taste encompassing language, dance, courtship, and lifestyle coalesced.[33] This development was inextricably linked to the hypercommercialization of popular culture during the 1920s when white-run media needed the content and energy that the black artistic tradition provided (i.e., the "jazz age"); yet this *black* musical tradition needed the access and the power of transmission that only a national media could provide. Whites and blacks participated and collaborated; yet the black-white tension existed not far removed from race.[34]

The early historical development of basketball and jazz derives from discernible historical conjectures. The creation of jazz and basketball occurred at almost precisely the same moment. Both jazz and basketball developed in distinct social places and diffused outward. Black basketball players were not more culturally inclined toward an improvisational sport (there was nothing about basketball that made it more *improvisational* than other sports such as boxing or football). Basketball was invented in 1891 by a Canadian-born "Muscular Christian," James Naismith, at the YMCA training school in Springfield, Massachusetts. The game was spread systematically by the YMCA during the late nineteenth and early twentieth centuries.[35] Music, dance, and sport "flowed into, out of, and within community gatherings, connecting participants to the community and to one another."[36] Unlike jazz, the route to black professional basketball was exceedingly narrow given that only a couple of leading teams carried only about eight players apiece.

Early black professional basketball performance emerged in Harlem as a result of black entrepreneurial interests and was closely linked to after-game dances. Guys and gals watched the Harlem Renaissance Five (the "Rens")— as well as teams such as Cumberland Posey's "Big Five" (the first openly professional team formed in Pittsburgh in 1913)—and afterward danced to the music of leading jazz bands (e.g., Count Basie, Duke Ellington, Chick Webb) at the most popular dance halls. Robert L. "Bobby" Douglas, an immigrant from the British West Indies, founded the Rens in 1923, allied with businessman William Roche who built the thrity-five hundred seat capacity Renaissance Casino and Ballroom to move out the tables and wheel portable goals onto the dance floor so that Douglas' team could provide basketball exhibitions for the throngs of people waiting to dance the night away (especially between Thanksgiving and New Year).[37] Ballplayers were probably among those who danced after games so that the diffusion of taste flowed from musicians to dancers to basketball players or from players to the dancers and musicians.[38] Roche also agreed to sponsor the team if the club adopted the *Renaissance* name as an advertisement for the casino. As Todd Gould has recently written, "to the sports world, it was the first all-black professional basketball team; to the music world, it was the oddest warm-up act in history."[39] Due to the lack of opportunity for black players to pursue their game, big-time basketball was a largely urban endeavor for a handful of performers in an underworld culture dominated by gangsters and gamblers.[40]

Like jazz, basketball emerged from a confluence of cultures. "African Americans were in transition from a rural to an urban environment," writes journalist Nelson George, "and in this time of change [they] developed new languages to describe their evolving condition." The black entertainment world was part of the larger gambling scene in major cities—ballplayers who maintained close relationships with musicians and gamblers (many of whom were musicians in their off-seasons or when they needed cash) were a major ingredient of this thriving subculture.[41] Louis Armstrong, Fats Waller, Count Basie, Cab Calloway, Lionel Hampton (an honorary member of the Kansas City Monarchsbaseball team) and other jazz stars were deeply interested in sports. Armstrong lent his name and financial support to a New Orleans baseball team, Armstrong's Secret Nine. Louis came to games dressed in "nines," a white hat, blazer, stiped tie, vest, white pin-striped pants, two-tone shoes.[42]

In this entertainment world, barnstorming teams provided the primary showcase of an evolving "black" style of play. Prior to 1950, the segregated entertainment industry rebuffed and marginalized performers who refused to accept Jim Crow, thereby prompting musicians and ballplayers to turn their rejection from mainstream culture into an assertion of black identity.[43] Barnstorming, a marker of vocational and economic marginality, provided entertainers (cultural producers) with strategies for imagining and contesting their eventual incorporation into the institutional and cultural mainstream. According to cultural historian Gaspar Gonzalez, traveling performers (all of whom lived on the fringes) created a demand for emergent performance styles that eventually rendered themselves obsolete.[44]

The founding of the Negro National League in 1920 ushered in an era of professional black ball that combined organized league play with barnstorming, which reached its heyday during the first half of the twentieth century as teams played other itinerant teams (as well as "all star" white teams) such that the racialized stereotypes were a key attraction. There are significant stylistic differences between white and black baseball prior to Jackie Robinson's integration of Major League Baseball. One contemporary journalist surmised that Negro Leagues' baseball was to white baseball what "the Harlem stomp is to the sedate ballroom waltz. . . . They play faster . . . [and] they think it a weakness to catch a ball with two hands and enjoy amazing dives into the bag to out foot runners. Players clown a lot, go into dance steps, [and] argue noisily and funnily." The "white ball" style of play—of home runs, playing by "the book," and keeping copious statistics—gave way to a faster, more daring "black" style of play (of deception, bunting, and speed) first by barnstorming Negro Leagues teams in interracial games (of which blacks posted an impressed 268–168 record), and thereafter, with the influence of former Negro Leagues players in Major League Baseball.[45] Keith Miller argues that the Negro Leagues baseball style, especially as animated by Jackie Robinson, embodied "African American cultural forms ('trickera-ton'—understood by African Americans and exoticized by whites) while appearing to embody the romanticized, Horatio Alger-like individualism so highly prized by whites." As such, prominent black players joined with bebop jazz musicians Dizzy Gillespie, Max Roach, and Bud Powell, as well as prominent writers Ralph Ellison, Zora Neale Hurston, Richard Wright, and other artists in a project of "exposing, interrogating, and critiquing dominant cultural forms, including America's favorite pastime." Bebop trumpeter Gillespie maintained that white bands (e.g., Jimmy Dorsey) were more strapped by a standardized, self-imposed racial bottleneck than the more unique, stylistic black bands of the 1940s and 1950s.[46]

In basketball, the Rens barnstormed out of necessity rather than by choice. They played every day and often twice on Saturday and Sunday against small-town eastern and midwestern semipro teams with an occasional tour through the south from November to mid-April traveling up to thirty-eight thousand miles a year to games in such distant outposts as Louisiana and Wyoming. Between the late 1920s and mid-1930s, the Ren won about 80 percent of their approximately 130 games a year (they compiled a 2318–381 record before the team folded in 1949). The Rens reached their apogee during the 1932–33 season winning 120 games against only eight losses and compiled an 88-game winning streak, based on speed, continuous ball movement, and relentless defense. In 1939 the Rens won 122 of the 129 games, and the New York *Evening Telegram* declared, "They are the champions of professional basketball in the whole world. It is time we dropped the 'colored' champion title."[47]

Following on the Rens' heels, the Harlem Globetrotters were the most innovative and successful team of the 1930s and 1940s. Formed as the Savoy Big Five in 1926 (the name derived from their nominal home court, Chicago's jazz haunt, the Savoy Ballroom) by a group of star former players from Chicago's all-black Wendell Philips High School, but later that year, Abe Saperstein assumed the coaching and promotional reins and in so doing renamed the team the Harlem Globetrotters ("Harlem" identified the team's African American identity and connected them to the great black intellectual and cultural renaissance; "Globetrotters" implied that they were well traveled). The Trotters dominated the pre-NBA basketball world. Between 1927 and 1939, the Trotters won 1793 and lost only 143; in addition to winning the 1940 World Basketball Tournament, they beat the Minneapolis Lakers in 1948 and 1949.[48]

The Trotters clowned during warm-ups, played serious basketball until they achieved a sizable lead, and then reverted to comedy routines (skit-like antics called "reems") so as to assuage lopsided scores. In much the same fashion as Louis Armstrong often wore the "coon's" mask in films and articulated an eloquent defense of musical "clowning," the Trotters adopted comedy for explicit business purposes, a marketing strategy that also affirmed the prevailing, racist attitudes of seeing black athletes as "natural" performers during a time when black men were regularly lynched for "eyeballing" white women, and America's favorite black movie star was "Stepin Fetchit." As journalist Nelson George put it bluntly, "the idea of five Black men rolling into a Midwestern town, kicking ass, and getting paid could not have been the easiest sell ever."[49] Saperstein, a pioneering sports promoter, incorporated comedy into what eventually became *the* defining style of the game. Unlike its regimented, deliberate white counterpart, the Trotters' rapid passing, dazzling dribbling, sharp shooting, and improvised one-on-one challenges exuded the same aesthetic as jazz and blues—*individual virtuosity within the context of an ensemble*. This style paralleled the jazz ensemble performance wherein the group plays the melody together, then each of the musicians does his own thing improvisationally, then the separate parts come together for a concluding section.[50] The popular song "Sweet Georgia Brown" is indelibly associated by people from around the world with the Trotters' style of play, along with jazz and dance motifs of black subculture in general— stereotypical black characteristics (tap dancing, comedy, laughing, relaxed cool pose) and the style of black sport in general.[51]

The Trotters' fast-break style was fundamentally different than the slower, horizontal, methodical game wherein until 1937 there was a mandated center tip-off after each basket. According to Peterson, the renowned fancy dribbling, trick shooting, and comedy routines of the Globetrotter style did not appear until the 1940s, after the Trotters won the 1940 World Championship (the apex of their years in "straight" basktball).[52] Saperstein's marketing talents attracted record numbers of spectators in search of competitive basketball mixed with amusing antics (i.e., sport as entertainment) and probably kept basketball alive on the nation's sporting landscape through the Great Depression.[53]

These strategies connected mid-twentieth-century sports marketing to an earlier era when, as David Nasaw writes, show businessmen entertainment impresarios such as Saperstein molded and maintained a "revised moral taxonomy of shows and audiences" so as to "keep their critics at bay and attract an audience from the diverse social groups in the city." In short, racial and gender discrimination within American (popular) culture sharply limited the media exposure of black athletes, female athletes, and black and various ethnic musicians, forcing them to conform to the cultural stereotypes and performance styles that music industry executives and sports promoters deemed to be "authentic." In so doing, they created alternative career paths as a creative strategy to negotiate with a business that had relegated them to the margins.[54]

The margins of pre–World War I American sports culture were truly dismal. Outside of several prominent barnstorming professional teams, black hoops were circumscribed at traditional black colleges (most of which were located in the South) where athletic facilities for African Americans were woefully inadequate. Given the segregated, poorly financed public schools (many without gyms and/or even outdoor dirt courts), unavailability of collegiate athletic scholarships, and no professional opportunities, basketball at black colleges remained little more than a diversion until after World War II.[55] Such obstacles were even more daunting for black, female basketball players. The exceptions were the powerhouse women's teams the Chicago Romas, led by Isadore Channels (also a star tennis player who won four ATA championships), and the Philadelphia Tribune, led by Ora Washington (another tennis star who won eight ATAs and twelve consecutive doubles titles but was barred from white tournaments). The Tribune conducted clinics during their southern tour and thereby popularized the game among young black girls in the segregated South.[56]

Black women developed this strenuous, full-court style of play not because they were *naturally* more athletic than their white "sisters" but rather, because they were *expected* to excel in physical, "mannish" sports due to the resiliency of stereotypes that black women were less feminine than white women.[57] Vertinsky and Captain conclude that "notions about the *natural* strength [my emphasis] and 'manly' athletic abilities of black women in running, jumping, and throwing activities—this despite that sport . . . was a luxury to the great majority of black women who needed to earn a living and raise a family in often very poor economic circumstances."[58] Sheila Scraton suggests that scholars need to "move towards analyses of sport that recognize the intersection of race, gender and class and that are located within *specific* historical contexts," recommending that scholars move toward analyses of sport that recognize the intersection of race, gender, and class located in specific historical contexts as a way to move away from essentialized either/or (gender/patriarchal or racialized discourses).[59]

"BLACK" CULTURE AND THE DIFFUSION OF A PERFORMATIVE STYLE

Cultural diffusion is always a vexing process for historians to document through traditional sources and methods. Basketball is no exception. Historian Stephen Fox assures us that basketball grew by "unrelated spontaneous generations, here and there, ballplayers making the game up as they went along." Aside from a few obscure magazines and annual yearbooks, the sport had no national media coverage or audience, no national pro league or college tournament. "In thousands of isolated pockets around the country," Fox concludes, "basketball players found and re-found [sic] basic techniques, all unaware of how the game was being played even in the neighboring pocket—much less in all the distant pockets. The sport bounced forward in the hands of numberless innovators, most of them now unknown and unknowable." If it is difficult to substantiate the timing of the sport itself, we must also confess that any documentation on the development of a distinctly *black* style of play is even more elusive and thus open to speculation and historical conjecture.[60]

The shift from an old horizontal game of picks and position to a more open, daring vertical style of play with the jump shot prompted more dunks, alley oops, and blocks. Fox reasons that like most basketball innovations, the development of the jump shot—by primarily white, rural boys who played on outdoor, dirt courts—materialized by players "fooling around in practice or shooting around" and then during a sudden moment, "an unexpected opening and a player pulls a move he has never done before." Curiously, Fox and John Christgau neglected to consider the contribution of black players to the development, perfection, and spread of the jump shot. Gena Caponi-Tabery provides credible evidence to argue that the jump shot "was part of a distinctively black style of play and began to appear about 1937" (simultaneously with jump tunes and the jitterbug) when the National Basketball Committee introduced a rule change that indirectly made the shot possible.[61] At the height of the civil rights movement, Boston Celtics coach Red Auerbach incorporated this black style into a team that dominated a newly integrated National Basketball Association (NBA) for over a decade. As Michael Novak captures the transformation, "basketball, once a game of the artillery, became a game of the cavalry. Watching the racially-integrated Celtics, nobody thereafter could watch or play the same way again."[62] Interestingly, though, it was a white guard named Bob Cousy whose improvisational style of play brought the style into the mainstream in much the same fashion as Chet Baker popularized the "cool" style of jazz (embodied by the Count Basie band and honed by Lester Young and Miles Davis) to white, working-class and lower-middle-class young jazz buffs to proclaim their estrangement from the post–World War II mainstream culture. An Oklahoma boy who played an elementary black, urban music, David Hajdu opines, "[E]mploying a black aesthetic without the liability of actual blackness." Hall of Fame sportswriter Leonard Koppett surmised that "black players were still few, so it was Cousy who displayed a truth that was already a cultural norm among the blacks and would be, eventually throughout the game—that in basketball, style is as important to the fan as the sheer result." Caponi-Tabery reaches a different conclusion. Although she is careful not to say that Cousy (and other whites) *stole* the black style, she maintains that like the dancers and musicians (as well as the nineteenth-century minstrel performers), "white players noticed the difference, practiced it, transported it to their own arenas, and transmitted it to white audiences . . . [who appreciated] the speed, showiness, and innovation of the African American style" before the time when "white coaches were willing to relinquish the slow, deliberate, ground-bound game they hoped to continue to control."[63]

PERFORMANCE, POSTMODERNISM, AND SPORT HISTORY

As a research avenue, "performance" poses thorny methodological and conceptual challenges to sport historians. The "primary" sources for early jazz and pre-1950s black basketball are elusive. Written sources are scarce, much of the oral testimony is contradictory and often impossible to corroborate; and the richest sources of all (black musicians and basketball players) have died and taken their recollections to the grave. With the exception of a few African American newspapers, there was virtually nothing about black basketball in the mainstream media prior to the early 1950s (some cryptic game summaries but few feature stories or editorials). One is forced to mine the skimpy newspaper coverage of pre-NBA professional basketball, an era that lacked ethnic and racial sensibilities in white-dominated sport where there were players nicknamed "Dutch," "Mick," "Wop," "Irish," and "Chief." Although jazz received more extensive contemporary media coverage than black basketball between the 1920s and the 1950s, based upon my reading of newspapers and sports magazines, information about nonwhite performers (and performance) is limited. Even in the heyday of jazz (1950s), Ralph Ellison recognized that the contemporary jazz pioneers were "local figures known only to small-town dance halls, and whose reputations are limited to the radius of a few hundred miles. . . . The riffs which swung the dancers and the band on some transcendent evening, and which inspired others to competitive flights of invention, become all too swiftly a part of the general style, leaving the originator anonymous." In reflecting upon the guitar style of Charlie Christian, Ellison was reminded of how obscure were the origins of jazz styles and the cultural conditions and tensions out of which various artists achieved their stylistic identities (even in 1958, just forty years after its emergence). Even today, we know the well-established landmarks in the history of jazz as entertainment (e.g., "Jelly Roll" Morton invented jazz while playing in a New Orleans bordello; swing was invented by Benny Goodman in the mid-1930s; bebop was invented by jazz rebels Monk, Gillespie, Parker, and Clarke at Minton's Playhouse in Harlem around 1941), yet, as Ellison observed, this type of "history" actually "ignores the most fundamental knowledge of the dynamics of [its] stylistic growth" whereby the musician's attainment of prominence is privileged over his/her early development in the South, "thus we are left with an impression of mysterious rootlessness, and the true and often annoying complexity of American cultural experience is oversimplified."[64] This is, perhaps, a consequence of the fact that a selective tradition started to be shaped (as well as a corresponding history) that identified individual jazz artists only when jazz began to be appropriated by the white middle classes.[65]

Ellison might reach a similar conclusion about the history of black base-ball whereby historians and enthusiasts have, since the early 1970s, exca-vated oral histories and preserved autobiographical and statistical evidence of early Negro Leaguers (and thereby corroborated the strong improvisa-tional performance style that prevailed prior to the formal integration of pro-fessional baseball). As such, their collective work provides a useful model for explicating the hidden, personal dimensions within oral history for under-standing otherhood in the sporting past.[66] As important as this research has been to the field of sport history, its legacy and implications are problemati-cal if engaged from a critical conceptual (e.g., cultural studies) perspective. The research on Negro Leagues baseball, based on formidable oral historical research, stimulated an explosion of media attention on the Negro Leagues and has thereby evolved from a historical curiousity to a topic of wide popu-lar interest (e.g., mass media articles, documentaries, films, photo exhibits, websites) culminating in Ken Burns' award-winning series *Baseball* (a cause of both celebration and regret). On the one hand, the Negro League narra-tive (culminating in Robinson's entry into Major Leagues baseball) drama-tizes the "promise" of sport in overcoming (segregationist) barriers in American culture; yet, on the other hand, it too easily reifies, as sport histo-rian Daniel Nathan observes, a feel-good, nostalgic "heartwarming tale of perseverance and redemption" that salves "our guilt-ridden collective con-science" about race relations at a particular historical/cultural moment of crisis (e.g., why do we need a liberal, uplifting narrative of improving race relations in sport in the 1990s?).[67]

So how and why did most sport historians miss the most exacting epis-temological critique of their field of the past decade? It is hardly news that the past only becomes "history" through historians' strategies of explanation (E. H. Carr acknowledged this over forty years ago before historians studied sport);[68] nevertheless, there has been relatively little awareness among sport historians of the *production* of the sporting past due to a strong empiricist ori-entation that privileged archival "facts" at the expense of a more self-reflex-ive historical imagination. Sport historians clutched onto the "tried and true" methods of mainstream social history and either ignored or missed the trenchant postmodernist critiques of social history (empiricist in both quali-tative and quantitative guises).[69] Most sport historians resisted engagement with the postmodern critique, mistaking its intellectual sensibility for a clearly defined method. But the postmodernist critique was more a general distrust of all methods and epistemological assumptions. No one method is accorded a privileged status. All approaches to the past (and knowledge) are partial. As Laurel Richardson explains, a postmodern position allows us "to know something without claiming to know everything. Having a partial, local, historical knowledge is still knowing."[70]

How might sport historians adopt a postmodern sensibility toward the stylized performances of black basketball and jazz without slipping into an essentialized view of race? Cultural studies scholar Cornell West asks whether postmodern debates can cast significant light on cultural practices of oppressed peoples or if such debates merely highlight "notions of difference, marginality, and otherness" in such a way that it further marginalizes actual people of difference and otherness, e.g., African Americans, Latinos, women, etc.? Sport historians should discard the conceptually passé (and morally bankrupt) notion of "race" for explaining social behavior and identity and thereby acknowledge that there are greater genetic or innate differences *within* perceived "racial" groups than *between* such perceived groupings.[71] Cultural studies scholar Paul Gilroy asks "[W]hat does this new perspective mean for people who have had to structure their institutions around the idea of 'race' and 'racial differences' in the daily lives?" In answering his own question, Gilroy assures skeptics (i.e., those wedded to the importance of race as an explanatory construct) that "the demise of 'race' is not something to be feared even among many racialized groups" in which "'race' and the hard-won, oppositional identities it supports" need to be reassured that "the dramatic gestures involved in turning against racial observance can be accomplished without violating the precious forms of solidarity and community that have been created by their protracted subordination along racial lines."[72]

If we discard race (and racialized explanations) from the conceptual framework, we can pursue a more nuanced, interdisciplinary, cultural aesthetic.[73] The new cultural studies scholarship on race and blackness challenges us to understand what it means to be socially constructed as "black" (which is as arbitrary and artificial as whiteness). An even more critical engagement would interrogate whether the racial identity of the user is fixed or fluid. For instance, are the sources of that identity biological, political, cultural, or some combination of all three? As Daniel Lionel Smith asks, when Wynton Marsalis plays a Haydn concerto, Dr. John plays the blues, Kathleen Battle interprets Handel, or Travis Tritt sings soul are those expressions of "black culture"? Moreover, "is participation in black culture a biological privilege, or can anybody join? Conversely, is black culture obligatory for black people, and does blackness preclude them from mastering non-black cultural modes?" In the absence of fundamental definitions and a more nuanced understanding of the ways in which race functions in popular culture, such questions "are impertinent . . . they cannot be answered," and as such, they should alert sport historians to the problematical nature of explanations based on either race or black culture.[74]

Such a conceptual approach requires what historian Joan Scott characterizes as "a genuinely non-foundational history, one which retains its explanatory power and its interest in change but does not stand on or reproduce naturalized categories." In this type of history, the historian operates as an interrogator who takes as his/her project "not the reproduction and transmission of knowledge said to be arrived at through experience, but the analysis of the production of that knowledge."[75] Following Foucault, Scott proposes historicizing history, "making history the very process of challenging facticity, of posing ideology against ontology, or recognizing the political status of experience." Scott compels us to ask not "what are the facts or what was the experience, but *whose* are they, where do they come from, and how do they operate *in* history, especially insofar as they cultivate the subjects *of* history?"[76]

Sport historians might, therefore, reorient their conceptual compasses to better appreciate why social groups develop distinctive styles of performance as well as how those distinct styles are to be analyzed. In combining performance and historical methodologies, performance studies scholars, for example, attempt to uncover new insights into the structure and function of many forms of cultural production. From their perspective, history is not something given (waiting to be discovered in "primary" sources) or as something made (the "facts") but an activity embodied in "performance," in the sense of action enfolded in the resources of representation and of representation as itself a form of action. As Della Pollock writes, "performance makes history *go away*, by exercising its representational tactics so vigorously that history can no longer be *seen*."[77]

NOTES

I wish to thank Paola Merli of DeMontfort University (UK) for her valuable criticisms and suggestions on an earlier version of this piece.

1. Todd Boyd, *Am I Black Enough for You? Popular Culture from the 'Hood and Beyond* (Bloomington: Indiana University Press, 1997) 145, 112, 29, 35.

2. James Lincoln Collier, *Jazz: The American Theme Song* (New York: Oxford University Press, 1995). For anthropologist Noel Dyck, what athletes exhibit in games and "what spectators watch and celebrate are *embodied* [my emphasis] sport techniques which unite the private realm of everyday body

practices with the public world of shared performances." Noel Dyck, ed., *Games, Sports, and Cultures* (London: Berg, 2001). See also Wayne Fields, "A Higher Plane," in *Body Language: Writers on Sport,* ed. Gerald Early, (Minneapolis: Graywolf, 1998), 36, 38. For an extended discussion of this see Chuck Wielgus and Alexander Wolff, *The In-Your-Face Basketball Book,* 2nd ed. (New York: Dodd, Mead, 1989), as well as Ralph Ellison's astute observation on jazz improvisation in *Shadow and Act* (New York: Vintage, 1964), 234 . British cultural studies scholar Andrew Blake takes this analogy a step further by suggesting that although jazz performers and audiences are intimately familiar with the instruments, tunes, melodies, and harmonies, they are united by the ways in which the players can perform within those conventions so as to actually transcend the rules. In other words, the virtuoso jazz musician, like the basketball player, can literally perform the impossible (or the previously unthinkable) but cannot be relied on to do so. Andrew Blake, *The Body Language: The Meaning of Modern Sport* (London: Lawrence and Wishart, 1996), 197–98. Blake's work also inspires us to adopt a wider view and situate this topic in a broader comparative context of the development of distinctive playing styles. C. L. R. James described a distinctive black West Indian style of cricket in his magisterial *Beyond a Boundary;* and in his work on South Africa, John Nauright has identified similar differences in styles of play between mixed race or "colored" rugby and cricket and the white versions of those games. See Nauright's *Sport, Cultures, and Identities in South Africa* (Leicester: Leicester University Press, 1997).

3. Dyck, *Games, Sports, and Cultures,* 24; Michael Novak, *The Joy of Sports: End Zones, Bases, Baskets, Balls, and the Consecration of the American Spirit* (New York: Basic Books, 1976), 100–01.

4. Olly Wilson quoted in Jacqui Malone, "'Keep to the Rhythm and You'll Keep to Life': Meaning and Style in African American Vernacular Dance," in *The Routledge Dance Studies Reader,* ed. Alexandra Carter (London: Routledge, 1998), 231; Early, "Why Baseball Was the National Pastime," in *Am I Black Enough for You?,* ed. Boyd, 112, 29, 35; see also Richard Majors and Janet Mancini Billson, *Cool Pose: The Dilemmas of Black Manhood in America* (New York: Touchstone Books, 1992).

5. For more on this historiographical neglect, see Gena Caponi-Tabery's excellent essay "Jump for Joy: Jump Blues, Dance, and Basketball in 1930s African America," in *Sport Matters: Race, Recreation, and Culture,* ed. John Bloom and Michael Willard (New York: New York University Press, 2002), 65–66.

6. The "black aesthetic"—a subject rich with insight into the process of confluence in an urbanizing society and a focal point in the pioneering literature of the 1970s through the 1980s although many scholars now see it as an essentializing concept. The work that launched the debate about this

concept was Addison Gayle, ed., *The Black Aesthetic* (New York: Doubleday, 1972). One might also explore how African American dance followed a sim-ilar trajectory within the development of the black artistic aesthetic. From the 1920s to the 1950s popular dances revolved toward African American styles—performed from a crouch—centrifugal, exploding from hips; gliding, dragging, shuffling steps performed to propulsive rhythm; importance of improvisation. See, for instance, Marshall and Jean Stearns, *Jazz Dance: The Story of American Vernacular Dance*, 2nd ed. (New York: DeCapo, 1994), 15.

7. Of the various forms of capital, Douglas Booth and John Loy iden-tify economic (e.g., wealth), cultural (e.g., artistic tastes), symbolic (e.g., prestige), linguistic (e.g., vocabulary), and bodily (physical attractiveness/prowess). See their astute overview of Bourdieu's work as it might be applied to sport in "Sport, Status, and Style," *Sport History Review* 30 (1999), 1–26.

8. Bourdieu, "Sport and Social Class," *Social Science Information* 17 (1978), 826.

9. John Fiske, "Cultural Studies and the Culture of Everyday Life," 162; Booth and Loy, "Sport, Status, and Style," 2, 5.

10. For an early exploration of this topic, see Jeff Greenfield, "The Black and White Truth about Basketball," *Esquire*, October 1975, 170–71, 248.

11. Ben Carrington and Ian McDonald, eds., *"Race," Sport, and British Society* (New York: Routledge, 2001), 8.

12. Birrell, "Racial Relations Theories and Sport: Suggestions for a More Critical Analysis," *Sociology of Sport Journal* 6 (1989), 213.

13. Vertinsky and Captain, "More Myth Than History: American Cul-ture and Representations of the Black Female's Athletic Ability," *Journal of Sport History* 25 (1998), 537–38.

14. Higginbotham, "African American Women's History and the Metalanguage of Race," *Signs* 17 (1992), 254; Carrington and McDonald, *"Race," Sport and British Society*, 2, 8.

15. Sammons, "'Race' and Sport: A Critical Historical Examination," *Journal of Sport History* 21 (1994), 205, 271; Paul Gilroy, *Beyond Race: Imag-ining Political Culture beyond the Color Line* (Cambridge, MA: Belknap, 2001), xvii; Patrick B. Miller, "The Anatomy of Scientific Racism: Racialist Responses to Black Athletic Achievement," *Journal of Sport History* 25 (1998), 140.

16. For more on developing an explicitly cultural studies approach to sport—a contextual sport studies—see David L. Andrews, "Coming to Terms with Cultural Studies," *Journal of Sport and Social Issues* 26 (2002), 110–19; see also Hartmann, "Rethinking the Relationship between Sport and Race in American Culture," 230.

17. Audrey Smedley, "Social Origins of the Idea of Race," in *Race in Twenty-first Century America*, eds. Curtis Stokes, Theresa Melendez, and Genice Rhodes-Reed (East Lansing: Michigan State University Press, 1999), 18.

18. The classic works on the early history of race in colonial America include Edmund Morgan, *American Slavery, American Freedom* (New York: Norton, 1975); Winthrop D. Jordan, *White over Black: American Attitudes toward the Negro, 1550–1812* (Baltimore: Johns Hopkins University Press, 1968); Gary B. Nash, *Red, White, and Black: The Peoples of Early America* (Englewood Cliffs, NJ: Prentice Hall, 1974); and George M. Frederickson, *The Black Image in the White Mind* (Middletown, CT: Weslayen University Press, 1971).

19. See Smedley, "Social Origins of the Idea of Race," passim, especially 18; Fields, "Slavery, Race and Ideology in the United States of America," 114. Elizabeth Hale traces the ways African American intellectuals and writers exposed the falseness of racial categories masquerading as natural and timeless, revealed the consciously constructed and historical nature of race, explored the essentially hybrid character of American culture, and sought alternatives to identities based solely on whiteness or blackness. These alternative possibilities never became central to America's self definition because turn-of-the-century Southern whites coordinated a cultural juggernaut that successfully implanted whiteness deep into dominant visions of regional and national identity in part by inventing images of blackness that served to bolster white supremacy and endow distinctions of race with a patina of timelessness. See Grace Elizabeth Hale, *Making Whiteness: The Culture of Segregation in the South, 1890–1940* (New York: Vintage, 1998). This concise overview of Hale's work comes from Carl H. Nightingale's incisive review essay, "How Lynchings Became High-Tech, and Other Tales from the Modern South," *Reviews in American History* 27 (1999), 141.

20. Jacques Barzun, *Race: A Study in Superstitution* (New York, 1937; 2nd ed., 1965), 16–17, 12–13, ix–xxii. See also Sammons, "'Race' and Sport," passim. Barzun maintained that "race-thinking" occurs when someone implies the truth of any of the following propositions: (a) "that mankind is divided into unchanging natural types recognizable by physical features (transmitted through the blood); (b) that the mental and moral behavior of human beings can be related to physical structures; and (c) that individual personalities, ideas, and capacities, as well as national culture, politics, and morals, are the products of social entities variously termed race, nation, class, family, whose causative force is clear without further definition or inquiry into the connection between the group and the spiritual 'product.'" Barzun, *Race*, 12–13. David L. Chandler, "In shift, many anthropologists see race as

social construct," *Boston Globe*, 11 May 1997, A30; see also, David Wheeler, "A Growing Number of Scientists Reject the Concept of Race," *Chronicle of Higher Education*, 17 February 1995, A8–9. As Patrick Miller notes, ultimately, for intellectual historians, cultural theorists, and social scientists, as well as journalists who hope to engage entrenched modes of racialist thought and to create a more expansive conception of culture, it may be well as a first step to adopt a new perspective regarding the texts that are devoted to innatist thinking. Central to this undertaking would be the compilation of a roster of phrases and pronouncements that clearly links academic racism, past and present. To be sure, as we strive to move beyond category, the idea of an index of racialist literature involves a troubling dimension. We might start erasing "racial" boundaries altogether. Miller, "The Anatomy of Scientific Racism," 140.

21. Henry Louis Gates Jr., *Loose Canons: Notes on the Culture Wars* (New York: Oxford University Press, 1993), 48–49. Sport historians have not devoted sufficient attention to the ways in which a central group of characteristics (what W. E. B. Du Bois termed "the differences of color, hair, and bone") became fixed and essentialized in one specie being; how power and exclusion derives from this essentialized sorting. The publication of Richard Hernstein and Charles Murray's *Bell Curve: Intelligence and Class Structure in American Life* (New York: Free, 1994) is but one prominent example of how pseudoscientific research continues to promote racism by claiming (through social scientific methods) to have found a genetically based deficiency in blacks on IQ tests.

22. Barbara Fields, "Slavery, Race and Ideology in the United States of America," 101, 114; Fields, "Ideology and Race in American History," in *Region, Race, and Reconstruction: Essays in Honor of C. Vann Woodward*, eds. J. Morgan Kousser and J. M. McPherson (New York: Oxford University Press, 1982), 144; Evelyn Brooks Higginbotham, "African American Women's History and the Metalanguage of Race," *Signs* 17 (1992), 255; and Gates, *Loose Canons*, 49. For an insightful overview of the development of African American history within the American historical profession, see Peter Novick, *That Noble Dream: The "Objectivity Question" and the American Historical Profession* (Chicago: University of Chicago Press, 1988), 473–91.

23. See Lee D. Baker, *From Savage to Negro: Anthropology and the Construction of Race, 1896–1954* (Berkeley: University of California Press, 1998); see also Gates, *Loose Cannons*, 50. On the recent controversy surrounding race and intelligence, see Steven Fraser, *The Bell Curve Wars: Race, Intelligence, and the Future of America* (New York: Basic Books, 1995). Miller shows how during the interwar period, anatomy and physiology were regularly invoked to explain African American athletic success. By the 1930s,

Miller writes, "generalizations from individual performances to group characteristics had come to dominate numerous renderings of the accomplishments of black prizefighters and sprinters," Miller, "The Anatomy of Scientific Racism," 128.

24. Miller, "The Anatomy of Scientific Racism," 120.

25. John Blacking, "Games and Sport in Pre-Colonial African Societies," and Sigrid Paul, "The Wrestling Tradition and Its Social Functions," in *Sport in Africa: Essays in Social History*, eds. William J. Baker and J. A. Mangan (New York: Holmes and Meier Publishers, 1987). See also Chinua Achebe's *Things Fall Apart* (Greenwich: Astor-Honor, 1959).

26. Stanley Crouch, *The All American Skin Game, or, The Decoy of Race* (New York: Vintage, 1995), 14, 19; Jim Cullen, *The Art of Democracy: A Concise History of Popular Culture in the United States* (New York: Monthly Review, 1996), 180. For an excellent, concise synthetic summary of the early fusion of blues and emergent jazz musical styles, see Bryan Palmer, *Cultures of Darkness: Night Travels in the Histories of Transgression* (New York: New York University Press, 2000), 343–69. Palmer employs the night as metaphor and unifying theme to look at dissident or oppositional cultures and movements of peasants, religious heretics, runaway slaves, prostitutes, pornographers, barflies, revolutionaries, gangs, and jazz musicians who lived outside the defining mainstream culture and how they shaped and were shaped by the transformation of capitalism.

27. Shane White and Graham White, *Stylin': African American Expressive Culture from Its Beginnings to the Zoot Suit* (Ithaca: Cornell University Press, 1998), 79, 83.

28. See British missionary George Basden's 1921 description of Nigerian dancing quoted in Blacking's essay in *Sport in Africa*, ed. William J. Baker and James A. Mangan (New York: Africana), 6.

29. See David Wiggins, "Sport and Popular Pastimes: Shadow of the Slavequarters," in *Sport in America*, ed. David Wiggins (Champaign: Human Kinetics, 1995), 51–68. Roger Abrahams' study of the corn-shucking contests on the nineteenth-century Southern plantation dramatizes the stylistic differences between the stiff, erect torso European dance tradition and the fluid, spontaneous hip movements that characterized African American dance. See his *Singing the Master: The Emergence of African American Culture in the Plantation South* (New York: Penguin, 1992). For more on this see Eugene Genovese, *Roll, Jordan, Roll: The World the Slaves Made* (New York: Vintage, 1974); Lawrence Levine, *Black Culture and Black Consciousness: Afro-American Folk Thought from Slavery to Freedom* (New York: Oxford University Press, 1977); Leon Litwack, *Been in the Storm So Long: The Aftermath of Slavery* (New York: Vintage, 1980); and William Barlow, *"Looking Up at*

Down": The Emergence of Blues Culture (Philadelphia: Temple University Press, 1989).

30. Abrahams, *Sing the Master*, xvii, xxiii; Wiggins, "Sport and Popular Pastimes," *passim*. For more on how this style developed within twentieth-century popular culture, see M. Anthony Neal, *What the Music Said: Black Popular Music and Black Public Culture* (New York: New York University Press, 1999), 7–8.

31. David Nasaw, *Going Out: The Rise and Fall of Public Amusements* (New York: Basic Books, 1993), 2; and Hale, *Making Whiteness*, 16, 38. For more on the jazz scene during the 1920s, see Lewis A. Erenberg, *Steppin' Out: New York Nightlife and the Transformation of American Culture, 1890–1930* (Chicago: University of Chicago Press, 1981); Kathy J. Ogren, *The Jazz Revolution: Twenties America and the Meaning of Jazz* (New York: Oxford University Press, 1989); Ann Douglas, *Terrible Honesty: Mongrel Manhattan in the 1920s* (New York: Macmillan, 1995). Film borrowed profusely from all the other popular art forms. From the silent film era of the early twentieth century through the 1950s, as Bogle documents, five character types dominated the representation of African Americans: Uncle Tom, brutal black buck, coon, and the tragic mulatto. Black women were primarily represented by Aunt Jemima or Mammy—an overweight, desexed, dowdy, and dark black actress. All were merely filmic reproductions of black stereotypes that had existed since the days of slavery. Not until the early 1970s did assertive black men make their way to the screen in regular fashion in films such as *Shaft*, *Super Fly*, and Melvin Van Peebles' *Sweet Sweetback's Baadasssss Song*. Only the occasional light-skinned actresses (e.g., Dorothy Dandridge, Claudia McNeil) were given lead roles and allowed sex appeal). See Donald Bogle, *Toms, Coons, Mulattoes, Mammies, and Bucks* (New York: Continuum, 1989), passim.

32. See Palmer, *Cultures of Darkness*, 358.

33. See Ben Sidran, *Black Talk* (New York: Holt, Rinehart, and Winston, 1971), 33; Eric Hobsbawm marveled at what he called the "extraordinary expansion" of jazz, which he surmised "has no cultural parallel for speed and scope except the early expansion of Islam."

34. See Douglas, *Terrible Honesty*. Hobsbawm wrote *The Jazz Scene* in 1960 under the pseudonym Francis Newton, This tension was personified by the "hot jazz" of Louis Armstrong and other leading black musicians juxtaposed against the more sedate, predictable swing of Benny Goodman and Artie Shaw; although it would be an oversimplification to assert that all black musicians played hot and whites played sedately and predictably given the exigencies of earning a living.

35. See William J. Baker's introduction to a reprint of Naismith's book, *Basketball: Its Origins and Development* (Lincoln: University of Nebraska

Press, 1996); see also William J. Baker and Steven W. Pope, "Basketball," in *Encyclopedia of World Sport*, eds. David Levensen and Karen Christensen (New York: Oxford University Press, 1999).

36. Caponi-Tabery, "Jump for Joy," 43.

37. Caponi-Tabery, "Jump for Joy," 43. Douglas was a leftist, black nationalist activist and a staunch supporter of the journal *Crusader*. See Ted Vincent's *Keep Cool: The Black Activists Who Built the Jazz Age* (London: Pluto, 1995), 156–59.

38. Caponi-Tabery, "Jump for Joy," 42. To support this hypothesis, she quotes college coach Clarence "Big House" Gaines who said of his players in the 1940s, "Those kids were all excellent dancers. To be a good basketball player you have to have an excellent sense of rhythm and good feet. The ones with slow feet were the first you cut."

39. Todd Gould, *Pioneers of the Hardwood: Indiana and the Birth of Professional Basketball* (Bloomington: Indiana University Press, 1998), 25. Historian Robin Kelley explains how such occasions were important in "constructing a collective identity based on something other than wage work" (e.g., low income, long hours, pervasive racism). Urban dance halls were places for working-class blacks to "recuperate, to take back their bodies" and in so doing, "challenge the dominant stereotypes of the black body." Robin Kelley, *Race Rebels: Culture, Politics, and the Black Working Class* (New York: Free Press, 1994), 169.

40. Romeo Doughterty, a prominent African American sports and entertainment journalist for the black nationalist newspaper, *The Crusade*, warned in 1921 that New York City amateur basketball must either create a structured protective association or see the gambling crowd ruin the game. See Vincent, *Keep Cool*, 81, passim.

41. Nelson George, *Elevating the Game: Black Men and Basketball* (New York: HarperCollins, 1992), 61. According to Sidran, for musicians, work was play—which explains why the money earned from playing was considered "fun money" and was often poured back into the gambling economy. See Sidran, *Black Talk*, 44.

42. Nelson George, *Hip Hop America* (New York: Penguin, 1999), 144. In recent years the Los Angeles Lakers have pursued late night, after-games partying with an old-fashioned devotion worthy of legends such as Babe Ruth and Wilt Chamberlain. "Sporting colorful suits and big jewelry, after a win or loss," a *Newsweek* writer observes the "favorite sons of a neon party town . . . strutted with the elite of black Hollywood and hip hop." See, for example, Allison Samuels and John Leland, "My White Father" *Newsweek*, 19 June 2000, 56.

43. Sidran, *Black Talk*, 82.

44. Gaspar Gonzalez, *Barnstorming American Culture: Traveling Entertainment as Work and Performance* (Knoxville: University of Tennessee Press, 2006), forthcoming.

45. John Holway, *Blackball Stars: Negro League Pioneers* (Westport: Greenwood, 1988), xiv.

46. Ted Shane quoted in Mark Ribowsky, *A Complete History of the Negro Leagues, 1884 to 1955* (New York: Citadel, 1995), 236. Black bebop musicians parodied popular melodies (and the accompanying "bureaucratized imagination") through "keyboard pyrotechnics" that enabled them to contrast their own "creativity to the dull conventions of the original white tune." Montye Fuse and Keith D. Miller, "Jazzing the Basepaths: Jackie Robinson and African American Aesthetics," in *Sport Matters*, eds. John Bloom and Michael Nevin Willard (New York: New York University Press, 2002), 120–21.

47. Robert W. Peterson, *Cages to Jump Shots: Pro Basketball's Early Years* (Lincoln: University of Nebraska Press, 2002), 96–97; the New York *Evening Telegram* quote was cited in George, *Elevating the Game*, 40. The Original Celtics' on-court antics added considerable color and sizzle to sportspages during the late 1920s. The *Cleveland Press*, for example, reported "every member of the Celtic squad handled the sphere as if it were a baseball. They threw the ball behind their backs, underhanded, overhanded, and every other way." Journalist Blinkey Horn reported in 1927 that the Celtics "spin the sphere around on the tips of their fingers like a trained seal juggles a huge rubber ball" and that they "fake passes in front and then adroitly whizz the ball behind them." Several players from the Original Celtics played in the NBL as the Cleveland Rosemblums (or Rosies), sometimes referred to as the "Houdinis of the Hardwood" for the ways in which they "passed the ball, pushed it under their jerseys, swallowed it, brought it back to light, and then made it disappear altogether." We might also include Frank Borgmann whose run and gun style brought a new dimension to the white professional game. For more on this white history of early professional basketball, see Murray Nelson, *The Originals: The New York Celtics Invent Professional Basketball* (Bowling Green: Popular, 1999).

48. Several noteworthy all-black high school and collegiate basketball teams nurtured this distinctive style that differed from the slow, deliberate game practiced by white teams, yet we know very little about the performance style of pre-World War II black college teams and even less about the diffusion of this style among high school and city league teams prior to 1960. Ira Berkow's book on the all-black Chicago DuSable Panthers high school team provides some clues about how the rapid diffusion of this evolving style of play transformed the game at the grassroots. Following in the footsteps of their racially mixed predecessor Phillips High School—a team that domi-

nated from the 1920s through the 1940s—the DuSable Panthers—renowned as the "young Trotters" of the mid-1950s—practiced to the jazzy theme song "Sweet Georgia Brown"; slam-dunked in deliberately intimidating pregame warm-ups; and astonished audiences with unorthodox dribbling, passing, and outside shooting displays. John McLendon (a Naismith student and first African American to earn a physical education degree at the University of Kansas in 1936) coached North Carolina College for Negroes in the 1940s and Tennessee A and I during the 1950s, a dynasty that dominated black college hoops prior to integrated competition. Employing the fast break prior to its popularization by the Boston Celtics, the Tennessee A & I was the first African American team to win a national title against white competition in any sport. See Art Rust and Edna Rust, *Art Rust's History of the Black Athlete* (Garden City, NY: Doubleday, 1985).

49. George, *Elevating the Game*, 49.

50. This style is not exclusive to jazz and blues given that other musical genres incorporate improvisation.

51. Snyder, "Responses to Musical Selections and Sport," 174. Without the constraints of a twenty-four-second shot clock, the offensive assault often began with a dribbling exhibition by Marques Haynes, who would then make a behind-the-back pass to Nat "Sweetwater" Clifton who dazzled the audience with magical ballhandling tricks performed to "Sweet Georgia Brown." From there, "Goose" Tatum clowned in the high post and coordinated a series of weaves that eventually opened up an easy dunk shot or reverse layup.

52. Peterson, *Cages to Jump Shots*, 107.

53. George, *Elevating the Game*. During the 1950s, the Trotters expanded their brand name image through television (e.g., *Ed Sullivan Show* in 1953), film (i.e., *The Harlem Globetrotters*, 1951; *Go Man Go*, 1953), and perhaps more significantly, through well-publicized world tours to Europe and Asia. In this sense, Saperstein popularized sport as entertainment and in some aspects anticipated the NBA's successful selling job of the 1980s and 1990s, in which the athleticism of star black athletes is packaged for a predominately white audience. See Lawrence W. Fielding, Lori K. Miller, and James R. Brown, "Harlem Globetrotters International, Inc.," *Journal of Sport Management* 13 (1999): 45–77.

Sociologist Gai Berlage has documented the striking similarities between the Trotters and the leading women's barnstorming team of the era, the All-American Red Heads, a team created by C. M. Olson in 1936 to promote his chain of beauty parlors. Olson scoured the country for the top AAU and high school players (including Hazel Walker, a seven-time AAU All American and perhaps most formidable player of the 1930s and 1940s). This "dream team" successfully disposed of the majority of men's teams with their repertoire of trick plays, gags, and stellar athleticism. Both teams gained wide public acceptance by mandating that players conform to racial and gender stereotypes of the dominant culture and promoting games as "shows," which placed the contests outside "true" sport into the realm of entertainment.

54. Nasaw, *Going Out*, 5; see also See Scott DeVeaux, *The Birth of Bebop: A Social and Musical History* (Berkeley: University of California Press, 1997).

55. Kelley, *Race Rebels*, 45. For more on this see Stephen Hardy, "Sport in Urbanizing America," *Journal of Urban History* 23 (1997): 675–708. As Caponi-Tabery notes, many black college basketball games ended with dance (connecting their venue with those of big-city ones), and due to the sparse number of high school and college gymnasiums, many black youth barred from participating in school activities played hoops at community centers. See Caponi-Tabery, "Jump for Joy," 41.

56. As historians Pamela Grundy and Rita Liberti document, the North Carolina scene was an important exception to the rule as competitive basketball became a popular sport at most of the African American colleges in North Carolina during the 1920s and 1930s. Turning the "biblical messages of racial equality into calls for female rights," Grundy found that black college women "bridged many of the boundaries between the energetic public action embodied in competitive basketball and the controlled refinement championed by [middle-class] physical educators," which provided another "venue in which to demonstrate female competence and encouraging an expansive sense of ability and accomplishment." Liberti discovered that to women at Bennett College, for instance, a "feminine ideal of black womanhood and participation in competitive athletics remained negotiable during the mid-1930s as one player remembered "we were ladies, too, we just played like boys." See Pamela Grundy, "From Amazons to Glamazons: The Rise and Fall of North Carolina Women's Basketball, 1920–1960," *Journal of American History* 87 (2000): 128–129; Rita Liberti, "'We Were Ladies We Just Played Basketball Like Boys': A Study of Women's Basketball at Historically Black Colleges and Universities in North Carolina, 1925–1945." Ph.D. diss., University of Iowa, 1998, 98. This era of black women's competitive basketball was short-lived due to the expanded prominence of female physical educators who crusaded against the "harmful" effect of intercollegiate athletics upon their athletic sisters. By the 1950s black women's college basketball had been almost completely eclipsed by sports days, gymnastic exhibitions, and intramural play.

57. Susan Cahn, *Coming on Strong: Gender and Sexuality in Twentieth Century Women's Sport* (New York: Free Press, 1994), 127–28.

58. Vertinsky and Captain, "More Myth than History: American Culture and Representations of the Black Female's Athletic Ability," *Journal of Sport History* 25 (1998): 545.

59. Sheila Scraton, "Reconceptualizing Race, Gender, and Sport: The Contribution of Black Feminism," in *"Race," Sport and British Society*, 178. Such a perspective raises basic questions: why the surge in black female athleticism, and why did this take root at traditionally black colleges (e.g. Tennessee State, Tuskegee, Shaw, North Carolina A and T)? When white collegiate women vacated particular sports, and athletic organizations withdrew their support, black female athletes stepped to the forefront. Moreover, traditionally black colleges in the South were primarily industrial schools that trained black women for skilled trades. The successful basketball and track programs, according to Martha Verbrugge, reflected a specific, not universal view of black female physicality . . . an athletic aesthetic not found at liberal arts colleges such as Howard, Fisk, or Spelman." See Verbrugge, "The Institutional Politics of Women's Sports in American Colleges, 1920–1940," *NASSH Proceedings*, 1996, 10.

60. Stephen R. Fox, *Big Leagues: Professional Baseball, Football, and Basketball in National Memory* (New York: Morrow, 1994), 17. Allen Guttmann has written the only book-length study of sport (ludic) diffusion. See *Games and Empires: Modern Sports and Cultural Imperialism* (New York: Columbia University Press, 1994).

61. Fox, *Big Leagues*, 16. Fox identifies six inventors of the jump shot all of whom emerged from the lower, grassroots levels of the game: John Cooper and Glenn Roberts (hailing from Kentucky and Virginia and playing their college ball in the 1930s); Belus Smawley and Kenny Sailors (North Carolina and Wyoming who played in the early 1940s); and finally, Joe Fulks— the first great star of the BAA in the late 1940s, who hailed from Kentucky and played at Murray State Teacher's College—is often credited as the main progenitor of the jump shot. For a more detailed exploration, see John Christgau, *The Origins of the Jump Shot: Eight Men Who Shook the World of Basketball* (Lincoln: Bison Books, 1999); Caponi-Tabery, "Jump for Joy," 39.

62. Novak, *The Joy of Sports*, 105.

63. Caponi-Tabery, "Jump for Joy," 56. In his youth, Baker was described as "the James Dean of Jazz," although according to Hajdu, "he was really its Elvis." "The Life and Death of Cool," *New York Times Book Review*, 30 June 2002, 9. Leonard Koppett, *24 Seconds to Shoot: An Informal History of the National Basketball Association* (New York: Macmillan, 1968). Without straying too far off course, the question is to what extent did such displays resemble the black athletic aesthetic? Sociologist Thomas Kochman argues that imitation and borrowing are done much more often by white rather

than black performers, which is why, in his view, blacks have bristled at the very thought of white performers getting the credit and reaping the benefits for simply reproducing black styles. Perhaps such differences in style are, as Jeff Greenfield noted nearly twenty-five years ago (in an *Esquire* article ahead of its time) "based on differences in cultural attitudes—not only about expressiveness, but also about competition, winning and losing, and even about the nature and definition of individuality within the context of team play."

64. Ellison, "The Charlie Christian Story," *Saturday Review*, 17 May 1958; reprinted in *Shadow and Act*, 233, 237–38. Such a conundrum is perpetuated, perhaps unwittingly, by recent biographers and documentary film directors, including Ken Burns in his widely celebrated PBS documentary on the history of American jazz. For a review of the Burns series strikingly resonant with Ellison's 1958 statements, see Whitney Balliett, "Louis, Miles, and the Duke," *New Yorker*, 25 December 2000 / 1 January 2001, 158–61.

65. I am indebted to Paola Merli for this point.

66. See, for example, Robert W. Peterson, *Only the Ball Was White: A History of Legendary Black Players and All-Black Professional Teams* (New York: Oxford University Press, 1970); and Donn Rogosin, *Invisible Men: Life in Baseball's Negro Leagues* (New York: Atheneum, 1983).The Whites' *Stylin,* provides an effective method for uncovering the nature of black style. Although they essentially ignore sports and athletics, they construct their study from all types of depictions in which African Americans presented their bodies in public.

67. Daniel A. Nathan, "Bearing Witness to Blackball: Buck O'Neil, the Negro Leagues, and the Politics of the Past," *Journal of American Studies* 33 (2001), passim, especially 467–69. For a sample of this nostalgic perspective, see the MLB's official website on the "Negro League Legacy," http://www. mlb.com/NASApp/mlb/mlb/history/mlb_negro_leagues.jsp. Not only have Negro Leagues stars "Satchel" Paige and Josh Gibson assumed iconic status but Jackie Robinson has become one of American culture's legendary heroes and poster boys for the "American Experience" despite the fact that two decades ago, there was a general ignorance and apathy about Robinson among even Major League baseball players. For a stimulating analysis of the "Robinson" phenomenon, see Gerald Early, "Performance and Reality: Race, Sports and the Modern World," *The Nation*, 10/17 August 1998, 11–20.

68. See Keith Jenkins, On *"What Is History"* (London: Routledge, 1995).

69. See S.W. Pope, "Sport History: Toward a New Paradigm," in *The New American History: Recent Approaches and Perspectives*, ed. S.W. Pope (Urbana: University of Illinois Press, 1997), 1–31; Hardy, "Sport in Urbanizing America."

70. See Syndy Sydnor, "A History of Synchronized Swimming," *Journal of Sport History* 25 (Summer 1998), 259–60; Richardson, "New Writing Practices in Qualitative Research," *Sociology of Sport Journal* 17 (2000), 8. For more on this perspective see Andrew C. Sparkes, *Telling Tales in Sport and Physical Activity*, (Champaign, IL: Human Kinetics), passim; and Robert H. Rinehart, "Sport and Personal Narrative," in *Qualitative Methods in Sport Studies*, eds. David L. Andrews and Daniel S. Mason, forthcoming. For a primer on postmodern history, see Keith Jenkins, *Rethinking History* (London: Routledge, 1991).

71. Shelley Fisher Fishkin, "Interrogating 'Whiteness,' Complicating 'Blackness': Remapping American Culture," *American Quarterly* 47 (1995), 456. For more on the historical development of whiteness in America, see Matthew Frye Jacobson, *Whiteness of a Different Color: European Immigrants and the Alchemy of Race* (Cambridge, MA: Harvard University Press, 1998); Catherine M. Eagan, "The Invention of the White Race[s]," *American Quarterly* 51 (1999), 921–29.

72. Gilroy, *Against Race*, 12–13; Smedley, "Social Origins of the Idea of Race," 19–20.

73. See Gena D. Caponi, "The Case for an African American Aesthetic," in *Signifyin(g), Sanctifyin', and Slam Dunking: A Reader in African American Expressive Culture*, ed. Gena D. Caponi (Amherst: University of Massachusetts Press, 1999), 9.

74. Daniel Lionel Smith, "What Is Black Culture?" in *The House That Race Built: Black Americans, U.S. Terrain*, ed. Wahneema Lubiano (New York: Vintage, 1997), 192, 180, 181. See also Cornell West, "Black Culture and Postmodernism," in *Remaking History*, eds. Barbara Kruger and Phil Mariani (New York: New Press, 1998; reprint); Celia Lury, *Consumer Cultures* (London: Routledge, 1996), 174–75; Ellis Cashmore, *The Black Culture Industry* (London: Routledge, 1997); and Hall, "What Is This 'Black' in Black Popular Culture," in *Black Popular Culture*, ed. G. Dent (New York: New Press, 1998; reprint).

75. Joan Scott quoted in Della Pollock, "Introduction: Making History Go," in *Exceptional Spaces: Essays in Performance and History*, ed. Della Pollock (Chapel Hill: University of North Carolina Press, 1998), 25. See also Joan Wallach Scott, *Gender and the Politics of History* (New York: Columbia University Press, 1988), passim, esp. pp. 7–10.

76. Ibid. For more on how historians should focus on the production of history, see Troulloit, *Silencing the Past*, 1–30.

77. Pollock, *Exceptional Spaces*, 27.

PART THREE

On the Future

CHAPTER 8

Beyond Traditional Sports Historiography

Toward a Historical "Holograph"

ROBERT E. RINEHART

Good questions are those of interest to the researcher.
—David Wiggins, "Social Historical
Methods in Sports"

[T]he difficulty of historiography is less to find answers than to find questions.
—Paul Veyne, *Writing History: Essay on Epistemology*

You're just a tourist with a typewriter, Barton.
I *live* here; don't you understand that?
—Ethan Coen and J. Coen, *Barton Fink*

A t the turn of the twenty-first century, the methodological issues that sport historians are grappling with align with the methodological issues that scholars from other disciplines—most especially history, but drawing from a variety of sources—seek to examine. There has been, in the past quarter century (at least) an emerging and specific sea change in how scholars, students, and other groups and individuals "see" scholarship. Due in large part to paradigmatic shifts with their roots in feminist, poststructuralist, cultural studies, and other significant modes of scholarship, the questions we ask, the answers we seek, and the ways of reporting upon and representing those individuals, events, and patterns we study are becoming more *overtly* personal than we have seen in many years. This has led to a reevaluation of that type of scholarship that admits to a personal realm—indeed, that privileges the personal as necessary and fundamental to "deep research." This type of research, drawing from both sociology and anthropology, welcomes an uncovering of its method, viewing contextual nuances as significant factors that affect the questions asked, the biases admitted, and the representational strategies utilized in historical research. As Sparkes notes, this type of research "draw[s] on personal experience with the explicit intention of exploring methodological and ethical issues as encountered in the research process. . . . Such writing is intended to show how each particular work came into being and to reveal the dilemmas and tensions contained in the process."[1]

While some "traditional" historians will no doubt take exception to the borrowing of methodology from sociology and anthropology (and other ways of knowing), to go beyond traditional sport historiography, researchers must try out new forms, new dynamics that may, in fact, answer historical questions in new and interesting ways. And sport historiography, while largely traditional in its methodology for many years, of course has admitted some types of "nontraditional" forms of reporting research into the margins of its "canon."

In this chapter, I primarily delve into three areas of so-called nontraditional sport historiography: (1) the questions that these nontraditional styles of "reporting" seek to answer; (2) the forms these reportings may take; and (3) the techniques and tools sport historians may use to get at more subjective forms of these historical "holographs." I am not trying to be cute with the term *holograph*, but rather I seek accuracy. When writing this chapter, I first thought *historical picture* might be the best term to describe what some history is about; then I tried out *historical snapshot*—but both of these terms seemed too static, too unchanging, too much in the tradition of a historical grand narrative. Berkhofer points out that what he terms the "Great Story" exists within the postmodern project:

> [A]n extreme view of the postmodern project produces its own reflexive problems. If postmodernism is a self-consciousness of a culture's own historical relativity with the consequent loss of the absoluteness of any Western account of history, then what about the history assumed in the Great Story of postmodernism? How can a postmodernist of this persuasion plot history? Is it a narrative of epistemological and ontological innocence lost or of epistemological and ontological sophistication gained? Should the story be emplotted as irony or as tragedy? If pastiche or montage is the preferred postmodernist mode, should not its Great Story, like all history, be plotted accordingly? Must not the narrative, like the subject, be fragmented and mimetic realism be subverted in and through the discourse?[2]

And of course he is correct. But Berkhofer simultaneously allows for, as Laurel Richardson puts it, knowledge of something without the knowledge of everything.[3] He writes that

> . . . proclaiming the death of . . . the grand metanarratives has not meant the death of Great Stories. Which and what Great Story matters greatly from the viewpoint of a person's politics, but from the politics of viewpoint all Great Stories present the same problems of textualization. Who is the Great Storyteller? From whose viewpoint is the Great Story told and emplotted either explicitly or subtextually?[4]

So I opted for the imperfect "holograph" as a more amorphous, fluid descriptor which comes closer to what my worldview sees as the reality of sport history research.

I first intend to explore the contested terrain that the term *nontraditional* makes in light of what is seen as "traditional," particularly in sport history, but informed by other, more general historiography. It is my contention that, while these terms are good starting points for further discussion, they in fact create a kind of false dichotomy for sport historians, and a too-rigorous focus upon them as polarized categories may miss the point of what *sport* history has been, currently is in practice[s], and may become. For example, clearly there are confessional-type strategies used within predominantly realist tales. Authors of traditional texts have learned that such forms of self-divulging as "bracketing" authorial biographies, strategies, and biases may be useful strategies to blend in with poststructural and postmodern sensibilities and that these "confessional" aspects may help to uncover and make more transparent the research strategies and problematics within sport historiography.[5]

There are, however, many parallels between traditional and nontraditional sport history. Berkhofer discusses what he terms "normal history," and in fact has created a viable diagram of "normal history," which includes the Past, Evidence, Facts, Synthesis, and History.[6] Certainly, good traditional sport history has appropriated the best of these aspects of normal history: it draws from a myriad of credible sources[7]; it establishes an arguably valid record of *a* past generally seen through the lens of the historian/writer[8]; it uses evidence to establish the claims its writers make. Sport history may, however, become constrained in the sense that vitality is lost due to its becoming overdeterministic; it may be faulted, in many cases, for being Eurocentric (or egocentric) while claiming general objectivity[9]; and its evidence may depend upon "the subject of analysis . . . [being] the isolated unit . . . These units exist in a world of like and unlike units, and their pattern of relations with each other makes each of them what they are."[10] In other words, traditional sport history may intend to create a snapshot effect, reducing highly complex interactions to in-focus moments that ignore interfering contexts.

Furthermore, traditional sport history may become enmeshed in many problems, including one that I term "historical nostalgia": in sport, those who recollect a past may tend to embellish it, or otherwise alter it, as much as or even more than those involved in reporting nonsport history.[11] Perhaps because there is a perception that the subject matter—sport—is relatively frivolous, there is the feeling that there is less at stake in fond recollection. Subjects may feel that they are expected to embellish—if they are former sports stars, their "stories" have been told so many times, to so many audiences, that they tend to improvise like a singer does when she has to sing her signature song yet another time—for this is a part of the context of fond reminiscence. It is an expectation of a sport culture that induces and promotes historical nostalgia.

If new, creative, even experimental methods are eschewed by scholars for a variety of reasons, but further, if new, innovative methods are discouraged, then sport historiography will likely continue to see the past as set and determined, uncontested, and part of a grand narrative. If "sport history" becomes proscribed in this way, then sport history, like history itself, may, to borrow from Pollock (1998), fall into the trap of

> locat[ing] [itself] within history as a linear, continuous design made up of periods and great events, [rather than] reflect[ing] on [its] place within a struggle for historical preeminence, to recognize [its] entailments in structures, codes, and discourses of power, and to explore [its] concrete and often discontinuous relation with embodied (local, family, institutional) histories.[12]

In Pollock's view, a "linear, continuous design made up of periods and great events" leads to a static view of history as that which has happened, not that which is currently constructed, that which is continually contested. It is a museumized history. It is a historiography that epistemologically reifies the world. It is one kind of history, one that is traditional and safe and canonized.

Certainly, Pollock demonstrates that what she terms "performative history" is fluid, constructed, and negotiated between actors and audience, between acted upon and actors, between a virtual myriad of spaces, individuals, and institutions to "produce" history. History is thus coproduced, continually recreated by and for new authors and audiences, written and changed with the objects of the history not a snapshot but rather a vibrant, changing matrix of evolving, contested concepts. This idea—the "coproduction" of history by the very writing of it and the concomitant relativistic and situated nature of historical "fact" finding—was hinted at by Louis O'Brien in a slim volume published in 1935:

> It should be perfectly clear, then, that historical truth may change, that of yesterday not necessarily being that of today or tomorrow, although at each moment it expresses the result of a critical examination of evidence which increases continually and is ever better understood. Historical truth is thus a dynamic rather than a static truth; it develops progressively without ever reaching a degree of absolute certitude.[13]

Writing nearly sixty years later, Richardson makes the point that "a postmodernist position does allow us to know 'something' without claiming to know everything."[14] But, of course, O'Brien wrote and studied history back in a time when

> all histories were narrative histories. Historians and their readers understood clearly what the relationships were among history, story, narrative, plot, voice, and viewpoint. A history was a true *story* about the past. Historians arranged their empirical evidence and facts into a *story* modeled upon the narrative conventions of nineteenth-century realistic novels. A plot was the author's arrangement of the actions in the story according to the chronological conventions of history-telling. Voice and viewpoint gave historians a synoptic, if not also an omniscient, outlook upon their subjects (emphasis added).[15]

So of course there is precedent to postmodernist or poststructuralist narrative—what is now termed "nontraditional"—sport history, albeit a narrative sport history that responds to some of the objections and concerns that both traditional sport history and other kinds of historiographical criticism have levied against narrativity. What the current narrativity attempts to respond to includes the idea of the narrator as omniscient, all-knowing observer; the fabrication of "story-like" conventions to give the history more impact; the use of current-day models to reinforce one's history for one's audience. Historians writing in nontraditional ways today try to explore some of these problematics, and often this is done using techniques derived from confessional or autoethnographic tales and forms.[16]

In some ways, it seems that what is now termed "nontraditional" sport historiography is a return to a generalized historiography that once embraced narrativity as conventional, then eschewed narrativity as too subjective, and now promotes an altered narrativity as a means of political and rhetorically strategic intent. A key point is the use of narrative as a strategic stance that not only pushes forward the idea of history as constructed and negotiated but that also provides a political stance toward *all* history as constructed and negotiated. Thus, those who claim objectivity for their histories will find in current narrativity a form of reporting that is decidedly more self-conscious and that seeks to make more transparent the myths of constructed "social science." The use of narrativity fits in with the worldviews of its purveyors, just as the use of "normal history" or "traditional," more static history methods fits in with the worldviews of those who promote its methodology.

Much of this dilemma comes from the alignment of history with social science. Earlier, history was most certainly aligned with the humanities; there was an understanding that history was written, that is, created, by the historian, including his or her biases, interpretations, and occasional flourishes for subjective effect. Berkhofer paints an admirable picture of why a return to such a historiography must be a part of the *solution* to a series of historical crises:

> To the crises of the decline of great narrative history for the popular audience, the multiculturalist challenge to Eurocentric history, and the loss of faith in grand themes or progress and liberation that provided moral and political guidance through history's lessons must be added the crisis created by the implication of literary and rhetorical theory for the very practice of history itself. The crisis posed by postmodernist theory makes problematic the appropriate subject matter of (a) history, the proper methods, the preferred philosophy of method, the appropriate role of politics in the profession, and even the best mode of representation.[17]

In the following pages, I explicate questions for research, a "mode of representation," and ways of reporting that are considered by many to be beyond typically traditional modes of representing sport historiography.

Perhaps the single thread that ties these three strands of nontraditional sport historiography together is the idea that history is not made up of singular "moments," well represented and finalized for posterity by the sport historian, but, rather, that sport history is contextual, colored by individual standpoints and agendas, contested, and malleable. The writer of traditional history may object to this stance, but for nontraditionalists, the very argumentativeness of "history" is what makes it exciting and alive. *The* history becomes *A* history, part of a larger series of contested and possibly changeable histories. Thus, the metaphor of *holograph* rather than *snapshot*, of situationally and context-determined histories.

POSING THE QUESTION(S)

Paul Veyne, writing about historiography through the ages, points out that "different kinds of events are unequally easy to perceive." By this, he indicates that *events* are seen differently than *movements* in the light of history: interpretation from the distance of temporal space qualitatively renders particular events less acutely than it does trends. He poses seven different reasons for this "unequal difficulty of perceiving events":

> First, the event is difference; but history is written from sources whose editors find their own society so natural that they do not divide it into themes. Second, "values" are not found in what people say but in what they do . . . Third, concepts are a perpetual source of misinterpretations . . . Fourth, the historian has a tendency to stop the clarification of the causes at the first freedom, the first material cause, and the first chance that come along. Fifth, the real offers a certain resistance to innovation . . . Sixth, the historical explanation is a regression to infinity; when we reach tradition, routine, inertia, it is difficult to say whether it is a reality or an appearance the truth of which is more deeply hidden in the shadow of the non-eventworthy. Finally, historical facts are often social, collective, statistical; demography, economics, customs.[18]

What these seven precepts hold in common is that they are all filtered through human agents. The perceptions of human agents are in some ways biased; that is to say, they are seated within that individual's own standpoint epistemology; they are skewed by individual filters.

The questions we derive from such epistemologies are, then, at the most fundamental, quite personal and biased and often colored by our time, by dominant ideologies extant within our own time frame. Our histories are driven by our own background, our own sensibilities, our own interests; and our questions similarly are interwoven with our ways of knowing, our abilities to problem solve, what has been successful for us in the past, and what larger agendas drive our seeking of knowledge.

Having agreed upon the individuality and ideosyncratic nature of historiographic intercourse (as well as its chameleon nature: witness how, in the following example, assumptions may be overturned, resulting in a "new" history of a formerly agreed-upon topic), I turn now to an exemplar of sharply divided and polemic prose. I will briefly examine Jean Baudrillard's *The Gulf War Did Not Take Place* as an exemplar of historical analysis deriving its thrust from the questions posed, from the seemingly outrageous and provocative (some would say absurdist) stance of whether the Persian Gulf War did, in fact, "take place." Admittedly polemical—and seated in both a play upon words and a deep rendering of contested terminology (for example, Baudrillard takes exception to the use of the term *war* when describing the United States-lead Gulf War during the early 1990s)—Baudrillard's treatise belies a "realistic" treatment of the conflict in favor of a contestation between the media-driven "virtual" war and the prior conceptions of war ("This imaginary object of media speculation was total war in the 1940s sense")[19] that most publics grew to expect.

(This shift in terms, of course, seems far off the track for a "sports-related" historiography; however, one must remember that Johann Huizinga, in his classic *Homo Ludens*, described war as a playful endeavor: "[A]ll fighting that is bound by rules bears the formal characteristics of play by that very limitation."[20] Supposedly, war is agon at its zenith. Further, Huizinga spells out the importance of differing viewpoints toward war as play while still stressing that rules must be agreed upon: "The Japanese samurai held the view that what was serious for the common man was but a game for the valiant.")[21]

Baudrillard argues cogently that, in the Gulf War, the virtuality of war has exceeded the reality of war. The conception of a "new history"/retreat of history is brought into tight focus of the Persian Gulf War. It is a new kind of history, one being written as it is contested. Thus, it is fraught with bias, and it is of course open to contested interpretation. Each "reader" of the war can have her own "war"; little in fact is agreed upon. However, while playing these virtual games, Baudrillard admits that

> the consequences of what did not take place may be as substantial as those of an historical event. The hypothesis would be that, in the case of the Gulf War as in the case of the events in Eastern Europe, we are no longer dealing with "historical events" but with places of collapse. Eastern Europe saw the collapse of communism, the construction of which had indeed been an historic event, borne by a vision of the world and a utopia. By contrast, its collapse is borne by nothing and bears nothing, but only opens onto a confused desert left vacant by the retreat of history and immediately invaded by its refuse.[22]

Clearly, Baudrillard is asking a very different question than the one that most readers will assume when they are confronted with the title of his series of essays. If a reader takes the statement that the gulf war did not take place literally, she believes Baudrillard to be absurd. If the reader asks similar questions as Baudrillard did (e.g., Has simulacra exceeded reality? What would "an Iraqi taking part with a chance of fighting . . . have been like[?] . . . [or] an American taking part with a chance of being beaten"[?]),[23] then the reader has a better opportunity to explore this sense of "virtual war" as opposed to conventional war. Baudrillard has shifted the terms. While this is disconcerting to a reader who is comfortable reading more conventional prose/history, it is also enlightening, and it leads to provocative, new questions.

So it is with historical sport writing, though there are few such polemical treatises extant. Provocative writing in historical prose is often dismissed as "not true sport history." The better answer might be to examine the questions of the writer, to examine the assumptions of both reader and writer, and to be open to new innovative ways of seeing the sport history world. Of course, this is the way that, in another example, T. S. Eliot in *The Wasteland* and James Joyce in *Ulysses* and *Finnegan's Wake*, the writer teaches the reader how to read the work in new and exciting ways.

Questions drive research. And, as Dave Wiggins stated, "Good questions are of interest to the researcher."[24] Baudrillard questions whether war between the two drastically disparate nations of the United States and Iraq, in the late twentieth century, is really war; Huizinger questions whether a play element exists within all civilized human endeavors: "[R]eal civilization cannot exist in the absence of a certain play-element, for civilization presupposes limitation and mastery of the self, the ability not to confuse its own tendencies with the ultimate and highest goal, but to understand that it is enclosed within certain bounds freely accepted."[25]

In both cases, fundamental questions—and assumptions—drive the research, drive the final form that the writing will take in representing human endeavor and achievement.

MODES OF REPRESENTATION

Though Paul Veyne sees as the "characteristic effort of the historian's profession and what gives it its flavor . . . astonishment at the obvious,"[26] this apparent delight at matters mundane might be characterized by the way in which historians *represent* "the obvious." For it is the representation, like the question, that forms the second part of the researcher's subjectivity during historical research.

Admittedly, Baudrillard represents the Gulf War from a largely Western perspective. Were he to have emplanted himself on the ground, with the presidential Guard, dodging a "smart bomb" here, a strafing there, he may have had a less esoteric bent to his story. His mode of representation is based upon his stance.

Likewise: if sport historians can derive delight and "astonishment at the obvious," they may also find it a challenging game to convey this to their audience. Conveying such an excitement might be a matter of learning to write more succinctly or of utilizing dramatic devices. Or the historian might choose to learn how to more effectively construct a representation of the event or person or trend or history, as Veyne writes:

> Below the reassuring surface of the account, the reader, from what the historian speaks about, from the importance he [sic] seems to attribute to particular sorts of facts (religion, institutions), can infer the nature of the sources he has used, as well as the gaps in them. That reconstitution finally becomes a reflex; the reader can guess where the badly filled gaps are; he [sic] is aware that the number of pages devoted by the writer to the different moments and aspects of the past is an average between the importance of those aspects to him and the richness of the documentation; he knows that the people said to have no history are merely people whose history is unknown and that the "primitive peoples" have a past, as everyone else has. Above all, he knows that from one page to the next the historian changes tense without warning, according to the tempo of his sources; that every history book is in this sense a fabric of incoherences, and it cannot be anything else.[27]

Historians, like any other writers, construct their written worlds. And these constructions, these modes of representation, may depend upon the richness of the sources, the interest of the historian, the depth of the questions that lead to other questions, the presumed audience,[28] or even some presumed pseudo-logical constraints.

For example: once, early in my academic writing career, while coauthoring a survey piece, I was instructed by the senior author to be sure to allot an equal amount of space to each section. Not equivalent, but equal. Precisely equal. The writing was laid out neatly, almost mathematically, yet it, in my mind, did not render the work that we were discussing in a fair and even-handed way. I thought, by giving each section equal space, we were impressing upon the reader that all the parts were of equal value and that the topics had all been researched equivalently. Such is the mode of representation, that *what* is written may often be overwhelmed by *how* it is constructed. Our construction of the survey piece was skewed toward total balance, and it gave the reader the impression that all subtopics were researched equally.

Those who see history as a photograph tend to argue that interpretive histories do not "get the true facts." This is the crux of the representational argument: as soon as the moment passes, there *are* no true facts. Interpretation of a singular past becomes interpretation of a series of pasts, each flavored with the individual writer's colorings. Joseph Amato, arguing against the use of literature to represent "reality," mostly because literature "pretend[s] to give form to what cannot be embodied,"[29] writes,

> Literature, as conscious and articulate representation, betrays reality. To a degree, it must, for the past is ever more than we can enumerate, fathom, or represent. The past never was one; it was made of many fleeting elements of place and mind. Consciousness cannot take it as a whole; it forever will be cut out of a fabric that was both inherited and anticipated. However rich historical documents are and however clever imagination can be, the past can be evoked and constructed only in a present whose own coherence and singularity is equally illusory.[30]

Amato also points out that literature can capture the "popular mind," thus rendering the historian's job the more difficult: "[A] popular work (however scintillating or dull, deep or shallow, dedicated to establishing or dispensing with historical context) becomes real."[31]

Though Amato seems to be decrying such use of fictive devices, I would argue that the "reality" of popular work becomes true for historical work. Interpretation can be more real than listings of facts, since interpretation involves the reader to the extent that the reader becomes embodied. The historian's work is not, Veyne argues, based upon scientific laws—"there are laws *in* history . . . but not laws *of* history"[32]—and much of what makes historical discourse interesting is arguable. Thus, the real itself becomes contested ground, and the modes of representation of historical events and fields are worked in their way through the contestation of the real.

Thus, Baudrillard takes us through the holographic feeling that exists for many Westerners that "the Gulf War [really] did not take place." It was not a war, in the conventional sense: it was unbalanced from the start of the verbal blustering. It was, as Baudrillard states, a contest between "two adversaries" who "have neither the same logic nor the same strategy, even though they are both crooks."[33] But Baudrillard admits that agony was suffered, that people (Iraqis) died, that Saddam Hussein "rendered more service to everyone" than anyone else:

> He reinforced the security of Israel (reflux of the Intifada, revival of world opinion for Israel), assured the glory of American arms, gave

Gorbachev a political chance, opened the door to Iran and Shiism, relaunched the U.N., etc., all for free since he alone paid the price of blood. Can we conceive of so admirable a man? And he did not even fall! He remains a hero for the Arab masses. It is as though he were an agent of the CIA disguised as Saladin.[34]

Baudrillard's is a history of questioning, of taking logics to their own logical end, and such a history utilizes a mode of representation that is mindful, oppositional, and, it must be admitted, fascinating.

(But is it history? Again, traditional historians will no doubt stand back in horror, shouting, "No, it cannot be!" Nontraditionalists might ponder a bit more and discuss whether Baudrillard "gets it right," in essence, whether his interpretations are more right than the superficial mediated "stories" coming out of the Gulf War. When history is a holograph, though, when history is contested turf and is created by each new generation, getting it right becomes a quite difficult concept. It is as if getting it right is a kind of temporal ethnocentrism, validated in one time period only to be debunked in the next.)

Similarly, sport historians may choose to utilize modes of representation that are, at first apprehension, naive and misinformed. Digging beneath the surface, asking the penetrating questions, learning how to "read" the text correctly as it was meant to be read, and then representing in nondominant ways those who answer may be the work of the nontraditional sport historian.

WAYS OF REPORTING

As historians, our writing "tells" stories. Just as former historians' stories "modeled upon the narrative conventions of nineteenth-century realistic novels,"[35] so too our transformations of histories model upon some kinds of writing styles. But which? And how self-consciously—that is, how mindfully—are we modeling certain types of writing styles? It seems to me that histories of historiography, after the fact, determine what kinds of models writers chose to use for their particular histories. Additionally, it seems that historians would be better informed to consciously choose models rather than merely be buffeted by their own time (although of course this will occur to some degree anyway). Their mindfulness, their conscious choice, may help them to write more clearly, more to the point, and may make their audiences gain knowledge and *understanding* of the histories they produce.

Hayden White has written about the "common constructivist character of both artistic and scientific statements."[36] While sport history hopefully has gotten somewhat beyond the schism created by the bifurcation of art and science, often reporting styles still reflect this dichotomous approach. But it does not have to be this way. White claims that one of the jobs the "current generation of historians" faces is "to aid in the assimilation of history to a higher kind of intellectual inquiry which, because it is founded on an awareness of the *similarities* between art and science, rather than their differences, can be properly designated as neither."[37]

The use of narrative, White argues, citing Jameson, is essential to historians (and others) making a break with history itself: "It is the authority of 'culture' that is to be distinguished from that of 'society' precisely by the universal translatability of the forms of its products. Enjoying a special place amongst these forms by virtue of its power to master the dispiriting effects of the corrosive force of temporal processes is narrative."[38]

Two of White's major projects have been to somehow site history within science and art and to discern what purpose history has. And within his answers to these questions lies the seed of the ways of representation that sport history (and history itself) may thrust itself in a "post-political age insofar as politics is conceived by its nineteenth century incarnations."[39] He muses, "could not the death of 'History,' politics, and narrative all be aspects of another great transformation, similar in scope and effect to that which marked the break with Archaicism begun by the Greeks?"[40]

For sport historians, a variety of narrative strategies may be attempts to pull themselves out of their own relics of history, but Sparkes suggests other, more interesting methods and ways of reporting historical narratives.

In the following section, I will discuss three classes of representation that may help historians to find voice for their "subjects" and convey the experience of lived lives. These are, using Sparkes' terms, "poetic representations," "ethnodrama," and "fictional representations."[41]

Sparkes' explication of "poetic representations," "ethnodrama," and "fictional representations" may prove to be fruitful for the nontraditional sport historian. In all of these methods alternative to various forms of prose reporting, writers need to understand that "simply writing in a different genre does not necessarily ensure a better product."[42] However, experimentation with different genres does ensure a relook at fundamental questions of research, at point of view, at representation practices (both failures and successes), at verisimilitude and authenticity, and at a variety of research problems that many traditional researchers learn in graduate school and then rarely interrogate again. Using a variety of genres—or experimenting with them as different "tales" of the same "data" set—leads the researcher to question basic assumptions of research.

Poetic representations may or may not use the informant's own words; they may elide "truth claims" that realist tales, for example, seek to uncover;

but, in the end, poetic representations "can be an evocative form of qualitative research communication" because they are meant to induce writer/reader interaction: good poetry has the capacity to pull the reader into the research process in such a way that the reader may actually vicariously live the experience.

An example of historical poetic representation, used to excellent effect, is "The Donner Party," by George Keithley, an epic poem of the pioneer wagon train calamity. Historical in fact, yet written evocatively (or, as White would have it, "a product of the historian's poetic talents"),[43] "The Donner Party" brings home to the reader the depths of despair, the moral uncertainty, and the resultant lifesaving cannibalism that the George Donner party experienced during the winter of 1846–47 near Lake Tahoe, California.[44]

Sparkes notes, in discussing such work as Laurel Richardson's "Louisa May's Story of Her Life,"[45] that Richardson points out a few advantages of poetic representation. First, there is an audience effect: the breaks on the page, the use of metaphor and repetition, and so on, deliberately reinforce "the facticity of the constructedness [of the text] . . . for both the author and the reader."[46] Second, historians might benefit by borrowing from such sociological constructions, for "representing the sociological as poetry is one way of decentering the unreflexive 'self' to create a position for experiencing the self as a sociological knower/constructor"[47] Third, "the poetic form . . . commends itself to multiple and open readings in ways that straight . . . prose does not."[48] Finally, the use of poetry may have the benefit of embodying lived experience more profoundly than prose.

Ethnodrama—the use of theatrical devices to create viable performances that elicit audience participation—is a fairly recent phenomenon in research circles. According to Sparkes, the use of ethnodrama is a direct response to the call by Denzin for performative texts.[49] Dramatic performance of sport history would clearly be an interesting creation; however the historian would have to avoid redundancy, since much of the drama would be based upon the already-constructed drama within sport itself.[50]

Dramatic reenactments of pedagogical, historical, and sociohistorical sport histories would seek to answer different questions than traditional sport history seeks to answer. As Culler, discussing "narratology," notes,

> recent criticism has enormously refined the Russian Formalists' distinction between *fabula* and *sjuzhet* . . . which investigate the potential of a great many different relations between narrative presentation or narrative order and plot order or story time. But . . . these . . . studies of the relations between the level of event and the level of narrative in fictional narratives . . . miss the kind of insight

afforded by studies which look at the relations between *fabula* and *sjuzhet* in non-literary cases.[51]

Of course, the "insight" is once again based upon the level of questions asked—in this case, between *fabula* (What happened?) and *sjuzhet* (How is it told?). Put slightly differently, White characterizes "narrative . . . as a form of discourse that may or may not be used for the representation of historical events, depending upon whether the primary aim is to describe a situation, analyze a historical process, or tell a story."[52]

Representing sport histories as ethnodramas would demonstrate a willingness to venture into a coproduced arena, where histories are enacted by groups of people; inclusive of a multiplicity of viewpoints, insights, and nuances of voice; and respectful of dynamical, shifting, holographic power relations.

The third type of sport historiography that is nontraditional in its representational mode is that of fictional representation. Perhaps one of the most debated topics in historiography, the use of fiction and fictional methods for "describ[ing] a situation, analyz[ing] a historical process, or tell[ing] a story"[53] begs a fundamental question: why is there such a discrete distinction between fiction and nonfiction? As Culler points out, "When one asks for a title in a bookstore, the clerk is likely to ask whether it is fiction or non-fiction, and bestseller lists have, *for reasons that remain obscure*, chosen 'fiction' and 'non-fiction' as the appropriate way of dividing the multifarious corpus of publications" (emphasis added).

Such a distinction disregards the continuum of choices that is made by writers and audiences daily. Such a distinction ignores "historical fiction"— indeed, such a distinction is meant to oversimplify decisions that should be made by readers as to effectiveness of the writing they are reading.

Of course, fictional methods are used as rhetorical devices all the time, even in so-called traditional sport history. The act of an author displacing a respondent's hesitant "uhm" with a cleanly elided, grammatically correct sentence is fictional; the act of trying to represent nonstandard English in idiomatic phraseology is both a political act and a fictional effort. The point is, such work is *constructed*. As such, all representations are fictions. However, there are distinctions that can be made: deliberate, imagined situations or relationships are probably seen as more fictional than those that make an effort to stick with the *fabula* itself.

The questions asked help to create the representation. If a story is meant to be told, and the narrative is meant to answer questions dealing with "how is life lived into existence" in a particular case, fiction might more readily represent the *truth* of the matter.[54]

Sparkes makes a distinction between ethnographic fiction and creative fiction, such that the former fits more along the continuum toward realist tales, and the latter would be placed wholly in the invented realm. Both types tend to represent lived experience, work to give a sense of how it happened, and utilize fictional methods such as temporal shifts (e.g., foreshadowing and flashbacks), multiple points of view, telling dialogue, and other devices that may more aptly mimic lived experience.

All three of these attempts at representing others in new, innovative ways seek to draw the reader closer to what might feel like unfiltered experience. Indeed, Denzin calls for visual representations, keying histories performatively by using videography. With new generations of historiographers, new methods will emerge that privilege visual rather than auditory, video rather than written, and so on. Whether these new representation attempts succeed or fail may largely be dependent upon prior assumptions the "writers" and "readers" bring to the effort. For example, how one perceives "truth claims" of histories may affect whether, indeed, *anyone* could succeed at "getting at the truth."

If the truth itself is holographic, then it appears that its representation should mirror the experience of that stance. There are many modes of representation, only three of which are poetic representation, ethnodrama, and fiction. Each of these types of representation, however, may be large stretches for traditional historiographers, but traditional sports historiography typically does not get at affect, experience, or verisimilitude nearly as well as these three modes of representation.

BEYOND TRADITIONAL SPORT HISTORIOGRAPHY

Sport historians tend to write similarly to general historians, their historiographies laden with what White terms "the usual chronological framework."[55] But he points out that "Burckhardt . . . broke with the dogma that an historical account has to 'tell a story,' at least in the usual, chronologically ordered way."[56]

To "tell stories" in new, interesting, reflective ways, historians need to discover and experiment with new modes of representation. They likely need to discard (if they have not already) the notion that they are telling a Great Story; they likely need to discover a sense of limitation of ambition, like Burckhardt, whose "intention was not to tell the *whole* truth about the Italian Renaissance but *one* truth about it, in precisely the same way that Cézanne abandoned any attempt to tell the whole truth about a landscape."[57] But they need to try out new modes, to see if new modes of questioning require new kinds of representations.

Hayden White writes that "artists and scientists alike are justified in criticizing historians, *not because they study the past*, but because they are studying it with *bad* science and *bad* art."[58] He calls for new forms of representation:

> There have been no significant attempts at surrealistic, expressionistic, or existentialist historiography in this century . . . for all of the vaunted "artistry" of the historians of modern times. It is almost as if the historian believed that the *sole possible form* of historical narration was that used in the English novel as it had developed by the late nineteenth century. And the result of this has been the progressive antiquation of the "art" of historiography itself.[59]

Similarly, sport historiographers might look at the dynamic between art and science, query new modes of questioning and representation, and play with new forms to see if they, indeed, interrogate issues differently in the twenty-first century than they did in the nineteenth century. Such a radical move might serve to revitalize the field in a variety of ways: new, younger scholars may find that their experimentations are welcomed into the academy; historical "data" may be seen in new lights; Great Stories may be found out for what they are—singular interrogations whose very construction paradoxically reduces any positivist stance toward objectivity.

Michel Foucault created a new type of historiography, one where the subject matter is "constructed by the discourses linked with various social practices and institutions."[60] His "genealogies," "histories," and "archeologies" typified an unnamable kind of historiographic writing, which drew from previous descriptive (traditional) histories, and primary and secondary sources from a variety of "discrete" fields.

Thus, Foucault's canon, but particularly *The History of Sexuality Volume I: An Introduction*; *Discipline and Punish: The Birth of the Prison*; and *The Archeology of Knowledge and the Discourse on Language* all create new forms, which of course treat the subject matter in new and innovative ways, which in turn the reader must learn to decode.[61] Randall Kennedy's *Nigger: The Strange Career of a Troublesome Word* attempts a similar task: to contextualize a subject matter in new (and provocative) ways.[62] To, as Culler writes

> show that what we take for granted as "common sense" is in fact a historical construction, a particular theory that has come to seem so natural to us that we don't even see it as a theory . . . theory involves a questioning of the most basic premises or assumptions of literary study, the unsettling of anything that might have been taken for granted: What is meaning? What is an author? What is it

to read? What is the "I" or subject who writes, reads, or acts? How do texts relate the circumstances in which they are produced?[63]

And sport, particularly, has the potential to break new ground for historiographers in that it focuses on the body, and the embodiment of history as it is inscribed on the body is a fresh and new way of conceiving the past, present, and future. Sport historiographers should take advantage of the turn in historiography and learn to embrace innovative new modes of representation, while proactively driving the research agenda toward a more fundamental discovery of the complex processes and constellations of factors involved in producing history.

NOTES

1. Andrew C. Sparkes, *Telling Tales in Sport and Physical Activity: A Qualitative Journey* (Champaign, IL: Human Kinetics, 2002), 59.

2. Robert F. Berkhofer, *Beyond the Great Story: History as Text and Discourse* (Cambridge, MA: Harvard University Press, 1995), 226.

3. Laurel Richardson, "Writing: A Method of Inquiry," in *Handbook of Qualitative Research*, eds. Norman K. Denzin and Yvonna S. Lincoln (Thousand Oaks, CA: Sage, 1994), 518.

4. Berkhofer, *Beyond the Great Story*, 227.

5. For more on types of tales used in qualitative research, see John Van Maanen, *Tales of the Field: On Writing Ethnography* (Chicago: University of Chicago Press, 1988); as applied to sport and physical activity, see Sparkes, *Telling Tales*.

6. See Berkhofer, *Beyond the Great Story*, especially 28–31.

7. I realize that I am making a case for "sport history" as an anthropomorphic entity. I assure the reader that in no way do I mean for this to be gendered (thus, the "it"), yet categorizing sport history as a type of person may allow us to explore some of the ways that sport history may touch individuals' lives, may be more praxis-oriented, may in fact be "performative" (see, e.g., Della Pollock, "Introduction: Making History Go," in *Exceptional Spaces: Essays in Performance and History*, ed. Della Pollock (Chapel Hill: University of North Carolina Press, 1998). In this way, of personalizing history, we may come to see history as alive and fluid rather than stagnant and dead.

8. And, of course, the use of "a" as opposed to "the" (or pluralized pasts) in terms of past is arguable: situated speakers may have a concretized, clear, comfortable past; but if we look at different groups of situated speakers

while simultaneously looking at individuals, it becomes clear that the past is contested terrain.

9. See, for example, Randall Collins, *Macrohistory: Essays in Sociology of the Long Run* (Stanford, CA: Stanford University Press, 1999, especially 2–3) for an extended criticism of Weber's extensive achievements as well as some of his flaws, including "a Eurocentric view: for all important purposes, the histories of what lies east of Palestine and Greece are taken as analytically static repetitions, while the only dynamic historical transformations are those of the West" (3).

10. Collins, *Macrohistory*, 6.

11. This, of course, is pure speculation on my part: however, see Richard C. Crepeau and Rob Sheinkopf, "'The Eddie Scissons Syndrome': Life Imitating Art Imitating Life," *Aethlon*, 8, no. 1 (1990), 175–84.

12. Pollock, *Making History Go*, 4.

13. Louis O'Brien, *The Writing of History* (adapted from Paul Harsin "Comment on Écrit L'Histoire") (Berkeley: University of California Press, 1935), 8.

14. Richardson, "Writing: A Method of Inquiry," 518.

15. Berkhofer, *Beyond the Great Story*, 26.

16. See Sparkes, *Telling Tales*, particularly chapters. 4 and 5.

17. Berkhofer, *Beyond the Great Story*, 25.

18. Paul Veyne, *Writing History: Essay on Epistemology*, trans. Mina Moore-Rinvolucri (Middletown, CT: Wesleyan University Press, 1971; reprint, 1984), 216.

19. Paul Patton, "Introduction," in *The Gulf War Did Not Take Place*, Jean Baudrillard (Bloomington: Indiana University Press, 1995), 7.

20. Johan Huizinga, *Homo Ludens: A Study of the Play Element in Culture* (Boston: Beacon, 1955), 89.

21. Huizinga, *Homo Ludens*, 102.

22. Baudrillard, *The Gulf War*, 70.

23. Baudrillard, *The Gulf War*, 61.

24. David Wiggins, "Social Historical Methods in Sport Studies," Seminar on Qualitative Methods in Sport Studies, University of Maryland, College Park, Maryland, 22 February 2002.

25. Huizinga, *Homo Ludens*, 211.

26. Veyne, *Writing History*, 7.

27. Veyne, *Writing History*, 16.

28. See Richardson, "Writing: A Method of Inquiry."

29. Joseph A. Amato, *Rethinking Home: A Case for Writing Local History* (Berkeley: University of California Press, 2002), 129.

30. Amato, *Rethinking Home*, 131.

31. Amato, *Rethinking Home*, 131.

32. Veyne, *Writing History*, 236.

33. Baudrillard, *The Gulf War*, 65.

34. Baudrillard, *The Gulf War*, 66.

35. Berkhofer, *Beyond the Great Story*, 26.

36. Hayden V. White, "The Burden of History," *History and Theory* 5, no. 2 (1966): 112.

37. White, "The Burden of History," 113.

38. Hayden White, "Getting Out of History: Jameson's Redemption of Narrative," in *The Content of the Form: Narrative Discourse and Historical Representation* (Baltimore: Johns Hopkins University Press, 1987), 144.

39. White, "Getting Out of History," 168.

40. White, "Getting Out of History," 168.

41. Most scholars agree on these terminologies, though the distinctions may not always be quite as clear as Sparkes reports them. See Sparkes, *Telling Tales*, chapters 6–8.

42. Sparkes, *Telling Tales*, 191.

43. White, "Getting Out of History," 27.

44. George Keithley, *The Donner Party* (New York: Braziller, 1972).

45. See Laurel Richardson, "The Consequences of Poetic Representation: Writing the Other, Rewriting the Self," in *Investigating Subjectivity: Research on Lived Experience*, eds. Carolyn Ellis and Michael G. Flaherty (Newbury Park, CA: Sage, 1992), 125–37.

46. Sparkes, *Telling Tales*, 110.

47. Richardson, "The Consequences of Poetic Representation," 136.

48. Sparkes, *Telling Tales*, 110.

49. Sparkes, *Telling Tales*, 127–28.

50. For a discussion of the sport-as-drama metaphor, both in sport studies and in popular culture, see Robert E. Rinehart, *Players All: Performances in Contemporary Sport* (Bloomington: University of Indiana Press, 1998), particularly chapter 2, "Dropping Hierarchies: Toward the Study of a Contemporary Sporting Avante-Garde."

51. Jonathan Culler, *Framing the Sign: Criticism and Its Institutions* (Norman: University of Oklahoma Press, 1988), 202.

52. White, "Getting Out of History," 26–27.

53. White, "Getting Out of History," 26–27.

54. See Robert Rinehart, "Fictional Methods in Ethnography: Believability, Specks of Glass, and Chekhov," *Qualitative Inquiry* 4, no. 2 (1998): 200–24.

55. White, "The Burden of History," 128.

56. White, "The Burden of History," 127.

57. White, "The Burden of History," 128.

58. White, "The Burden of History," 127.

59. White, "The Burden of History," 127.

60. Jonathan Culler, *Literary Theory: A Very Short Introduction* (Oxford: Oxford University Press, 1997), 6.

61. See Michel Foucault, *The Archeology of Knowledge and the Discourse on Language* (New York: Pantheon Books, 1972); *Discipline and Punish*, trans. A. Sheridan (New York: Vintage Books, 1979); *The History of Sexuality*, trans. R. Hurley (New York: Vintage Books, 1980).

62. Randall Kennedy, *Nigger: The Strange Career of a Troublesome Word* (New York: Pantheon Books, 2002).

63. Culler, *Literary Theory*, 4–5.

CHAPTER 9

Contact with God, Body, and Soul

Sport History and the Radical Orthodoxy Project

SYNTHIA SYDNOR

In 1998 I composed a critique of sport history in the form of a postmodern essay entitled "A History of Synchronized Swimming."[1] In the essay, I wanted to challenge sport historians to go beyond easy alliances with social history and sociological models, and I wanted to explore practically how a specific sport history might look when disparate ideas labeled as postmodern such as those dealing with aesthetics, language and performance, or the thought of Michel Foucault informed it. Arching over these goals was my desire to expose the discourses of modernism, science, and the Enlightenment as they influenced, formed, and policed fields such as sport history with their assumed truths and hegemony.

As I tried to accomplish in the "Synchronized Swimming" essay, postmodern thinkers criticized the Enlightenment project but offered no solution out of the postmodern dilemma they identified. If postmodernity is, as Zygmunt Bauman has aptly described, modernity censuring and assessing itself—a minute version of which I tried to contribute in my essay, then what follows postmodernity? In this chapter, I introduce and discuss an academic sensibility known as radical orthodoxy that I believe is one academic paradigm that has the capacity to further the postmodern project in sport history in significant ways. Radical orthodoxy thought holds that a theological sensibility and a sense of the sacred lie at the root of all knowledge work and that the task of understanding and revitalizing such relationships is part of postmodernism's project that has yet to be fulfilled. Radical orthodoxy claims that for all humans to live in the world is sacramental/liturgical and that postmodernism offers a language to recover for our time the world before and beyond the secular.[2] Specifically, in terms of the academy, radical orthodoxy thinkers claim that only theology can embark upon and realize postmodern hope. Postmodernism is celebrated as a space in which "God emerges from the white-out nihilism of modern atheism . . . we [wait] patiently, [watch] constantly, [trace] endlessly the invisible as the visible, the divine as the corporeal . . . The task of understanding those relationships is part of postmodernism's project."[3]

For radical orthodoxy, the mystery of God is at the root of all knowledge work, and radical orthodoxy thinkers make a radical claim that all disciplines—science, social sciences, humanities and so on—are theological, that the "ultimate" social science[4] and humanities is theology. This theology is not a theology that is fused to scientific or secular discourse as any other academic discipline but a radical "lived narrative which . . . projects . . . represents . . . and gives content to the notion of 'God'. And in practice, providing such a content means making a historical difference in the world."[5] Most significantly, radical orthodoxy seems to answer questions of what is to follow postmodernism and how are the critiques of society that postmodernism aptly provided to be rectified. That is, radical orthodoxy holds that the standpoints that emerge from specific disciplinary theories and methodologies become more profoundly capable of truth, love, and beauty when they are based on other corporealities that are outside of modernity's Enlightenment project.

Radical orthodoxy is a poetics that goes beyond objectivity and subjectivity to theoretically challenge the world and the modern and postmodern critiques of that world. Radical orthodoxy has as its premise that "discourses about anything—language, the body, perception—can have meaning only if they acknowledge their participation in the transcendent."[6] Thus sport history informed by radical orthodoxy would go beyond science and cultural interpretation and push its discussion and performance into spaces such as those dealing with morality, holiness, the sacred, truth, and beauty. Also, some of the classic and current theoretical themes pursued by scholars working in sport history may be illuminated in new ways when viewed through the lens of radical orthodoxy. To explore this amazing idea—that we have to acknowledge and converse about our participation in the transcendent—in the following pages, I attempt to (1) overview the major thinkers and works of radical orthodoxy; (2) attend to the problem of understanding and critiquing radical orthodoxy in terms of sport history; (3) explore the thematic question, can the languages and practices of one's religious faith be intellectually linked to reason and disciplinary knowledge such as sport history?

Radical orthodoxy began and was so named at Cambridge in the early 1990s in the work of theologians Graham Ward, Catherine Pickstock, and

John Milbank. It grew into a Routledge book series and is examined in a sim-ilar series published by Duke University Press. Ward was Dean of Peterhouse, Cambridge (and is currently professor of contextual theology and ethics; director of the Center for Religion, Culture, and Gender at the University of Manchester, England; and editor of the Oxford University Press journal *Lit-erature and Theology*). Catherine Pickstock, Cambridge University philoso-pher, was a student of John Milbank (who now holds a chair in religious studies at the University of Virginia). These three scholars used postmodern theory to reclaim theology and the sacred as central to all of the arts and sci-ences, to the spirit as well as to the mind.[7]

The radical orthodoxy sensibility engages the ideas of such work as that of Hans urs von Balthasar, Barth, Hegel, Bataille, Freud, Lacan, Lacoste, Lyotard, Fredric Jameson, Clifford Geertz, Victor Turner, Slavov Zizek, Judith Butler, Luce Irigaray, Jean-Luc Marion, Emmanuel Levinas, Jacques Derrida, Michel Foucault, Michel de Certeau, Roland Barthes, and Gayatri Spivak and draws on earlier philosophers such as Augustine, Gregory of Nyssa, Saint John of the Cross, Bonaventure, William of Ockham, and Thomas Aquinas.[8] Radical orthodoxy thinkers are influenced by this pre-modern, theological, and philosophical scholarship that they understand as a way to truth and knowledge in our new times. They say that their work is postsecular—"turning again to the premodern to find what they judge modernity has forgotten."[9] Radical orthodoxy is "written by Jews, Christians and atheists; indebted to Plato, the Bible and Augustine; haunted by Hei-degger, Levinas, Foucault and Derrida; dealing with jazz, the Shoah, the eco-logical crisis, the American prison system and many other topics."[10]

Can the languages and practices of faith (or nonfaith) be intellectually linked to reason, intellect, and disciplinary knowledge? Lacoste, one of the foundational thinkers used by the radical orthodoxy school of thought, refers to the "liturgical status of knowledge";[11] as being valuable in itself. Ward, Pickstock, and Milbank seem to describe their project as for those who take philosophy seriously, for those who constantly interrogate philosophy with ways of thinking and writing about God, in coming to understand the truth of our existence. In radical orthodoxy it is argued that "truth is at once the-oretical and practical . . . ; that truth is a matter of faith as well as reason, and vice versa."[12]

As doctors of philosophy, our grand calling is to converse about, create, and disseminate knowledge concerning the human condition. As sport his-torians, we should seriously engage thematic questions such as the following: "can the languages and practices of one's belief/nonbelief be intellectually linked to reason and disciplinary knowledge? How does the journey of the mind to God (in)form / (de)form ways of being in the academy? Hopefully, dialogues within our journals and seminars that move between, within, and around the diverse epistemologies of sport history will explore if, and how, higher disciplinary knowledge—as structured in academic fields/disciplines of study—is compatible with higher knowledge of God. I do not mean fundamental evangelical commentary on sport, nor do I mean that sport historians are to necessarily study religion, rituals, or cult in regard to sport. I mean in part for sport histories to contemplate the meaning of life, what in the world sport has to do with this. We are doctors of philosophy, and philosophy is "inside theology."[13] We should be directed by questions such as, Why are we doing this? Who governs/controls what we do? What is the value of what we do? How does what we do mirror the unwritten and taken-for-granted beliefs, norms and values of the particular times and places in which we live? Sport is certainly a huge cultural institution in the world today—in some parts of the West, sport interest and participation in sport far surpasses involvement in religious activities. For this reason alone, it is crucial for scholars of sport to continue to investigate the hold that sport has upon humans and to seek to understand what it is about sport that fulfills humans (in authentic or inauthentic ways?) and has such a long existence in human community. Indeed, its originators preface radical orthodoxy as a "theological imperative" that "coincides with an increased presence of theology in the domain of public debate."[14]

The earliest work of radical orthodoxy, John Milbank's *Theology and Social Theory: Beyond Secular Reason*, has three major discussions in light of questions such as I pose above and concerning the compatibility of knowledge of God with academic fields. First, Milbank shows how secularism constructed and is constructing the discourses of liberalism such as greatly influence our studies of sport in the past decade. Second, Milbank argues that the fusion of theologic and scientific discourse restrict religion to a purely private realm and thereby creates an "ontology of violence"—unjust economic and social practices. And last, Milbank tries to demonstrate that Hegelian and Marxian dialectics and liberation theology come closest to deconstructing the secular, but then are "re-recruited" by scientific politics and the political economy. Milbank's initial project was to lay the theoretical foundations for sacramental living, and he concludes *Theology and Social Theory* with philosophical foundations for this. As can be seen from this very brief overview, the very discourses that Milbank criticizes are those that frequently frame sport histories and are considered the "height" of critical theories of sport. I think that sport history, any discipline—all earthly activities and practices for that matter—can only aim toward revealing and honoring God, of journeying toward God and the sacred. There is nothing left for us to do on earth except this. God is the ur-history of Walter Benjamin, the history that "seizes us at a moment of danger,"[15] a history that is not history at all but that hints at the eternity and timelessness of what we are a part. History—including sport history—is God's action in the world. God speaks to us through the events of history. Especially, as historians then, we must reflect upon the meaning of our times, upon its wonders, horrors, beauty, and evil.

The radical orthodoxy school of thought specifically claims that theology reconceived and reworked in a poststructuralist way can truly fulfill the postmodern project "because it proceeds groundlessly"; along with Ward, the twenty-some authors of one of the other early works of radical orthodoxy, *The Postmodern God*, contemplate what such a postmodern theology might look like. They describe radical orthodoxy as another corporeality, a new spacing; a desire for the Good; a language deeply glorifying and distancing of God; a new language to describe God, love, and *agape* and to critique current strands of Christianity. For example, the work of thinkers such as Foucault, not usually seen as compatible with Christian theology, are used by radical orthodoxy to assert that Christian theology is itself not politically innocent but a cultural and historically situated product and more specifically that it is Christianity itself that gave rise to and constituted the "historical trajectory" of lustful craving of desire "implicated in an economy of lack" that came in modernity to erase the Trinitarian, christological theology of eros.[16] As Milbank rehearsed in *Theology and Social Theory*, theology, aware of itself as socially constructed and complacent in the invention of nihilism, can deconstruct itself and move on to an "other city": "Even today, in the midst of the self-torturing circle of secular reason, there can open to view again a series with which it [vision of ontological peace] is in no continuity: the emanation of harmonious difference, the exodus of new generations, the path of peaceful flight."[17]

Who walks this path of peaceful flight? At the end of the recent *Cities of God*, Ward defines postmodern theologians as everyone: "mother, brother, lover, son, child, church-member, neighbor, cousin, taxpayer, resident, employer, colleague," making a call that "the theologian's task is to keep alive the vision of better things—of justice, salvation and the common good—and work to clarify the world-view conducive to the promotion of those things. As such, the theologian prophesizes, amplifying the voice of the accuser."[18]

To apply this to sport history, "cities of God" are being constantly given to us to live in and to build, and these cities of God are built of intellectual works, including that of sport. If all have the capacity to be theologians, then that also means that it is not only "scholars" who author sport history; anyone can share title pages of sport history. The foundations of these works, these cities, are sacramental understandings of love, peace, justice, and community (that in radical orthodoxy are distinct from social, historical or political understandings of these terms[19] as we may currently comprehend them).

For example, a sport history that showcases an athletic feat or individual's sport story that pushes beyond the limits of romanticized biography, typical prose, or cultural studies of sport, to provoke the reader/ viewer to "touch" God, understand sacrifice or mortification, might be small examples of such sport histories. These would not necessarily be in the genre of article, book, chapter or review, but be performative creations that blend artistic and musical compositions with virtual reality and computer/graphic design. Examples are Cirque du Soleil performances or artistic video of a snowboarder trailed by a tremendous avalanche. The call of radical orthodoxy also urges us to once again contemplate "play" and "fun," mysteries rooted in sport.

For the radical orthodoxy school, scholars live in the world liturgically by always being in the process of journeying toward God in radical new ways whose practices, narrations, methodologies, and theories are grounded in disparate fields, which "condense" around certain sites of cultural metaphors. Instead of "simply composing sociologies of postmodernity," radical orthodoxy takes up Zygmunt Bauman's challenge of actually making a new postmodern sociology. The contemporary and future city and the use of postcolonial theorists such as Homi Bhabha are especially important as intellectual and emotional sites for radical orthodoxy, just as these have been useful frames for doing urban sport history and postcolonial sport projects. Ward, Milbank, and Pickstock specifically seek to construct a new Christianity through which humans live in "interdependent bodies" in "cities of habitation" bearing witness to Christ, pouring out love alongside non-Christian others. Ward explains that this new Christian dogmatic is not a reinvention of the Christian faith but an unfolding of the revelation of God.[20] Of such liturgical living Ward describes:

> I approach cautiously, through critical self-awareness facilitated by postcolonial theorists. I can and do remain a Christian, but my body is continually mapped onto other bodies; bodies which have no theological affiliations (political groups, cinema clubs, community welfare programs) and bodies that are involved in practices of faithful living in theologies not my own.[21]

In his recent *Cities of God*, as in the quotation above, Ward does not make Christianity an identity statement; what it is to be a Christian is "weak and hermeneutical." The Old and New Testaments of the Bible are read in postmodern, mystical ways that move beyond the literal and historical toward spiritual meaning of the text "not proceeding according to ordinary analogies";[22] Augustine and Aquinas are especially held as exemplars of this strategy in works of radical orthodoxy. With such premodern ideas scholars can create "rhizomatic orders . . . fluid, fluent, fluctuating; hybrids giving birth to new complex discourses . . . discourses which cannot be bound (or seized upon) by one academic discipline, owned by one academic department."[23]

The ongoing debates in sport history that demand of particular projects, but is this *sport history*? (versus *sport philosophy-sociology-psychology-anthropology*) as well as the disciplinary gatekeeping of various journals in sport studies (that are focused on rigid definitions of *sport history*) and fixations on sport authenticity, uncritical athlete biographies, sport trivia, and sport "origins," are examples of topics that radical orthodoxy thought may assist to deconstruct and/or highlight the problematics of sport history.

For radical orthodoxy, the hope of coming communities illuminates theories of hybridization, intermixing of discourses, and new holistic relationships in thinking manifested particularly in the work of Serres, Irigaray, and Wender.[24] "What kind of theological statement does the city make today?" Ward asks in opening his *Cities of God*, explaining that to examine the city is to understand what it is to be human in the image of God.[25] What time is this in which we stand? What am I called to be and do? What is the will of God? are questions postmodern beings can ask, as well as personal questions that "veer off into the larger theological fields of dogmatic inquiry," doctrines of salvation, end times, nature of being made in image of God, and so on. When we yearn toward other spatialities suggested by radical orthodoxy, we are practicing a theological, multigendered worldview/space of communion/liturgical space that may heal nations and produce a renaissance of redemptive thought, art, poetry, and language.[26] In his excellent books *Landscapes of Modern Sport* and *Sport, Space and the City*, John Bale ventures in this direction of probing sport in terms of other spatialities.[27] Another wonderful example is Ian Borden's *Skateboarding, Space and the City: Architecture and the Body* in which interpretations of skateboarding as a "production of space, time and social being" are used to reimagine the city, "to rethink architecture's manifold possibilities."[28]

Ward, Milbank, and Pickstock go to great length in their writings to explain the theories and methodologies (and the shared characteristics of these theories that guide their writing) that will help us to answer such questions. These shared characteristics include concepts that are very familiar to and widely used in sport history: "thick description" from Clifford Geertz; knowledge as a theory of discursive practice; the world constituted in terms of sexual difference, the idea that we have not explanation but persuasion when it comes to understanding the human condition; and, as mentioned earlier, a premise that "weak, hermeneutical," reflexive thinking best narrates the human condition. A difference between radical orthodoxy and sport history is that radical orthodoxy claims that theoretical "circularity" is not just about "critical method, but does itself have theological import" in that it reaffirms the structure and mystery of faith.[29] Furthermore, based on explicit understandings of standpoint epistemology, for radical orthodoxy scholars, the need to theorize is a requirement of responsibility in relation to others: "The theologian's task cannot be one which provides the solutions. The matrices of power—economic, political, cultural and historical—that brought about and continue to produce alienation, solipsism, incommensurate and unequal differences, are complex."[30]

To generally summarize so far: radical orthodoxy understands that thinking, being, and acting within the theoretical framework of theology is as close as we can get to living liturgically, journeying toward God, living in cities of God; in this way, radical orthodoxy, using classic, foundational Judeo-Christian theology and philosophy, contemporary social anthropology, postcolonialist thought, and critical theory: (1) critiques the positivism of the Enlightenment, which impedes routes to the divine; (2) analyzes the whole of culture itself with respect to the "grammar of the Christian faith;[31] (3) reads the "liturgical status of knowledge"[32] and the signs of the times; (4) acts or comments upon them from a Christian standpoint; (5) explores (as did humans before the Enlightenment) interconnections between language, society, and the sacred.

The radical orthodoxy school poetically explores interconnections (which are sometimes labeled as "metaphors" or "analogies") between symbolic production and interpretation in language, power, the sacred, and society in ways that are perhaps not new but are fresh and significant dialectical understandings of diverse cultural signs in the world such as "evident in dreams, in literature, in ideologies, in institutions and social transformations."[33] Sport certainly falls within the realm of important cultural signs that are associated with ideologies, institutions, and social transformation. (Although he never mentions sport) Ward says, for example, that reading such cultural signs is a "fundamental gospel teaching," and in this way, he magnifies the idea that to be part of the Christian tradition is to read cultural signs.

In reading culture, radical orthodoxy not only points out postsecularism, but it also specifically critiques the current popular ontologically soft yearning for the sacred and pure such as may be seen in the contemporary commodification/ commercialization of angels, new ageism, "native" spiritualism, and "the manufacture of new urban mythologies, a longing for transcendence, the fabrication of cosmologies, and a desire to become divine while being constantly reminded of Hiroshima, the German death camps and continuing exploitation."[34]

It is clear that in sport history, we have been obsessed with studying such empty transcendental yearnings and urban mythologies. See our many studies that are focused upon historicizing and interpreting the deification of superstar athletes such as Michael Jordan; research that seeks to contextualize "girlpower" through sports in terms of society and politics; studies that trace fads of the developed West related to Eastern martial and meditative arts and body practices; and research that studies quests for immortality and transcendence through extreme sports and back-to-nature/primitive activities. Radical orthodoxy thought allows sport historians to ask, what in postmodernity allows for social, cultural, historical, and personal systems of belief that popularize and commodify things such as bodily holism (e.g., video and DVD marketing of yoga); sport celebrity, virtual, computer-simulated games, and video-cyber sports; touristic pilgrimages to sport festivals (Olympic Games, Superbowl, Formula 1 racing, World Cup soccer), and sport-related sites (for example, sports halls of fames and revered sporting landscapes marked as tourist sites such as Dyersville Iowa "Field of Dreams"); and eroticisms of new sport (as in World Wide Wrestling Federation (WWF), American XFL Football League and televised voyeurism of athletes)? In our studies, theses, and conclusions of these, we might boldly answer that the developed world's obsession/fascination with these sport-related productions and representations is the result of individual and societal emptiness that is only fulfilled by God. Augustine said: "Oh Lord . . . our heart is unquiet until it rests in you."[35] This is in sharp contrast to the sport "pilgrim" who believes that his family troubles will be healed if he plays "catch" with his sons at the "Field of Dreams" mecca (a 1989 movie set).

In *Cities of God*, although he never considers sport, Ward specifically forwards that such longings for holism and contact with the divine are escapes from actuality of embodiment and rejections of corporeality and that although these are "shot through with theological colouring," and "re-enchant the world," these vacant practices are "not towards or away from anything" but an "erotic ontology founded upon absence," that the "larger the pseudo-space the deeper the political and social aphasia." The radical orthodoxy school criticizes this secular desire for total knowledge, "interconnectedness, love, participation, incarnation, and shared liturgical practices that are theorized, photographed, appealed to, and traced" as "caught up in a massive drift of signification." Although theology is public discourse again, such a "theological imaginary" is "impious, earthly, profane, unrighteous, distorted representations of the divine, parodic simulacra of theological truths."[36] The excellent studies and critiques of baseball card collecting as a kind of quest for "total knowledge" such as by John Fiske and Charles Springwood[37] could be colored and expanded with a radical orthodoxy sensibility. John Fiske is fascinated by the consumption of baseball and its interpretation by scholars. His baseball card collecting ethnography, which is grounded in Pierre Bourdieu's thought, privileges the baseball card, and by extension, baseball knowledge, as a physical sign of knowledge, a kind of cultural capital. "The possession and collection of cards [baseball knowledge] is the material evidence of acquired and accumulated knowledge . . . knowing the player by owning the card is a way of owning the player."[38] In today's technologically cold, fast-moving world in which families are distant from one another and masses of people have little economic capital, the baseball card collection—as well as the collection of facts, ethical analyses, and sport trivia—empowers owners with control, clear boundaries as to beginnings and ends, and a way to define themselves. Baseball erudition "reduces the public, the monumental and the three-dimensional into the miniature, that which can be enveloped by the body."[39]

That is, while sport historians have dealt with and especially point to and describe the postmodern nihilism reflected in contemporary sporting practices such as those associated with obsessive collecting of sports memorabilia, they have rarely pushed their analyses into theological realms nor offered solutions to the ways that modern humans have become accomplices to the hegemony of capital and to the infinite accumulation of simulacra and positivism. Instead, sport history interpretations commonly situate sport conjuncturally in cultural, political, and economic articulations. Radical orthodoxy melts away such analyses into a certain way of "doing" philosophy that ends up at the borders of theology; the relations between philosophy and religion, reason and faith, are elided.[40] Thus, to reiterate, in radical orthodoxy, sport history, philosophy, anthropology, and all academic/disciplinary undertakings are not reduced to human disciplines or sciences but are raised to the level of *theological* reflection, which have redemptive qualities and build analogical worldviews.

Tropes developed in postmodern theory, such as those having to do with alterity and *bricolage*, are also especially thematic of radical orthodoxy thinkers, who use these to rupture classificatory schemes of modernity[41] and initiate new signs of identity and innovative sites of collaboration and contestation in the act of defining the idea of society itself.[42] Radical orthodoxy especially explores ideas of nothingness, voidness, and liminality,[43] themes that have been worthy of note to sport studies in the last decade, especially influenced by Victor Turner's conception of liminality. For instance, based upon Johan Huizinga's work, sport is much studied as a liminal "in-between," "on the threshold" play space, a "sacred sphere" in which players and spectators are free, outside of reality, and able to take on roles outside of everyday life. Using ideas of radical orthodoxy, sport historians might return to and explore the ideas of Josef Pieper on human play as a most valued and sacramental activity on earth.

Appropriated from postcolonial theory, anthropology, and gender studies—and central to theories of radical orthodoxy—understandings of liminality, the other, the hyphen, and alterity might rupture the classificatory schemes of modernity and help to found a new ethics of the other found only in a "holy middle."[44] That is, these are theoretical ways for sport historians to put into practice the forgetting of difference; for radical orthodoxy, the overcoming of difference is a final exaltation of the human condition. The Christianity of the radical orthodoxy project is prefaced as a practice of alterity and fluid boundaries of alterity are the places of action[45] with athletic performance and spectatorship as offering a glimpse of infinite beauty as some sport philosophers have proclaimed. Radical orthodoxy leads one to envision sport as a cultural site that may have transformative sacramental qualities in which the effort and discipline of sport can be experienced as purification, sacrifice, and immolation.[46] Such a rendering begins to blur the boundaries of dance, music, and performance with sport, a happening that clearly has been generated in postmodernity, especially as regards extreme or x-sports. Clearly, this is applicable to sport history where attempts for solutions to difference have been central to research related to sport, play, games, sexism, ageism, racism, and disability. What are the possibilities and constraints of utilizing radical orthodoxy to organize and undergird such sport history projects?

John Milbank forwards that Christianity can become "internally postmodern in a way that may not be possible for every religion or ideology."[47] Radically, it is claimed that the need to theorize might be a necessity of being Christian. Yet, how might "nonbelievers" or non-Christian others critique this seemingly hegemonic, imperialistic stance that I have outlined, since many will not begin with the faith that I have used to read radical orthodoxy? From the epilogue of *Cities of God*, Ward, using Homi Bhabha, (a postcolonialist thinker) answers that Christendom and Christian hegemony are over but that Christianity is a cultural "in-between" liminal space continually honing a "deepening sense of the rich interpretive openness of the [Christian] narrative."[48]

Milbank, Ward, and Pickstock, as well as the ideas that are forwarded as classical groundings of radical orthodoxy, distinguish their particular elucidation of Christianity and a certain kind of theology as engaging the world and the search for truth to be more fully realized than that of other traditions. No other religious tradition has approached the sophisticated depth of generated knowledge, academic discovery, and dialogue and theoretical and practical application with the world as that of this Judeo-Christian philosophical tradition (whose primary thinkers were listed at the beginning of this chapter). Colonialism, persecutions, and the atrocities of Christianity are seen as human sins and weaknesses of human institutions that people must constantly struggle to overcome and right as they journey toward God. The radical orthodoxy perception of Christianity is instead of radical newness: Christianity in postsecularism has a rich interpretive openness. The radical space of Christian theology "provides the terrain for elaborating strategies of selfhood—singular or communal—that initiate new signs of identity, and innovative site of collaboration and contestation in the act of defining the idea of society itself."[49] Ward elaborates on this new theology:

> The Christian community always waits to receive its understanding, waits to discern its form. It is a community that produces and occupies a space transcending place, walls and boundaries, a liturgical, doxological space opening in the world onto the world. It is a community whose admission of not-knowing, whose admission of different modes of knowing, substantiates its wisdom. Not that the pursuit of knowledge is wrong. We must continually strive to understand, for it is not just we, but the faith we live that seeks understanding, seeks clarification in the movement towards true judgment. But we must recognize that our knowing, thinking and representing is time-bound, situated and therefore, incomplete, open to what is more and more limited by that which cannot yet arrive—the question of tomorrow. The suspension of time, space and materiality demands the suspension of judgment. We do not know how the story ends and we do not know how far we have come in the plot . . . We do not know what we say when we say "Abba," "Lord," "Christ," "salvation," "God." We see so few of our connections with other lives. We see so few of the consequences of our smallest actions.[50]

Radical orthodoxy writings bask in the "divine love of a theological cosmology of older, reappropriated analogical and *Logos* theologies." Analogical relations are complex relational, semiotic, "personal, ecclesial, and global" correspondences and participations among history, salvation, and bodies ("physical, social, political, theological") that are always in the act of becoming and always "dependent upon a creating God, an active God"—not in past or future, but in present. As shown above, for radical orthodoxy leading thinkers Ward and Milbank, "the city is the foremost site of analogical conceptions of embodiment."[51] Since embodiment has been a continuing theoretical and methodological trope in sport history, the ideas of radical orthodoxy on this topic are provocative.

Important to the study of embodiment and to body culture studies in our field, radical orthodoxy borrows from and then furthers the theories of performance of Butler and Irigaray. From the lens of radical orthodoxy, humans comprehend the God who is always beyond human thought and speech (merely) through premodern and modern language/naming (and thus, following Foucault, "disciplining") with binary (sometimes biological essentialist) labels such as "male/female," "homo-/hetero-sexual." Using postmodern theology as exemplified in radical orthodoxy, sport historians might be able to go beyond and outside of such modern reductionist ideas and in so doing begin to understand the gendered body as woven into the Eucharistic[52] and ecclesial body of Christ as a complexity of erotic multiple social and political bodies.[53] As postfeminist sport historians do, radical orthodoxy reads the body as "displaced" erotic civic community; radical orthodoxy thinkers further this displacement to be Christ-as-body-of-the-Church-as-erotic-community.[54] In analogical relations, in the erotic community, human beings are in communion through loving, erotic exchange. It is crucial to point out that this "erotic" is not narcissistic, idolatrous, or "sleazy" as the label may connote in today's culture. The erotic as the displaced body of Christ cares only about the other and mimics the love of God.

The Eucharistic fracture, union, and dispersal are key (and at the same time, controversial) metaphors for radical orthodoxy in terms of understanding eros. We are bodies/ a body that is bounded by divine love.[55] This difficult teaching of radical orthodoxy, which builds on Irigaray and Butler's theories of gender and cultural performance, is controversial because its logic leads radical orthodoxy thinkers to argue that same-sex marriages should be sanctioned within the church. In contrast, bodies are male and female: two innate, complimentary distinctive sexes whose differences are ordained from the beginning of time for purposes of procreation, chastity, and/or nuptial fulfillment of the Trinitarian domestic church. Radical orthodoxy seems to understand bodies as more fluid than this, and for this reason, it is at odds with many orthodox Christian thinkers, including myself. Whether we align with radical orthodoxy thinkers on this point or not, it is an important idea of radical orthodoxy that the civic erotic ecclesial sacramental body is "not yet whole, not yet healed"; the final healing will come with the end. In the meanwhile, we "rehearse the end with every theological analysis undertaken, with every practice (academic or otherwise) a time when there is no fracture."[56] This impression of the body as metaphorically "not yet whole, not yet healed" seems central to the project of sport history.

This means that by using radical orthodoxy thought in sport history studies, everything would stand as, and be interpreted in, analogical relation to the Word of God made flesh—to the Eucharist—which is a way that signification becomes knowledge. Thus, and very important, the universality of sport, the intense human interest in sport/competition/play over the span of human history, and the huge role that sport plays in filmic, televisual, and consumer media today would be explained as a crucial way that humans commune—play—and erotically exchange with others. That this is difficult for us to understand and authentically live out liturgically is because of the "decline of the theological understanding of the social"[57] and erotic. When theological understanding is not present in culture at large, we have secular parodies of these analogical relations including the libido-, pornographic-driven nature of sport.

Radical orthodoxy asserts that when the theological is erased, and desire takes its place, then erotic communities are no longer civic and religious communities. When God is remote and in the background, the modern society/mind constructs social atomism and narcissistic erotic acts (such as x-sport, paintball, World Wide Wrestling Federation, sport spectacles, fantasy baseball teams, violent video games, sport gambling) as entertainment, for "desire does not foster participation, sharing, co-operations."[58] People no longer belong to the body of Christ but to an artificial, "external corpus" of stimulating distinctively "now" and sometimes dangerous experiences.[59] Such practices mimic analogical connectedness—a goal of radical orthodoxy—but these are simulacra, empty copies of things for which there are no originals. Take a new kind of fitness workout called "Cardio-Strip," which originated at the gym Crunch Fitness in Los Angeles. Cardio-Strip incorporates exotic dance moves, pseudostripping, and lap dances. While the activity seems to be "about learning to love your body,"[60] sport historians working within the radical orthodoxy paradigm would understand this activity as an example of an artificial corpus mimicking analogical connectedness.

Radical orthodoxy is also relevant to sport historians' work on sport tourism: in the tradition of the long line of critical work on tourism of Dean MacCannell, Jonathan Culler, and James Clifford,[61] radical orthodoxy critiques postmodernity's obsession with touristic experiences: "To enjoy the instant is to experience the thrill, the buzz of being there."[62] "Salvation becomes a secular matter, effected through obedience to a material, but socially and linguistically constructed authority"; a modern "godless" space.[63] Radical orthodoxy helps to untangle the social practices of the "been there, done that" mentality of sport tourism. It would see the unsatiated desire for tickets to Olympic Games and Super Bowls and to travel to sports' ever-newly invented cultural "back spaces"—for example helicopter skiing and athletes' bedrooms and intimate lives—as exemplars of secular salvation.

Also, radical orthodoxy sees that "when this [godless] space is seen through postmodernist thought for what it is—founded upon the virtual and the simulated—" it collapses into "endless" "secular and nihilistic drift of desire."[64] Ward specifically uses Hegel to show that the civic/the state can actually be a Trinitarian, ethical, free community, a "divine idea as it exists in the world,"[65] but that Hegel's idea has been "taken up in ways that advanced the secularization of the social, rather than returned it to the provenance of the theological and cosmological."[66]

With Benedict Anderson, Slavov Zizek, and Zygmunt Bauman, Ward critiques the contemporary fascination with, and highly charged eroticism of, cyberspace cybersex, global cities, and virtual communities. Certainly this critique is important to sport historians' perceptions of virtual sport and computer games, violent and pornographic sport, and the narcissism that is cultivated in body culture and athletics. Important to his overall argument, for Ward, these would be perceived as "idolatrous versions of the Church as the erotic community *par excellence*."[67] Allen Guttmann's *Erotic in Sports* can be read as a whole tome devoted to revealing and tracing the history of sport in terms of eros. Guttmann uses Freud, Arthur Schopenhauer, and Georges Bataille in defining eros as "the mighty force that holds all the world together" and all that is not death.[68] Guttmann's earlier *From Ritual to Record: Sport and the Modern World*[69] might also insightfully critique the ideas of radical orthodoxy.

Why did analogical worldviews collapse, and how did modernity come to try to bridge them with idolatrous dualisms such as the modern/postmodern sport practices we critique and study?[70] As described above, radical orthodoxy reads the liturgical interchange before the distribution of the Eucharist—the fraction—as a way to understand "true" analogical natures. This understanding can be useful for sport historians interested in sport diffusion; in folk sport including that of newer sports such as skateboarding and sky surfing; in utopic and/or dark embellishment of American and transnational sport; and in architectures and technologies of sport in the third millennium. Aquinas and others help create "a genealogy of presence" that critiques the phenomenological understanding of sacramental presence in the study of these topics and themes. Since our lives are

> hidden with Christ in God . . . our bodies occupy a space in Christ's body. Our desire is to understand and be conformed to that which we know we are, and yet also—because we have not the mind of Christ—know what we are not. We are not Christ-like; our redemption is the formation of that Christ-likeness which is ours truly insofar as we occupy this place *en Christoi*.[71]

In their intricate discussion in their 2001 *Truth in Aquinas*, Pickstock and Milbank further expand on the idea of the Eucharist as central to the formation of Christ-likeness and to an analogical worldview. As closely as I can understand and articulate it, their argument goes as follows: truth is most of all in the Eucharist, where philosophy, pure intuition, incarnation, and divine understanding are liturgically consummated as fully as can be on earth. "Outside the Eucharist, there is no stable signification, no anchoring reference, no fixable meaning and so no truth [as postmodern theory holds.]"[72] To get out of this postmodern dilemma, the supreme organ of intelligence for humans becomes "touch," which is understood by Milbank and Pickstock in a metaphorical way to encompass all human sensation, vision, and creation. This "touch," which is in a sense our work as scholars, can radically select, mold, or alter what it grasps. In order to understand anything of the truth of things (such as topics of sport history), and to get beyond the aphasia and aporia of our learning and work in the academy, we must somehow touch and be touched by God. We come closest to accomplishing this through partaking of the Eucharist. This sense of touch enables us to journey toward God in unwritable, unthinkable ways that put us outside the postmodern project, toward a real "truth" that helps us—to put it quite simply—to make the world a better place and to honor the God who created us. Milbank and Pickstock state that this "truth is immediately accessible to the simplest apprehension, and yet amendable to profound learned elaboration."[73] This truth is theological yet refers to and expands all academic disciplines and knowledge. Pickstock further explores this weighty idea in her book *After Writing: On the Liturgical Consummation of Philosophy*, in which she begins with the words, "This essay completes and surpasses philosophy in the direction, not of nihilism but of doxology . . . I suggest that liturgical language is the only language that really makes sense . . . [T]he event of transubstantiation in the Eucharist is the condition of possibility for all human meaning."[74]

The possibility for all human meaning to know and "touch" truth is passed on to colleagues, students, and the world as a "driving energy," "a gift" (as Pope John Paul II often described). Writing from the 1920s through 1940s, Edith Stein (who seems a precursor of radical orthodoxy thinkers) in her famous essay "Ways to Know God," shows how the thought of the premodern philosopher Pseudo-Dionysius, urges us to understand that "the intellect can never be set at ease in its search for the truth."[75] Dionysius held that the search for truth leads to "The Good," which is the perfect name for God. "The Good" is not solitary, but communicates love whose highest perfection is reached when the mind contemplates God.[76] Stein's theology, by way of the Pseudo-Dionysius, deconstructs formulaic trivia-laden sport history. Stein writes, "The higher the knowledge, the darker and more mysterious it is, the less it can be put into words."[77] I have found that that higher knowledge comes from trust in the Eucharist. Pickstock opens up this idea in the last paragraph of *Truth in Aquinas*:

> Such everyday trust . . . becomes the precondition for finding truth . . . We are still knights looking for the Grail, just as we are still Israel on pilgrimage. Since knowledge consists in desire, we must affirm that the aporia of learning is resolved all the time in the promise of everyday human practices. We are usually unaware of this recollection, and yet in a way we do have a certain inchoate awareness of it. Thus we see that the Eucharist as disclosure of truth

through touch and sign is itself desire. Although we only know via desire, or wanting to know, and this circumstance also resolves the aporia of learning, beyond this we discover that what there is to know is desire itself: desire which has already actuated all that for which we long.[78]

A liturgical sport history, that is, a sacramentalism that would pervade all of sport history, as well as worldviews grown from the premises of radical orthodoxy, would exult in greater dissemination of thought within academe and society as a whole (such as sport histories that are performative, "beautiful" transcendent creations that blend artistic and musical compositions with virtual reality and computer/graphic design and those whose genres and materials we cannot now imagine). And more so than other disciplinary strategies, radical orthodoxy allows the theorization and development of methodologies and epistemologies to deal with the critique and interpretation of new sites of history (such as the internet, space stations, and robotic/cyborg/virtual sport). Our process of historical inquiry into sport can be enriched by desiring the ideas of the sacred/ mysterious/invisible not only having to do with new historical sport developments but also in previous understandings of older forms, practices, and representations of sport, competition, and play.

Emmanuel Levinas writes that modern thinkers used modern shapes/names to "reduce the God who comes to mind to merely what the mind can think."[79] Levinas' "God and Philosophy" understands the human condition as an "ancient trauma" of awakening to a philosophical state in which we begin to be conscious of Truth-God-the Infinite-Immanence. For Levinas, philosophy itself, which compels disciplines such as sport history, is the way that humans voice and become conscious of God. Thus, using Levinas' idea, we would understand sport history as an earthly, rudimentary language in which humans grasp at voicing the unspeakable, the unsayable, and the unknowable. After the postmodern comes the postsecular, a time of being awakened to a philosophical state in which we begin to be conscious in our academic work of God whom however unknowable, we are called upon to know, love, and serve.

The effort of loving and serving God as I fulfill my vocation as a professor means for me that ultimate knowledge begins and ends with God. I believe that all things come from God and that "the desire for God is written in the human heart."[80] In all that they do (and not limited to "religious" activities or to those who consider themselves religious), humans are participating in divine life—to live in the world is sacramental/liturgical because all things of the world derive from God. Consequently, all knowledge work, including that of sport history, are ways that humans voice, become conscious of, and journey to union with the infinitely perfect God. How do I as a scholar working within sport history illuminate this vital concept? After postmodernism, I have turned to radical orthodoxy as a theoretical frame for this segment of my journey. Theologian David S. Cunningham states that the writings of radical orthodoxy are "complex and difficult; they require patience and stamina. They are intended primarily for academics and their practical implications are not always obvious. Such implications will have to be teased out and made explicit."[81] In this chapter, I have attempted to begin to tease out the theoretical and practical implications of radical orthodoxy for sport history.

    To conclude, I recall a favorite quotation from Arthur Machen: "[E]very branch of human history if traced up to its source and final principles vanishes into the mystery of God."[82] Indeed. What is left for us to do in the academy and in sport history? I have recommended that we invigorate our journey in sport history by contemplating the place of theology—of God—via sophisticated thought called "radical orthodoxy" that might rupture easier epistemological and ontological frameworks upon which we rely. Over two decades ago, "postmodern" thought forced us to do this. Radical orthodoxy now aids sport historians (and for that matter, an endless variety of disciplines and intellectual traditions) to "proceed by grace."[83] Most significantly, radical orthodoxy makes a call drawn logically and in great detail from solid philosophical and poststructuralist foundations. The call is for our research, writing, and academic doings to become "incarnate . . . by making us all messengers who live out absolutely our messages."[84] Yet can we as academics/messengers blend attainment of higher knowledge of theology with attainment of excellence of the discipline of sport history? This kind of higher knowledge—in which we journey to God—seems in some ways to differ distinctly from higher knowledge of sport history. Can these discourses of faith and reason ever be intermingled? Radical orthodoxy holds that this and more is possible, and I have written this chapter to provoke sport historians to think about the obligation that they have to build sacramental sport histories and perform scholarly vocations that are filled with transcendent reality and significance.

NOTES

I am grateful for support of this project from the Illinois Program for Research in the Humanities Reading Group Initiatives and Wojtek Chodzko-Zajko, head of the University of Illinois Department of Kinesiology. I am especially indebted to the Reverend Fr. Dwight P. Campbell for his direction and to he and Professors John Gueguen, Kenneth Howell, and Carl

Nelson for their discussions of radical orthodoxy. I take full responsibility for the contents, mistakes, and omissions of the present work.

1. Synthia Sydnor, "A History of Synchronized Swimming," in *Special Issue: The Practice of Sport History*, ed. Steven Pope, *Journal of Sport History* 25 (1998): 252–67.

2. Graham Ward, "Introduction, or, A Guide to Theological Thinking in Cyberspace," in *The Postmodern God: A Theological Reader*, ed. Graham Ward (Malden, MA, and Oxford: Blackwell, 1997), xxxix.

3. Ward, "Introduction," xxi–xxii, xliii.

4. John Milbank, *Theology and Social Theory: Beyond Secular Reason* (Malden, MA: Blackwell, 1990), 6.

5. Milbank, *Theology and Social Theory*, 6.

6. David S. Cunningham, "The New Orthodoxy?" *Christian Century*, 17-24 November 1999. Online http://www.religion-onl;ine.orgl.cgi...earchd. dl1/showarticle?item_id=821, 12.

7. Some of the important founding works of radical orthodoxy include Ward, *The Postmodern God*; Catherine Pickstock, *After Writing: On the Liturgical Consummation of Philosophy* (Malden, MA and Oxford: Blackwell, 1998); John Milbank, Graham Ward, and Catherine Pickstock, eds., *Radical Orthodoxy* (London and New York: Routledge, 1999); Graham Ward, *Cities of God* (London and New York: Routledge, 2000); John Milbank and Catherine Pickstock, *Truth in Aquinas* (London: Routledge, 2001); Graham Ward, ed., *The Blackwell Companion to Postmodern Theology* (Oxford: Blackwell, 2001). See also David Batstone, Eduardo Mendieta, Lois Ann Lorentzen, and Dwight N. Hopkins, eds., *Liberation Theologies, Postmodernity and the Americas* (London and New York: Routledge, 1997); Lewis Ayres and Gareth Jones, eds., *Christian Origins: Theology, Rhetoric and Community* (London and New York: Routledge, 1998); Paul Heelas (with the assistance of David Martin and Paul Morris), ed., *Religion, Modernity and Postmodernity* (Oxford: Blackwell, 1998); Thomas A. Carlson, *Indiscretion: Finitude and the Naming of God* (Chicago and London: University of Chicago Press, 1999); Michel Certeau, "How Is Christianity Thinkable Today?" in *Theology Digest* 19 (1971): 334–345; Nancy Murphy, *Anglo-American Postmodernity: Philosophical Perspectives on Science, Religion and Ethics* (Boulder and Oxford: Fortress, 1997); Mark C. Taylor, ed., *Critical Terms for Religious Studies* (Chicago and London: University of Chicago Press, 1998); Edith Wyschodrod, *An Ethics of Remembering: History, Heterology and the Nameless Others* (Chicago and London: University of Chicago Press, 1998). See also these web pages:

http://www.will.uiuc.edu/WILL_Contents/AM_Contents/AM_Focus_5 80_Webcasts.htm

http://www.religion-online.org/cgi-bin/relsearchd.dll/showarticle?
item_id=821

http://www.usnews.com/usnews/issue/000828/religion.htm

http://www.killingthebuddha.com/dogma/gods_own3.htm

http://www.firstthings.com/ftissues/ft0002/articles/reno.html

http://www.findarticles.com/cf_0/m1571/2_16/58617328/print.jhtml

http://www.time.com/time/magazine/article/0%2C9171%2C110101121
7-187579%2C00.html

http://chronicle.com/free/v46/i42/42a02001.htm

http://www.abc.net.au/rn/relig/spirit/stories/s65244.htm

http://www.art.man.ac.uk/RELTHEOL/staff/gward/cv.htm

8. In the United States, *Time Magazine* and *U.S. News* have show-
cased radical orthodoxy. The *U.S. News* piece on radical orthodoxy was
titled "Academia's Getting Its Religion Back"; in December 2001, *Time Magazine* called radical orthodoxy a "giddy exploration of theology's vast, recovered social responsibilities." The *Chronicle of Higher Education* describes this
new theology as "the vanguard of a larger movement that may well become
the biggest development in theology since Martin Luther nailed his 95
theses to the church door." See Jay Tolson, "Academia's Getting Its Religion
Back," *U.S. News*, 8 August 2000, http://www.usenews.com/usnews/issue/
000828/religion.htm; David Van Biema, "God as a Postmodern: Radical
Orthodoxy," *Time Magazine*, 17 December 2001; Jeff Sharlet, "Theologians
Seek to Reclaim the World with God and Postmodernism: The Subtle Passion of 'Radical Orthodoxy' Emerges as an Intellectual Force," *Chronicle of
Higher Education*, 23 June 2000, http://chronicle.com/free/v46/i42/
42a02001.htm. See also Rachel Kohn, "Rejecting Modernity: Radical
Orthodoxy," Archive 9944 of Radio National *The Spirit of Things* interview
with radical orthodoxy theorists, http://www.abc.net.au/rn/relig/spirit/sto-
ries/s65244.htm; James Lucier, "Pickstock Chooses Radical Orthodoxy,"
Insight on the News, 10 January 2000, http://www.findarticles.com/cf_0/
m1571/2_16/58617328/print.jhtml; R. R. Reno, "The Radical Orthodoxy
Project," *First Things* 100, February 2000, pp. 37–44; Charlotte Allen, "The
Postmodern Mission: Is Deconstruction the Last Best Hope of Evangelical
Christians?" *Lingua Franca: The Review of Academic Life*, December/January
2000, pp. 46–59.

9. Wayne Hankey, "Denys and Aquinas: Antimodern Cold and Postmodern Hot," in *Christian Origins*, ed. Ayres and Jones, 139–40.

10. Fergus Kerr, frontispiece quotation in Ward, *Companion*.

11. Jean-Yves Lacoste, "Liturgy and Kenosis, from *Expérience et Absolu*,"
in *Postmodern God*, 253; Ward, "Introduction," xxxiii–xxxiv; Craig James,
"Georges Bataille (1897–1962): Introduction," in *Postmodern God*, 13;

Emmanuel Levinas, "God and Philosophy," in *Postmodern God*, 67; Certeau, "Christianity," 155, 157; Jacques Derrida, "How to Avoid Speaking," in *Postmodern God*, 179.

12. Milbank and Pickstock, *Truth in Aquinas*, xiii.

13. "Milbank, John, An Interview by Jeff Sharlet, in *The Chronicle of Higher Education* (Research and Publishing), 23 June, 2000. http://www.brow.on.ca/Articles/MilbankRev.htm

14. Pickstock, *After Writing*, xii.

15. Walter Benjamin, *Illuminations*, ed. H. Arendt and trans. Harry Zohn (New York: Schocken Books, 1936; reprint 1968), 255. The exact quote from his "Theses on the Philosophy of History" follows: "to articulate the past historically does not mean to recognize it 'the way it really was.' (Ranke) It means to seize hold of a memory as it flashes up at a moment of danger."

16. Lacoste, "Liturgy and Kenosis," 172.

17. Milbank, *Theology and Social Theory*, 434.

18. Ward, *Cities of God*, 260.

19. Ward, *Cities of God*, 226, 233.

20. Ward, *Cities of God*, 253, 20–21.

21. Ward, *Cities of God*, 257.

22. Ward, *Cities of God*, 211.

23. Ward, *Cities of God*, 212, 214.

24. The following quotes relevant to these authors are highighted by Ward, *Cities*, 205–44; Michel Serres, *Angels: A Modern Myth* (Paris: Flammarion, 1993); Luce Irigaray, *An Ethics of Sexual Difference* (Ithaca: Cornell University Press, 1993); Wim Wenders, *The Logic of Images: Essays and Conversations* (London: Faber, 1991).

25. Ward, *Cities of God*, 1.

26. Paraphrased from Ward, *Cities of God*, 3, 205, 214–15, 221–24, 226.

27. John Bale, *Landscapes of Modern Sport* (Leicester, London, New York: Leicester University, 1994); Bale, *Sport, Space and the City* (London: Blackburn Press, 2001).

28. Ian Borden, *Skateboarding, Space and the City: Architecture and the Body* (New York: Berg, 2001), 1.

29. Ward, *Cities of God*, 259, 21.

30. Ward, *Cities of God*, 260.

31. Ward, *Cities of God*, 8.

32. Lacoste, "Liturgy and Kenosis," 253.

33. Ward, *Cities of God*, 13.

34. Ward, *Cities of God*, 223.

35. Augustine, *Confessions* (New York: Vintage Spiritual Classics, 1997), trans. Maria Boulding 1.1.1.

36. Paraphrased from Ward, *Cities of God*, 224, 250–51; 228–29.

37. John Fiske, *Power Plays, Power Works* (London and New York: Verso, 1993); Charles Fruehling Springwood, *From Cooperstown to Dyersville: A Geography of Baseball Nostalgia* (Boulder, CO: Westview, 1995); Synthia Sydnor, "On Baseball and Desire . . ." Paper presented at the annual Philosophic Society for the Study of Sport Conference, September 1997, Oslo, Norway.

38. Fiske, *Power Plays*, 86. See also 81–93.

39. Susan Stewart, *On Longing: Narratives of the Miniature, the Gigantic, the Souvenir, the Collection* (Baltimore and London: Johns Hopkins University Press, 1984), 137.

40. Ward, "Introduction," xxxvii, xv–xlvii.

41. For example, Frederich Christian Bauersmith, "Aesthetics: The Theological Sublime" in Ward, *Cities*, 209–16.

42. Homi Bhabha, *The Location of Culture* (London: Routledge, 1994).

43. Jean-Luc Marion, "Metaphysics and Phenomenology: A Summary for Theologians," in *Postmodern God*, 292.

44. Edith Wyschogrod, "Saintliness and Some Aporias of Postmodernism From *Saints and Postmodernism*," in *Postmodern God*, 341–55.

45. Frederick Christian Bauerschmidt, "Michel de Certeau (1925–1986): Introduction," in *Postmodern God*, 138; Michel Certeau, "How Is Christianity Thinkable Today?" in *Postmodern God*, 151.

46. See, for example, David Sansone, *Greek Athletics and the Genesis of Sport* (Berkeley: University of California Press, 1988).

47. John Milbank, "Postmodern Critical Augustinianism: A Short *Summa* in Forty-two Responses to Unasked Questions," in *Postmodern God*, 267.

48. Ward, *Cities of God*, 257–58.

49. Ward, *Cities of God*, 257–58.

50. Ward, *Cities of God*, 258–59.

51. Ward, *Cities of God*, 3, 2, ix, 23.

52. The Eucharist is the Christian sacrament of Holy Communion in which the priest, acting in the person of Christ, transubstantiates bread and wine into the body and blood of Jesus Christ and distributes it to the faithful. The Eucharist, in which Christ's love makes contact with the soul, re-presents the ongoing sacrifice and resurrection of Jesus Christ; it places the receiver in a state of sanctifying grace and enables spiritual growth.

53. Ward, *Cities of God*, 23.

54. Ward, *Cities of God*, 202.

55. Pickstock, *After Writing*.

56. Ward, *Cities of God*, 237.

57. Ward, *Cities of God*, 126.

58. Ward, *Cities of God*, 129.

59. Ward, *Cities of God*, 129.

60. Gisela Williams, "Grab Your Tassels," *In Style*, March 2002, p. 282.

61. James Clifford, "Traveling Cultures," in *Cultural Studies*, eds. Lawrence Grossberg, Cary Nelson, and Paula Treichler (New York and London: Routledge, 1992), 96–116; James Clifford and George Marcus, eds., *Writing Culture: The Poetics and Politics of Ethnography* (Berkeley and Los Angeles: University of California Press, 1986); Jonathan Culler, *Framing the Sign: Criticism and Its Institutions* (Norman and London: University of Oklahoma Press, 1988); Dean MacCannell, *The Tourist* (New York: Schocken, 1976); MacCannell, *Empty Meeting Grounds: The Tourist Papers* (London and New York: Routledge, 1992).

62. Ward, *Cities of God*, 170.

63. Ward, *Cities of God*, 131.

64. Ward, *Cities of God*, 138.

65. Ward, *Cities of God*, 140.

66. Ward, *Cities of God*, 141.

67. Ward, *Cities of God*, 151.

68. Allen Guttmann, *The Erotic in Sports* (New York: Columbia University Press, 1996), 171–75.

69. Allen Guttmann, *From Ritual to Record: The Nature of Modern Sports* (New York: Columbia University Press, 1978).

70. Ward, *Cities of God*, 165.

71. Ward, *Cities of God*, 173.

72. Milbank and Pickstock, *Truth in Aquinas*, 109.

73. Milbank and Pickstock, *Truth in Aquinas*, xiii.

74. Pickstock, *After Writing*, xii, xv.

75. Pseudo-Dionysius: *On the Divine Names, III, 1*, found in Bonaventure, *The Journey of the Mind to God*, ed. Stephen F. Brown, trans. Philotheus Boehner; "Introduction and Notes" (Indianapolis: Hackett, 1956) xviii; Edith Stein, *Knowledge and Faith*, trans. Walter Redmond (Washington DC: ICS, 1993), 32.

76. Pseudo-Dionysius: *Names, III, 1*, xviii.

77. Stein, *Knowledge and Faith*, 87.

78. Milbank and Pickstock, *Truth in Aquinas*, 111.

79. Robert Gibbs, "Emmanuel Levinas, [1906–1995]: Introduction," in *Postmodern God*, 51.

80. *Catechism of the Catholic Church* 27 (Ligouri, MO: Ligouri, 1994).

81. Cunningham, "The New Orthodoxy?" 16.

82. Arthur Machen, *The Novel of White Powder,* quoted in *The Hand of God: Thoughts and Images Reflecting the Spirit of the Universe,* ed. Michael Reagon (Atlanta: Templeton Foundation, 1999), 150.

83. Ward, *Postmodern God,* xliii.

84. Ward, *Cities of God,* 215.

CHAPTER 10

Time Gentlemen Please

The Space and Place of Gender in Sport History

PATRICIA VERTINSKY

INTRODUCTION

"It is not I who speak, Gentlemen, but History who speaks through me."

—"Fusel de Coulanges," *Revue Historique*

Gender is a determining factor in cultural production.[1] The gradual inclusion within sport history of a focus upon gender, which in turn has pressed the academy to pay attention to a wider and deeper version of the history of sport and physical education, is to be celebrated. In particular, the conflation of feminism and certain elements of postmodernism has stimulated new approaches to sport history and comparative examinations of the education and training of the body. Yet, in the current debate around modernism and postmodernism, feminists cannot help but point out how both modernism and postmodernism remain so frequently, so unimaginatively, patriarchal.[2] Perhaps nowhere is this more true than in the world of sport scholarship where Western white males have traditionally controlled the production of knowledge and the parameters of the debates around both modernism and postmodernism—or more appropriately *postmodernisms*. As Bonnie Smith points out in relation to the profession of history, "no matter what the changes from realism to modernism, or modernism to postmodernism, from claims of truth to claims of explanation, masculinity continues

227

to function as it did in the 19th century . . . The profession's unacknowl-
edged libidinal work—the social ideology that draws us to value male pleni-
tude, power and self-presentation—is but rarely glimpsed in the mirror of
history."[3] This chapter, therefore, will discuss the changing space and place
of gender in sport history and the role (and relative success) of feminism in
identifying the inadequacies of the modernist project in its dominant form
and embracing some aspects of postmodern thought to nudge the gender
agenda forward in sport history. My approach is not designed to deny the
possibility of progress and change held out by modernism but rather to highlight the postmodern potential of incorporating multiple voices and perspectives into the study of sport history and to encourage challenges to the
longstanding notion of science and society as a patriarchal hierarchy with a
claim to truth.

MALE ANXIETY AND THE END OF SPORT HISTORY

Echoing the "end of history" debate propelled by Francis Fukuyama in 1992,[4]
it has become the fashion lately for self-identified sport historians, mostly
male, to bemoan the impending death of a sport history subdiscipline, inca-
pable of self-criticism, substantive debate, and the kind of (healthy?)
internecine warfare common in such organizations as the MLA and AHA.[5]
Historians generally, suggests Mark Poster, have been socialized by the discipline of history to avoid questions about the meaning of their own work,
acceding too readily to the injunction to produce work that adds to the font
of knowledge rather than questioning its worth.[6] In sport history, there is not
enough critical assessment of the good, the bad, and the ugly, says Colin
Tatz.[7] Sport historians avoid reflecting upon questions about the meaning of
their work, concurs Murray Phillips, especially where theoretical and conceptual issues are concerned.[8] "We rarely step back and ask basic questions
about why and how we do things . . . [T]here has been a conspicuous reti-
cence for thorough, searching review and evaluation," adds Steve Pope
(quoting David Thelan), in his special *Journal of Sport History* issue on *The
Practice of Sport History*.[9] In their rush to embrace the class/gender/race
mantra, he says, as well as the promises of postmodernism, many sport historians have effectively lost their ability to communicate with a broader audience. To achieve this aim, Pope commissioned a series of articles around the
use of visuals, film, museum artifacts, and the internet, which might revitalize the practice of sport history teaching and return it "closer to the playing
field."[10] Eschewing scholarly detachment he begged sport historians to bring
their work into popular culture, to join perhaps "that playpit for the

unattended urchins of other disciplines" that Tony Judt warned about long ago in relation to social history.[11]

It is not clear in this particular gambit what purpose Synthia Sydnor's postmodern article is designed to serve (although she is the lone female representative among the special issue authors). In a provocative writing of the history of synchronized swimming (rivaling the scholar Philippe Tamizey de Larroque who used at least five hundred footnotes per article),[12] she cleverly uses postmodern tropes to show how sport history displayed in this manner can only be understood within the academy whose practices Pope finds so confining.[13] In this respect, Doreen Massey might have a point that "much postmodernism is less about communication and more about self-presentation."[14] However, it can suggest that Sydnor and a number of other feminist sport historians are less shaken by talk of an "end to history" and have been open to those aspects of postmodernity and poststructural analyses that promise a more reflective understanding of sport history and the significance of women and gender relations within it.[15] Where Fukuyama's "end of history," (lacking any competitor for liberal capitalism) seems to be over, as if world history were a football game, feminists, along with Poster, can read it as a sorry masculinist tale—(recognizable as) the end of the white, male metanarrative, the end of the heroic bourgeois epoch, the end of an unselfconscious (muscular) patriarchy that has nothing left to accomplish.[16]

In another relatively recent critique, this time aimed at British sport historians, Jeff Hill got it right that British sport history is mired in methodological conservatism, thoroughly attached to the "real" labor of gathering, sorting, and representing the facts. Without proposing the complete abandonment of the archives, he suggested that some of the theoretical aspects of postmodern influences might be usefully embraced and harmonized with the areas of empirical enquiry that were coming onto the sports historian's agenda.[17] He also got it right (though a good deal later than a number of female sport historians, and well toward the end of his lengthy critique), when he pointed out that one of the most overlooked aspects of British sport among historians is "the place in it of women." Nor, he added, could matters of gender any longer be assumed to be of interest only to women.[18] The problem, as he saw it, was that "gender comes trailing clouds of theory" and that sport feminists have a proclivity to draw eclectically upon groupings of ideas and political positions that place gender at the center of analysis. Such an approach, he felt, could draw sports history away from its conventional methodology.[19] Hill went on to consider whether feminist critiques of historical practice and postmodern theories could or should destabilize such methodological conservatism and/or whether they could enrich studies of sport through greater attention to important issues around meaning and identity.

DISCOVERING WOMEN IN AND THROUGH SPORT HISTORY

This is a task in which a number of sport historians interested in women's studies and gender relations have been involved for many years, though not without difficulty. In 1983, the editor of the *Journal of Sport History* addressed the prospects and promise of sport history and lamented that "despite the fact that sport has been embedded in, and contoured by, patriarchal relationships, we have still to see an adequate analysis of women and sport."[20] This was partly due to the everpresent obstacles faced by women's history and sport history itself in gaining acceptance to history's established domain. In its early development, the dominant Western sport historiography was largely descriptive rather than analytic, and researchers assumed that historical evidence existed independent of the historian; that the past could be constructed from that evidence, and that a change over time was both inevitable and progressive.[21] Historians operating in this empiricist, descriptive approach examined "modern" sport in a way that served as the classic, even paradigmatic definition of sport.[22] The modernization model was not a panacea for sport historians, said Nancy Struna, but it worked best with urban, middle-class people who were the dominant constructors of the rational scientific world that was central to the process it framed.[23]

By the 1970s and 1980s, sport historians were carving out a specific niche for their field within the general discipline of history as part of history's rapprochement with the social sciences. They took their philosophical, theoretical, and methodological cues largely from social history, which, according to Eric Hobsbawm, was powerfully shaped and stimulated not only by the professional structure of other social sciences, and by their methods and techniques, but also by their questions. Social history, as he famously put it, was "the history of society," requiring a commitment to understand all facets of human existence in terms of their social determination.[24] Sport, physical education, and gender relations clearly had an important role in this definition, and historians of women began to assume that their scholarship would come to fit into the field of history as a whole.

Yet even as social history flourished, women's history (along with women's sport history) was slow to find acceptance.[25] Looking back at his survey of the development of social history during the 1970s, Eric Hobsbawm writes of his astonished embarrassment at making no reference whatsoever to women's history. Nor, he adds, did the most distinguished males in the profession notice their blindness to this aspect of their work.[26] Certainly sport historians of the time, who increasingly found their place within the intellectual home of social history and adopted its methodological innovations, typically wrote through a male lens, and largely about men's sporting and athletic achievements. This was hardly surprising since in Western iconography the knowing subject, along with the historically important objects the mirror serves up for scrutiny, is usually male.[27] After all, sport is one of the few ways in which the male body is continually represented, examined, worshipped, all too often to the exclusion of the female-body-as-active.[28]

One of the promises of postmodernism is that it allows fuller appreciation of those historically banished to the margins, such as women. Hence women-centered historians first worked to counteract Virginia Woolf's earlier complaint about women's virtual exclusion from the historical record.[29] Their aim was to redress the high costs of a history predicated on the silence and invisibility of those who have been hidden from history. From an initial preoccupation with the need to rediscover and render visible the contributions of women reformers and heroines from the past (which was in itself an important contribution to the discourse of collective identity that made the women's movement possible in the 1970s), they went on to embrace revisionist interpretations in exploring and documenting the diverse nature of women's historical experience, bringing to light a plurality of viewpoints. In the domain of sport history, Nancy Struna was among the first to ask prescient questions about "that field of ours which intersects with women's history—women's sport history." She called for scholars to move beyond compensatory measures and to explore themes such as identity, conflict, and the relativity of equality. "Has our literature moved beyond the parochial to the universal questions which historians ask; has it begun to suggest what ultimate difference women's sporting experience makes in our total understanding of the human experience; is it contributing to theoretical debate and methodological innovation?"[30]

As women's sport history developed, its promoters increasingly questioned the strategy of viewing women and men through a separate spheres perspective for its tendency to emphasize difference rather than elucidating the reciprocity between gender and society. In any case, simple recognition does not necessarily bring empowerment, as David Harvey has bluntly pointed out.[31] A generic, male-oriented sport history tended to align itself with those specializations emerging from the social history parent (hallowing the male sporting experience). Both suffered, in some respects, from restrictive assumptions derived from uncritically applying a contemporary characterization of sport as male, modern, and athletic to the past. The premise of women's history was that hierarchical social, economic, and political contexts rather than biology, history rather than nature, created women. Hence questions posed about "women" called forth responses selectively—to some degree they isolated the female subject from the social relationships that created her and presumed that woman existed in certain ways. "Tell me about a woman always to some extent meant, tell me about someone who will be recognizable to me as a [sporting] woman."[32]

GENDERING SPORT HISTORY

The discernible shift during the 1980s from women-centered investigations and the analysis of sex roles to the study of gender roles involving both men and women began from the poststructural premise that identities are made in relationships.[33] As gender became increasingly evident as a useful category of analysis across the humanities and social sciences it was persuasively argued that events and processes that had traditionally preoccupied historians must now be revisited from a gender perspective.[34] Gender, said Joan Scott, offered a good way of thinking about history[35] (just as gender offered a good way of thinking about sport and sport history.)[36] Her influential views underscored the historian's active role as producer of knowledge while attempting to understand the production of knowledge and power as multiple and conflictual processes engendering theories of "multiplicity" rather than theories of "the woman." Bonnie Smith went further in claiming that the entire development of modern scientific methodology, epistemology, professional practice, and historical writing was inextricably tied to gender relations and to evolving definitions of masculinity and femininity.[37] It became clear that if gender inequalities were to be examined and challenged then a more comprehensive understanding was required of where power was held in the relationship. This entailed a multidimensional emphasis on social processes that was at the core of poststructural theory. Not only women but also men and the construction of dominant masculinity/ies had to be understood and explored.[38] Connell's theory of the gender order as a dynamic system of power relations in which multiple masculinities and femininities were constructed, contested, and altered continually was fundamental to this analysis.[39]

Once sport historians began to look for ways in which the concept of "gender" legitimized and constructed social relationships they were able to develop clearer insights into the reciprocal nature of gender and society, and a series of excellent works elucidated this.[40] Even historians who persisted in treating sport as a predominantly male domain no longer winced at the possibility that it was, and is, a gendered domain.[41] Male feminist scholars such as McKay, Messner, and Sabo built on the framework developed by feminist analyses of women and sport to demonstrate the fundamental importance of gender in men's sports.[42] A wealth of studies have followed, though often with an emphasis on the diversity among men rather than the privileges of dominance shared in male sport.[43]

In 1991, Roberta Park edited a special issue of the *Journal of Sport History* that displayed the growing maturity of scholarship in the area of gender relations and sport history. Dedicated to balancing male and female perspectives, she sought to include both male and female constructions, interests, and events and to extend gender analyses to race, ethnicity, class, location, and aging. Following Connell and others she showed that it is not enough to simply juxtapose social categories of gender, class, and race and apply them to sport. They must be woven together by an inductive analysis of sport, beginning with the most basic element of sport, the human body, and an investigation of its social meanings.[44] "Bodies," Park pointed out "are used to convey a host of deep-seated cultural beliefs and values."[45] She thus underscored how a version of historiography that acknowledged gender might encourage new perspectives on the sporting practices of the past, since the practice of gender history, which engages the interpretive possibility that manliness and womanliness are socially constituted and continually construed, goes all the way down to the body itself.[46]

In 1994, when I reviewed a decade of changing enquiry in women's sport history and gender relations in the *Journal of Sport History*,[47] it was clear that shifts from scientific to literary paradigms among social scientists, from an emphasis on cause to one on meaning, as well as critiques of science, empiricism, and humanism by poststructuralists were coalescing to present fresh lines of enquiry for feminist sport historians. A recognized focus was on seeking ways of representing gender as both a constitutive element of social relationships and a primary way of signifying relationships of power. Clearly, gender was a determining factor in cultural production and was also so in relation to its interpretation. Reclaiming sporting experience was a significant task, but it was important to see how the forging of experience was itself an outcome of social processes. Experience was now understood to be formed through discourses that had to be analyzed in order to view the workings of power.[48] In the end, said Joan Scott, there is no way to detach politics—the relations of power, systems of belief, and practices—from knowledge and the processes that produce it.[49]

In the same decade review, I also discussed how the new genre of body history, exemplified by Ludmilla Jordanova, Barabara Duden, Londa Schiebinger, Thomas Laqueur, Sander Gilman, and others raised provocative issues for sport historians about how the sporting body had been inscribed with the stigmata of gender, as well as age, race, class, and ethnicity.[50]

Gender is the way bodies are drawn into history; bodies are arenas for the making of gender patterns.[51] Thus the inclusion within sport history of a focus upon gender—which in turn forces a focus on the body and bodily practices—has pressed an increasing number of sport historians to pay attention to a much wider and deeper version of the history of sport and physical education. It has illustrated how athletics, physical culture, and exercise, which intentionally and explicitly give prominence to the body, offer rich and untilled soil for historical investigations of icons and metaphors of male as well as female bodies. And it has invited attempts to draw up a new geography, a historical landscape in which the transformative effects of feminist theorizing about the gendered body (and other categories of difference such as race, class, and ethnicity) led historians to people space in different ways and shift the boundaries. In concert with the continuing reception of Foucault's attention to the body as the primary site for the operation of modern forms of power, and as the object of processes of discipline and normalization, a fruitful array of new tools and perspectives has become available to historians of sport, physical culture, and exercise.[52]

POSTMODERN PROMISES AND PITFALLS

"Postmodernism has knocked the subject from its pedestal, which makes discussion of identity awkward. There are simply too many fragments to hold at one time to produce a mass sufficient to be called a definitive subject. One is tempted to quit very early in the project."[53] Feminist historians, notes Catriona Parratt, were among the first to both entertain and critique postmodern theories, whose assaults on history's empirical claims, empiricist certainties, and the modernist credo of progress perturbed the very philosophical and conceptual grounds on which social history and sport history stood.[54] Social history was taken to task for its universalizing claims to be the key to the whole of historical understanding as well as the centrality some believed it had given to class as a category of analysis.[55] Encouraged to direct greater attention to language, discourse, and ideology, sport historians were directed to seek meaning rather than explain causes and to take more seriously themes hitherto neglected or marginalized by traditional historians. The anti-essentialist stance of postmodernists also helped to stress that there were no fundamental truths about the nature of men and women. Indeed, said Poster, the topic of women provided a good occasion for examining the whole relation of the historian to the truth because women have been figured in Western history as other to the truth—as outside the couplet truth-real. Only a postmodern understanding of the individual as complex, unstable, and constructed could allow for a proper historical grasp of minority experience.[56] On the positive side, therefore, the use of postmodern theory by sport historians promises "to replace unitary notions of 'women' and 'feminine identity with plural and complexly constructed conceptions of social identity, treating gender as one relevant strand among others, attending also to class, race, ethnicity, age and sexual orientation."[57]

But, warned Parratt, where gender was the focus of analyses in the new historicism, sport historians were also in danger of obscuring, marginalizing, or even erasing women. Indeed it was quite possible to focus on gender in sport history and ignore women completely, since the history of sport could be said to be centrally a history of gender, of masculinity in which women have hardly figured at all.[58] And, she continued, while attention to theory about gender offered a powerful way of exposing and attacking the oppositions and hierarchies on which gender relations are based, it also posed the danger of abandoning concern with the lives of "real women." Sporting women of color and ethnicity, working women, lesbian women, aging women, and those with disabilities were among those who had remained hidden from history and whose voices needed to be heard as authentic and legitimate. If the turn to theory, like the turn to gender with which it is connected, entailed abandoning the study of all of these women's experiences, she said, then historians of women's sport and leisure should be warned to make it with caution.[59]

Colin Howell posed further issues in relation to postmodernism and gender in *Sport History Review* while admitting that it was in the hands of feminist scholars that postmodernism had usefully established itself as a form of social criticism and contributed a great deal to the broader movement for gender equality.[60] Obviously postmodernism has its attractions, he said, though dangers lurked in abstract theorizing and unfettered idealism,[61] and in particular in the postmodern flight from materialism.[62] In a trenchant critique of sport history methodological preoccupations he underscored the importance of recognizing how postmodernism is itself connected to broader historical forces at work in the contemporary world and that it must be seen as serving a multitude of ideological purposes.[63]

Certainly there has been intense historiographical debate around postmodernism that continues to be seen by the neoconservative historian as a fundamental threat to the preservation of tradition and the status quo, a threat calling into question the seemingly universalist principles of the West.[64] Postmodernism, accuse Appleby, Hunt, and Jacob in their provocatively titled *Telling the Truth about History*, cannot provide models for the future when it claims to refute the entire idea of offering models for the future.[65] Seeking the path of moderation, Richard Evans points out:

> Postmodernism in its more constructive modes has encouraged historians to look more closely at documents . . . and to think about texts and narratives in new ways. It has helped open up many new subjects and areas for research while putting on the agenda many topics which had previously seemed to be exhausted. It has forced historians to interrogate their own methods and procedures as

never before and in the process has made them more self-critical. It
has led to open acknowledgement of the historians' own subjectivity . . . [and] it has shifted the emphasis of historical writing back
from social-scientific to literary models and in so doing has begun
to make it more accessible to the public.[66]

Yet so extensive and contentious has the debate around postmodernism
become that in some respects it may be unproductive to continue to engage
in the modernism/postmodernism debate. Even mere "ism" is a misunder-
standing and the death of history, said Heidegger in *What Is a Thing?*[67] Any
attempt to define the word necessarily brings forth both positive and negative dimensions, though it has to be seen as a useful attempt to denaturalize
some of the dominant features of our ways of life.[68] Part of postmodernism's
power, says Eagleton "is the fact that it exists . . . it is the period we are living
in . . . though how far down this goes, whether it is wall-to-wall is a matter
of debate."[69] Certainly it has become a concept to be wrestled with, for as
Laclau points out, postmodernism cannot be a simple rejection of modernity;
rather it involves a different modulation of its themes and categories.[70] It
might be more useful to simply think about postmodernism as a dominant
cultural trend; a convenient label for a set of attitudes, values, beliefs, and
feelings about what it means to be living in the twenty-first century;[71] a frag-
mented, decentered, uncertain, yet flexible and exciting contemporary
scene. This is Jameson's notion of the cultural logic of late capitalism in the
transforming nature of a globalizing society—though he does hold fast to a
Marxist grand narrative.[72] This of course poses some problems for those feminist sport historians who believe that what Lyotard called an "incredulity
toward metanarratives"[73] is an essential notion toward accepting a multiplicity of viewpoints and diverse subject positions in the histories they write.

Then there are those who would disavow both postmodernism and
modernism altogether, "who would avoid the competition—invented by the
word *postmodern*—in which people try to define the modern era, something
that began in the past and is now apparently over, posted into history."[74] In
We Have Never Been Modern, Bruno Latour mocks the arrogance and angst
of Western academics in their despair over modernity and the end of history.
Postmodernism is a symptom, not a solution he says.[75]

Haven't we shed enough tears over the disenchantment of the
world? Haven't we frightened ourselves enough with the poor
European who is thrust into a cold soulless cosmos, wandering on
an inert planet in a world devoid of meaning? Haven't we shivered
enough before the spectacle of a mechanized proletarian who is
subject to the absolute domination of a mechanized capitalism and

a Kafkaesque bureaucracy, abandoned smack in the middle of language games, lost in cement and formica? Haven't we felt sorry enough for the consumer who . . . is manipulated by the powers of the media and the post-industrialized society? How we do love to wear the hair shirt of the absurd, and what even greater pleasure we take in postmodern nonsense![76]

What we have to realize, he points out is that "Modernization has never occurred. There is no tide, long in rising, that would be flowing again today. There has never been such a tide. We can go on to other things—that is return to the multiple entities that have always passed in a different way."[77]

For Latour, then, not only have we never been modern, but disenchantment (with a modernity we have never known) cannot therefore be our fate, nor postmodernity our future. I think, however, that Poster offers a more useful view. "At this point," he says, "it has become clear that what is at stake is not so much the nature of the past and the status of discourses about it, as a change in the present and the consequent impossibility of maintaining earlier forms of discourse about the past."[78] This works well for gender sport history, which is by definition an unfinished project, always/already in the making.

SETTING OUR SIGHTS ON THE BODY

The notion of embodiment is crucial to the feminist enterprise. From my own perspective, and in the attempt to bring issues of gender and the body most fully into sport history in the twenty-first century I think we have to settle (even if with some discomfort) upon aspects of postmodernism and postmodernist strategies that promise to be most useful in seeking new cognitive maps and new strategies of analysis in our historical work.[79] Rapid technological development does seem to be leading to a period of cultural life that does not fit within modernist horizons—or modernist buildings either.[80] Contemporary arguments about postmodernism do press us into important understandings about the nature of power and raise provocative issues about gender politics that need to be faced with greater generosity and imagination than in the past. To be sure, postmodernism has not adequately theorized agency, nor has it provided strategies of resistance that would correspond to feminist ones.[81] Yet feminisms, says Hutcheon, have made postmodernists think, not just about the body but also about the female body; not just about the female body but also about its desires and about both as socially and historically constructed through representation.[82] For feminist sport historians it is the particular conflation of feminism and postmodernism with their common interest in representations of the sporting body and the construction of the gendered subject that has provided rich soil for interdisciplinary enquiry and fresh research approaches. And since a central concern of feminism has been the reintroduction of the body and categories of the body into the realm of the political, it is within this nexus that some of the most interesting and potentially useful comparative studies around physical or body cultures, sport, and the spatial-temporal training and disciplining of the body are appearing in the sports history literature.[83] Through the lexicon of postmodernity the body has stolen the spotlight as something to grasp, something that has a history worth telling in an increasingly somatic society.

NOTES

1. Doreen Massey, *Space, Place and Gender* (Oxford: Polity, 1994), 238.

2. Massey makes this complaint in *Space, Place and Gender* where she critiques the work of David Harvey and Edward Soja as being fundamentally antifeminist, 212.

3. Bonnie G. Smith, *The Gender of History: Men, Women and Historical Practice* (Cambridge, MA: Harvard University Press, 1998), 235.

4. See for example, Francis Fukuyama, *The End of History and the Last Man* (New York: The Free Press, 1992). Fukuyama argued that liberal democracy may constitute the end point of mankind's ideological evolution, the final form of human government, and as such constituted the end of history—or at least, history understood as that kind of single coherent evolutionary process outlined by Hegel and Marx.

5. Modern Language Association and the American Historical Association.

6. Mark Poster, *Cultural History + Postmodernity: Disciplinary Readings and Challenges* (New York: Columbia University Press, 1997), 48–49.

7. Colin Tatz, "History Lessons," *Sporting Traditions* 16, no. 1 (1999): 15–22.

8. Murray Phillips, "Deconstructing Sport History: The Postmodern Challenge," *Journal of Sport History* 28, no. 3 (2001): 327–44.

9. Steve W. Pope, "Sport History: Into the Twenty-First Century," *Journal of Sport History* 25, no. 2 (1998): i.

10. Pope, "Sport History," vi. He quotes David Thelan, "The Practice of American History," *Journal of American History* 81 (1994): 933.

11. Tony Judt, "A Clown in Regal Purple: Social History and the Historians," *History Workshop Journal* (Spring 1979): 66–94.

12. Smith, *The Gender of History*, 213.

13. Synthia Sydnor, "A History of Synchronized Swimming," *Journal of Sport History* 25, no. 2 (1998): 252–67.

14. Massey, *Space, Place and Gender*, 219.

15. Sport history is not only not in decline, says Charlotte Macdonald, but has all the more to say to a world in which sport has never been more important and more valued. And of all the identities that sport brings into being, the masculine one is most recurring and consistent across sport, culture, and time. Charlotte Macdonald, "The End of Sport History?" *Sporting Traditions* 16, no. 1 (1999): 107.

16. Fukuyama, says Poster has apparently not read a single work of feminist theory. *Cultural History*, 63–64. As Mascia-Lees and others comment, "when western white males who traditionally have controlled the production of knowledge can no longer define the truth . . . their response is to conclude that there is not a truth to discover. F. E. Mascia-Lees, P. Sharpe, and C. Cohen, eds., "The Postmodernist Turn in Anthropology: Cautions from a Feminist Perspective," *Signs* 15, no. 1 (1989): 33.

17. Jeffrey Hill, "British Sports History: A Postmodern Future," *Journal of Sport History* 23, no. 1 (1996): 15. Postmodernism, especially for a historical tradition such as that of the British so steeped in empiricism, poses a fundamental question about the historian's craft, namely, can the sources be treated as a point of access to the social reality presumed to lie beyond them?

18. Hill, "British Sports History," 13.

19. Hill, "British Sports History," 14.

20. Jack Berryman, "Preface," *Journal of Sport History* 10, no. 1 (1983): 5.

21. Nancy Struna, "Social History," in *Handbook of Sport and Society*, eds. Jay Coakley and Eric Dunning (London: Sage, 2000), 189.

22. As Struna points out, Allen Guttmann's *From Ritual to Record: The Nature of Modern Sport* (1978) was one of the most influential discussions of the historical basis for and characteristics of modern sport. Following Max Weber, Guttmann emphasized the formative context shaped by the rational scientific worldview of the nineteenth century.

23. Nancy Struna, "Sport History," in *A History of Exercise and Sport Science*, eds. John D. Massengale and Richard H Swanson (Champaign, IL: Human Kinetics, 1997).

24. Eric Hobsbawm, *On History* (London: Weiderfield and Nicholson, 1997), 76.

25. Geoff Eley, "Playing It Safe, Or How Is Social History Represented?" *History Workshop Journal* 35 (Spring 1993): 206–20.

26. Hobsbawm, *On History*, 71.

27. Smith, *The Gender of History*, 2.

28. Andrew Blake, *The Body Language: The Meaning of Modern Sports* (London: Lawrence and Wishart, 1996), 161.

29. Virginia Woolf, *A Room of One's Own* (New York: Harcourt, Brace and World, 1929), 43–59.

30. Nancy Struna, "Reyond Mapping Experience: The Need for Understanding the History of American Sporting Women," *Journal of Sport History* 11, no. 1 (1984): 129, 121.

31. David Harvey, The Condition of Postmodernity: An Enquiry into the Origins of Cultural Change (Oxford: Blackwell, 1990).

32. Joy Parr, "Gender History and Historical Practice," *The Canadian Historical Review* 76, no. 3 (1995): 362.

33. Elaine Showalter, ed., *Speaking of Gender* (London: Routledge, 1989), 2.

34. Joan Wallach Scott, "Re-Writing History," in *Behind the Lines: Gender and the Two World Wars*, eds. Margaret Higonet, Jane Jenson, Sonya Michel, and Margaret C. Weitz, (New Haven: Yale University Press, 1987), 22.

35. Joan Wallach Scott, *Gender and the Politics of History* (New York: Columbia University Press, 1988), 34.

36. Elliott J. Gorn and Michael Oriard, "Taking Sports Seriously," *Chronicle of Higher Education* (24 March 1995): A52.

37. Smith, *The Gender of History*.

38. Jim McKay, Michael A. Messner, and Don Sabo, eds., *Masculinities, Gender Relations and Sport* (Thousand Oaks, CA: Sage, 2000), 2.

39. R.W. Connell, *Gender and Power: Society, The Person and Sexual Politics* (Stanford, CA: Stanford University Press, 1987).

40. There are many examples. For a few of the earliest, see Sheila Fletcher, *Women First: The Female Tradition in English Physical Education, 1880–1990* (London: Louds, 1984); Kathleen E. McCrone, *Playing the Game: Sport and the Physical Emancipation of English Women, 1870–1914* (Lexington: University Press of Kentucky, 1988); Helen Lenskyj, *Out of Bounds; Women, Sport and Sexuality* (Toronto: Women's Press, 1986).

41. Nancy Struna, *Social History*, 19.

42. Michael A. Messner and Don Sabo, eds., *Sport, Men and the Gender Order: Critical Feminist Perspectives* (Champaign, IL: Human Kinetics, 1990), 2.

43. R. W. Connell, "The Big Picture: Masculinities in Recent World History," *Theory and Society* 22 (1993): 610–12.

44. Roberta J. Park, Special Issue on Sport and Gender, *Journal of Sport History* 18, no. 1 (1991). See my article on gender for a later discussion of these developments, "Gender Relations, Women's History and Sport His-

tory: A Decade of Changing Enquiry, 1983–1993," *Journal of Sport History* 21, no. 1 (1994): 19–20.

45. Roberta J. Park, "Physiology and Anatomy Are Destiny! Brains, Bodies and Exercise in Nineteenth Century American Thought," *Journal of Sport History* 18, no. 1 (1991): 63.

46. Parr, "Gender History," 355–56.

47. Vertinsky, "Gender Relations."

48. This did leave questions, however, about the difficulty of disentangling the discursive aspects from the moments of experience and agency in the shaping of identity. Kathleen Canning, "German Particularities in Women's History/Gender History," *Journal of Women's History* 5, no. 1 (1993): 106.

49. Joan Scott, "Women's History," in *New Perspectives on Historical Writing*, ed. Peter Burke (Cambridge: Polity, 1991), 65.

50. See Vertinsky, "Gender Relations," 22 for a discussion of these works.

51. R. W. Connell, "Debates about Men, New Research on Masculinities," in *The Men and the Boys* (Cambridge: Polity, 2000).

52. See for example the excellent work of David Kirk in exploring how forms of bodily practices such as physical education in schools can be located as sites for the surveillance of bodies. David Kirk, *Schooling Bodies, School Practice and Public Discourse, 1880–1950* (Leicester: Leicester University Press, 1998). David Kirk, "Schooling Bodies through Physical Education: Insights from Social Epistemology and Curriculum History," *Studies in Philosophy and Education* 20 (2001): 475–87.

53. Eileen Schlee, "The Subject is Dead, Long Live the Female Subject," *Feminist Issues* 13, no. 2 (1993): 69.

54. Catriona M. Parratt, "About Turns: Reflections on Sport History in the 1990's," *Sport History Review* 29 (1995): 4.

55. Rosemary Deem and other feminist sociologists argued that those who were willing to take gender into account did so only if it could be accommodated without shifting the focus too far from class; that is, class was the most important struggle, and gender was simply something for women to worry about. Rosemary Deem, "Together We Stand, Divided We Fall," *Sociology of Sport Journal* 5 (1988): 341–54. For a larger discussion of this debate see M. Ann Hall, *Feminism and Sporting Bodies* (Champaign, IL: Human Kinetics, 1996).

56. Poster, *Cultural History*, 54.

57. N. Fraser and L. Nicholson, "Social Criticism without Philosophy: An Encounter between Feminism and Postmodernism," *Theory, Culture and Society* 5 (1988): 391.

58. Parratt, "About Turns," 8.

59. Parratt, "About Turns," 8–9. This was also the message of M. Ann Hall, *The Girl and the Game: A History of Women's Sport in Canada* (Toronto: Broadview, 2002).

60. Colin Howell, "On Metcalfe, Marx and Materialism: Reflections on the Writing of Sport History," *Sport History Review* 29 (1998): 96–102.

61. These are the views of Bryan Palmer in *Descent into Discourse: The Reification of Language and the Writing of Social History* (Phildadelphia: Temple University Press, 1990). For example he says that "all this theory stuff is bankrupt because it ignores experience in favor of discourse, dissolves agency into textuality, substitutes nihilism for social commitment. Language is not life." iv.

62. In a counter argument Massey, in *Space, Place and Gender*, says, "let us by all means discuss gender within the frame of materialist enquiry but we have to be sure what it means—it is far wider than an emphasis on the power of money and capital circulation," 243.

63. Howell, "On Metcalfe, Marx," 99.

64. It is worth noting that Nobel Prize–winning economist Amartya Sen had no trouble demonstrating the hollowness of the West's claim to an exclusive access to the values that lie at the foundation of rationality and reason, science and evidence, liberty and tolerance, rights and justice. Amartya Sen, "East and West: The Reach of Reason," *New York Review of Books* (July 2000): 33.

65. Joyce Appleby, Lynn Hunt, and Margaret Jacob, *Telling the Truth about History* (New York: Norton, 1994), 237.

66. Richard J. Evans, *In Defence of History* (London: Granton Books, 1997), 248.

67. Martin Heidegger, *What Is a Thing?* (first published 1935–36) trans. W. B. Barton, Jr. and Vera Deutsch (South Bend, IN: Regnery/Gateway, 1967).

68. Linda Hutcheon, *The Politics of Postmodernism* (London and New York: Routledge, 1989).

69. Terry Eagleton, *The Illusions of Postmodernism* (Oxford: Blackwell, 1996), ix, 20.

70. Ernesto Laclau, ed., *The Making of Political Identities* (New York: Verso, 1994).

71. Dave Robinson, *Postmodern Encounters: Nietzsche and Postmodernism*, (Cambridge: Icon Books, 1999), 25.

72. Fredric Jameson, *Postmodernism or, The Cultural Logic of Late Capitalism* (Durham, NC: Duke University Press, 1991).

73. Jean-Francois Lyotard, *The Postmodern Condition*, trans. Geoff Bennington and Brian Massumi (Minneapolis: University of Minnesota Press, 1984).

74. Ian Hacking, *The Taming of Chance* (Cambridge: Cambridge University Press, 1990), 206.

75. Bruno Latour, *We Have Never Been Modern*, trans. Catherine Porter (Cambridge: Cambridge University Press, 1993), 74.

76. Latour, *We Have Never Been Modern*, 114–15. My thanks to Hart Caplan for bringing these passages to my attention.

77. Latour, *We Have Never Been Modern*, 76.

78. Poster, *Cultural History*, 67.

79. I thank Leslie Roman for suggesting this notion of "settling with discomfort."

80. See for example, Brian Pronger, *Body Fascism: Salvation in the Technology of Physical Fitness* (Toronto: University of Toronto Press, 2002); Patricia Vertinsky and Sherry McKay, *Disciplining the Body in the Gymnasium: Memory, Monument and Modernism* (London: Routledge, 2004); Douglas Booth, *Australian Beach Cultures: The History of Sun, Sand and Surf* (London: Cass, 2001); Andrew Sparkes and Martti Silvenoinen, eds., *Talking Bodies: Men's Narratives of the Body and Sport* (Jyvaskyla: University of Jyvaskyla, 1999).

81. Hutcheon, *The Politics of Postmodernism*, 168.

82. Hutcheon, *The Politics of Postmodernism*, 143.

83. It may seem ironic, say Dworkin and Messner, that the institution of sport that has continued to contribute to the reconstitution of hegemonic masculinity throughout the twentieth century has become a key site for the development of a critical feminist scholarship on gender. In fact it is the very centrality of the body in sport practice and ideology that provides an opportunity to examine critically and illuminate the social construction of gender. Shari L. Dworkin and Michael A. Messner, "Just Do . . . What? Sport, Bodies and Gender," in *Revisioning Gender*, eds. M. Ferree, J. Lorber and B. Hess (Thousand Oaks, CA: Sage, 1999).

Conclusion

MURRAY G. PHILLIPS

> Postmodernism entices us with the siren call of liberation and creativity, but it may be an invitation to intellectual and moral suicide . . . If we have survived the "death of God" and the "death of man," we will surely survive the "death of history"—and of truth, reason, morality, society, reality, and all other verities we used to take for granted and that have been now problematised and deconstructed. We will even survive the death of postmodernism.
>
> —Gertrude Himmelfarb, "Postmodernist History"

Some readers of this book will share Himmelfarb's skepticism and disdain for all things postmodern. At the heart of her concerns are the challenges made by postmodernism to the fundamental way we produce knowledge, and, as pointed out in the introduction, there are certainly well articulated concerns about postmodernism and postmodern history. Himmelfarb's position is an extreme reading of the postmodern view of history that portrays it in a revolutionary way leading to the demolition of history. Ironically there are some historians from the other end of the epistemological spectrum, the antifoundationalist end, like Keith Jenkins, who agree with Himmelfarb. After exploring postmodern history in three books and advocating these approaches as the best way to represent the past, Jenkins in *Why History?* contended that history may have little to offer contemporary culture.[1] He concluded more recently: "in a really tangible sense postmodernism thus seemed to me to signal the end of at least these sorts of conceptualizations of history and, maybe, even the end of thinking historically at all."[2] There are, of course, less demonic readings of postmodern history as articulated by Himmelfarb, and less cataclysmic readings as expressed by Jenkins, that promote

245

critical reflection and analysis as well as significant change, but not total destruction of the discipline. I hold the latter view.

As a supporter of engagement with postmodern approaches to history there are, nevertheless, at least two concerns worth briefly addressing. One common issue is that postmodern historians are very good on critique, of making traditional history look lame and inept, and poor on producing a body of historical works that portray its goals. A valid point, until the 1990s. An early example of postmodern history is Robert Rosenstone's *Mirror in the Shrine* (1988).[3] Rosenstone experiments with narration in the first person through the author's subjects, in the second person addressing the reader and even the historical characters. His narrative also includes "a biographer" who comments on the challenges of creating the book.[4] Authorial self reflexivity is a dominant feature of his book. Another landmark book utilizing postmodern historical practices is Richard Price's history of eighteenth-century Surinam.[5] *Alabi's World* is a compelling story of slavery constructed from the perspectives of Dutch colonial authorities, Morovian missionaries, slaves, and the historian. The contributions of these voices are represented in the text in different typefaces and are intended to "decenter the narrative, to fragment the power of the author's inevitable authority, and to draw the reader more directly into the process of interpretation."[6] It is history through multiple, complex, and competing voices. Published shortly after *Alabi's World* is Greg Dening's *Mr Bligh's Bad Language*.[7] Dening's award winning book about the South Seas gives equal voice to Tahitians and Europeans while showing how stories about the *Bounty* have been represented differently over time. Among many things, *Mr Bligh's Bad Language* illustrates how histories are imbued with the presuppositions, attitudes, and values of the people who create them.

These examples, along with a few others, hardly form an expansive corpus of work.[8] The launch of *Rethinking History* in 1997, however, provided a critical and receptive professional space for historians wanting to experiment more radically than was acceptable in established historical journals. As the editors explain: "*Rethinking History* challenges the accepted ways of doing history and rethinks the traditional paradigms, providing a unique forum in which practitioners and theorists can debate and expand the boundaries of the discipline."[9] A selection of articles from this journal has been subsequently published in a collection entitled *Experiments in Rethinking History*.[10] Not only does this collection provide a wide range of creative, confronting and, in Jenkins' parlance, "disobedient" histories to illustrate postmodern historical practices but each author has added an informative, personal, and theoretical reflection some years after the original articles.[11] While it is true that postmodern historical literature is not abundant, there are enough works to refute the charge that under the "postmodern dispensation much of the discipline of history would resolve into talking *about* historian's writings rather than producing them."[12]

The second and more contentious attribute of postmodernism is expressed by two prominent sport historians and shared by many other historians.[13] Postmodern history, as Colin Howell contends, provides a slippery slope down to a "descent into discourse"[14] and as Richard Holt suggests "we get nothing more than a dazzling kaleidoscope of impressions where anything can be construed to mean anything."[15] Is anarchic nihilism the outcome of postmodern forms of history? As I have intimated, this is an understandable but ultimately unwarranted concern.

Nihilism is not the outcome for a number of reasons. Postmodern historians do not dispute factual statements. George Herman "Babe" Ruth died in 1948, the USSR did not attend the 1984 Los Angeles Olympic Games, and women were officially admitted to the surf lifesaving movement in 1980 are established factual statements in sport history. Narratives constructed about these facts such as the importance of "Babe" Ruth to baseball in America, or the rationale for the USSR boycott and its impact on the Olympic Games, or the role of women in the surf lifesaving movement in Australia, however, are totally different scenarios. These narratives, as Hayden White contends, are contrived by the historian through a process of troping, emplotment, argument, and ideological implication.[16] While White's analysis has been challenged on a number of fronts, postmodern historians do agree with the general thrust that history is primarily a literary enterprise that produces many contrasting, competing and contradictory stories about the past.[17]

In order to make this point with a nonsporting and a sporting example, let us consider one of the most seminal twentieth century events, the Holocaust, and a debate on surf lifesaving in Australia that I have contributed to. Historians have written about the Holocaust from different perspectives. There are histories of the Holocaust from the perspectives of the victims - the Jews, Catholics, Gypsies, Polish, and others—and from the German perpetuators who carried out the atrocities. These histories tell different stories about the Holocaust and, in some cases, produce radically different conclusions. The perpetuators of the Holocaust, for example, have been portrayed by historians as either manipulated by the structure of the Nazi regime or willing accomplices with a deep-seated mindset of anti-Semitism.[18] Similarly in surf lifesaving, the role of women has attracted contrasting views. Ed Jaggard contends that women tolerated and resisted years of discrimination to emerge as fully fledged members and eventually were the saviors of the movement who arrested the steep decline in membership.[19] Alternatively, Douglas Booth emphasizes the pain, suffering, and agony of these women over almost a century and the lack of reconciliation with male members of the movement.[20] Booth's tortured souls are Jaggard's heroic women.[21] Neither view of the Holocaust or surf lifesaving is necessarily right or wrong but alerts us to the literary dimension or what has been termed the poetics of history.[22]

But there are limits to historical representation. Holocaust denial is a celebrated example. According to Robert Eaglestone, author of *Postmodernism and Holocaust Denial*, the Holocaust debate triggered an insightful review of historical method. David Irving, historian and Holocaust denier, brought libel charges against Deborah Lipstadt, on the grounds that she had destroyed his reputation as a historian. The debate was not primarily about what archive Irving had used but how he used the archive to create, develop, and falsify his argument. He was found in the court proceedings to have manipulated, misused, and misconstrued archival material to make the case that the Holocaust, as commonly conceived, did not exist.[23]

Ultimately the court trial and the associated historical debate were very informative about some of the concerns raised about postmodern history. First, the debate supports the importance placed on the worldview or what White has termed the "ideological implication" of the historian in the production of history. Marxist historians believe in the merits of Marxism, liberal historians support tolerance as a worthwhile trait, feminist historians question patriarchy, and they all write their histories under these guises. "It is because of this that history is always history for a particular reason which supports, without necessarily stating it explicitly, a certain cause or worldview."[24] Irving's worldview was anti-Semitic and racist and so was his historical work.

Second, the concerns that postmodern history leads to a "decent into discourse" or produces a "dazzling kaleidoscope of impressions where anything can be construed to mean anything" are misleading. It needs to be emphasized that the Holocaust deniers do not use postmodernism to construct their cases; they are traditional historians who selectively use information to support racist positions while deliberately masking their ideological agenda. It is a misleading reading of postmodern history if you propose that "recognising history as a narrative construction might somehow trivialize the horrors of the Nazi Holocaust or allow its deniers the freedom to peddle their lies?"[25] Similarly, while Jaggard and Booth can legitimately write competing versions of the history of the surf lifesaving movement in Australia, there are limits to historical representation. How seriously would Jaggard and Booth be taken if they denied the existence of women as members, competitors, and administrators in surf lifesaving in Australia? Anarchic nihilism is not the winner.

This rationalization may appease concerns about postmodernism and encourage some experimentation with historical practices, but there are many academics, such as Beverly Southgate, who contend that historians do not have much choice. "The postmodern challenge to historical study can't just be ignored. Ostriches may choose to think that postmodernity is another passing phase that will have left the historical desert and moved on by the time they get their heads out of the sand; but postmodernity is a condition, and it's the one we're privileged (or condemned) to live in." His critique continues with concerns that are shared by many historians: "The time for unreflective study of the past—with no thought, that is, for why we're doing it, or what it is we're doing—has passed; it's 'history.'"[26] While Bale, Booth, Hill, Parratt, and Pope might be reluctant to be branded as postmodern historians, their contributions in this book certainly advocate Southgate's appeal for critical, reflective, and innovative examinations of the past in the place of traditional history, which has been at the epicenter of sport history.

It will be interesting to see if sport historians adopt the ostrich mentality and keep their heads in the sand. As indicated in the introduction of this book, particularly in the main journals of the subdiscipline, this has been the approach over the last couple of decades. This stance is probably an unwise course of action, not because postmodernism is a chic academic fad but because the critique of traditional history is based on a very diverse, yet comprehensive range of theoretical knowledge driven by Roland Barthes, Jean Baudrillard, Jacques Derrida, Michel Foucault, Fredric Jameson, and Jean-François Lyotard who have collectively challenged and reshaped the humanities.[27] If the ostrich mentality is continued, a case has to be coherently argued to address the following: Why is the subdiscipline of sport history exceptional to other areas of the humanities? And what is special about sport history that makes it immune from the challenges posed by Barthes, Baudrillard, Derrida, Foucault, Jameson, Lyotard, and subsequently by Hayden White, F. R. Ankersmidt, Keith Jenkins, Alun Munslow, and others? This case has yet to be comprehensively made.

Or to stretch the analogy further, will sport historians imitate camels slowly moving through the desert taking on board some issues, rejecting others, and finding some middle ground between postmodern and traditional historical enterprises? There are certainly a growing number of historians who are articulating well-argued positions that combine dimensions of postmodern and traditional history. Joyce Appleby, Lynn Hunt, and Margaret Jacob, for example, have enunciated positions on realism, truth and objectivity to create concepts such as "qualified objectivity" and "practical realism."[28] Likewise Richard Evans, from a practical historical position, and C. Behan McCullagh, more from a philosophical position, have engaged with the postmodern debate and rationalized approaches that situate the process of historical production midway between traditional historical practices and postmodern history.[29] McCullagh after reviewing issues of the truth of historical descriptions, cultural relativism, and historical interpretations argued that "historical synthesis, then, is not just a matter of arranging information about the past in any manner which pleases the historian . . . History is not entirely objective, but it is much less a product of subjective preferences than philosophers sometimes assume."[30] More recently, Mary Fulbrook has argued against naïve empiricism by recognizing the theoretical dimension of all historical pursuits but also criticizes the postmodern position that historians simply impose narratives on the past. According to Fulbrook, some historical answers are more adequate than others.[31] In a similar vein Hutchins, Oriard, and Vertinsky in this collection describe sophisticated mediations between the modern and postmodern that reflect the broader movement to develop nuanced views on the historical process in the wake of postmodernism. These responses from historians and sport historians alike are important because they align with the objectives of this book: to get sport historians to engage with contemporary debates about history, to encourage them to consciously position themselves in relation to the central issues prompted by postmodernism, and to promote the importance of reflecting on the literary or poetic dimensions of producing history.

Finally, there will be the permanent desert dwellers that wholeheartedly embrace the tenets of postmodernist history and add to the *moment* in sport history that was initiated by Synthia Sydnor at the end of the last millennium and continued by Sydnor and Rinehart in their contributions in this book. Sydnor's and Rinehart's examples point to what postmodern history looks like. Postmodern history examines, experiments, and trials new ways of dealing with the past. As Rosenstone contends, postmodern history promotes the ideas of historians writing in the first person, of playing with the voices of historical figures, of utilizing the language and imagery of fiction, comic strips, poetry, and even tarot cards, of representing the past through humour, mystery, parody, and pastiche.[32] Postmodern history is radically and critically disobedient of traditional history.[33] It challenges the concept of the unified, rational, and knowing historian at the centre of traditional history and opens up opportunities for exploring the subjectivity of historians as authors. It challenges, as Munslow argues, accepted equations such as factualism with actualism, author with authority and, most importantly, history with the past. It challenges conventional hierarchies including objectivity over subjectivity, causation over chaos, and fact over fiction.[34] Postmodern history reverses the priority of content over form and supplants the empirical-analytical (traditional history) with the narrative-linguistic (postmodern) version.[35]

For sport historians to dabble in postmodern historical forms, the gate-keepers of the subdiscipline—principally the editors of the journals and those with links to the main publishers—need to support experimentation, innovation, and antifoundational work. If the gatekeepers of the profession need any encouragement they should consider the opportunities created by postmodern history. Postmodern histories have the potential to include aspects or dimensions of the past that have been previously excluded, to express relationships to the past that are impossible under the traditional history model and, to share more broadly, understandings of the past appropriate to our contemporary condition.[36] Postmodern histories can tell meaningful stories about the past, a past more reflective, as Mark Poster argues, of the condition of postmodernity in which we live.[37] Accepting a greater breadth of approaches of historical work will no doubt provoke discussion, reflection, and debate—an objective of this book—surely a worthwhile attribute for the growth, development, and maturation of any subdiscipline.

NOTES

1. Keith Jenkins, *Why History? Ethics and Postmodernity* (London: Routledge, 1999).

2. Keith Jenkins, *Refiguring History: New Thoughts on an Old Discipline* (London: Routledge, 2003), 2.

3. Robert A. Rosenstone, *Mirror in the Shrine: American Encounters with Meiji Japan* (Cambridge, MA: Harvard University Press, 1988).

4. Robert A. Rosenstone, "Introduction: Practice and Theory," in *Experiments in Rethinking History*, eds., A. Munslow and R. A. Rosenstone (New York: Routledge, 2004), 3.

5. Richard Price, *Alabi's World* (Baltimore: John Hopkins Press, 1990).

6. Price, *Alabi's World*, prologue.

7. Greg Dening, *Mr Bligh's Bad Language: Passion, Power, and Theatre on the Bounty* (Cambridge: Cambridge University Press, 1992).

8. Other commonly cited sources include Natalie Zemon Davis, *The Return of Martin Guerre* (Cambridge, MA: Harvard University Press, 1983); Simon Schama, *Dead Certainties (Unwarranted Speculations)* (New York: Knopf, 1991); and James Goodman, *Stories of Scottsboro* (New York: Pantheon, 1994). See, for a summary, Karen Halttunen, "Cultural History and the Challenge of Narrativity," in *Beyond the Cultural Turn: New Directions in the Study of Society and Culture*, eds., V. E. Bonnell and L. Hunt (Berkeley: University of California Press, 1999), 165–81.

9. http:/www.tandf.co.uk/journals/titles/13642529.

10. Alun Munslow and Robert A. Rosenstone, eds., *Experiments in Rethinking History* (New York: Routledge, 2004).

11. Jenkins, *Refiguring History*, 6.

12. M. C. Lemon, *Philosophy of History: A Guide for Students* (London: Routledge, 2003), 375.

13. For this concern amongst historians see Joyce O. Appleby, Lynn A. Hunt, and Margaret C. Jacob, *Telling the Truth about History* (New York: Norton, 1994); Richard J. Evans, *In Defence of History* (London: Granta, 1997); C. Behan McCullagh, *The Truth of History* (London: Routledge, 1998); Gertrude Himmelfarb, "Postmodernist History," in *Reconstructing History: The Emergence of a New Historical Society*, eds. Elizabeth Fox-Genovese and Elisabeth Lasch-Quinn (New York: Routledge, 1999), 71–93; Bryan D. Palmer, *Descent into Discourse: The Reification of Language and the Writing of Social History* (Philadelphia: Temple University Press, 1990); Keith Windschuttle, *The Killing of History: How Literary Critics and Social Theorists Are Murdering Our Past* (San Francisco: Encounter Books, 2000).

14. Colin D. Howell, "On Metcalf, Marx, and Materialism: Reflections on the Writing of Sport History in the Postmodern Age," *Sport History Review* 29, no. 1 (1998): 97.

15. Richard Holt, "Sport and History: British and European Traditions," in *Taking Sport Seriously*, ed., L. Allison (Aachen: Meyer and Meyer, 1998), 18.

16. Hayden White, *Metahistory: The Historical Imagination in Nineteenth Century Europe* (Baltimore: John Hopkins University Press, 1973).

17. See, for example, Keith Jenkins, *On "What is History?": From Carr and Elton to Rorty and White* (London: Routledge, 1995), 134–78 and Alun Munslow, *Deconstructing History* (London: Routledge, 1997), 140–62.

18. Robert Eaglestone, *Postmodernism and Holocaust Denial* (Cambridge: Icon, 2001), 30–34.

19. Ed Jaggard, "Writing Australia's Surf Lifesaving History," *Journal of Sport History* 29, no. 1 (2002): 15–23.

20. Douglas Booth, "The Dark Side of Surf Lifesaving," *Journal of Sport History* 29, no. 1 (2002): 7–13.

21. Murray G. Phillips, "A Critical Appraisal of Narrative in Sport History: Reading the Surf Lifesaving Debate," *Journal of Sport History* 29, no. 1 (2002): 25–40.

22. For detailed discussions of the poetics of history see Robert F. Berkhofer, *Beyond the Great Story: History as Text and Discourse* (Cambridge: Belknap Press of Harvard University Press, 1995).

23. For an excellent summary see Eaglestone, *Postmodernism and Holocaust Denial.*

24. Eaglestone, *Postmodernism and Holocaust Denial*, 34.

25. Keith Jenkins and Alun Munslow, eds., *The Nature of History Reader* (London: Routledge, 2004), 14.

26. Beverley Southgate, *History: What & Why? Ancient, Modern, and Postmodern Perspectives* (London: Routledge, 2001), 158.

27. For a recent synopsis of the contribution of these intellectuals to postmodern history see Lemon, *Philosophy of History*, 359–70.

28. Appleby, Hunt, and Jacob, *Telling the Truth about History*, 241–70.

29. Their positions are clearly outlined in Evans, *In Defence of History* and McCullagh, *The Truth of History*.

30. McCullagh, *The Truth of History*, 10.

31. Mary Fulbrook, *Historical Theory* (London: Routledge, 2002).

32. Rosenstone, "Introduction," in *Experiments in Rethinking History*, 2.

33. Jenkins, *Refiguring History*, 6.

34. Alun Munslow, "Introduction: Theory and Practice," in *Experiments in Rethinking History*, 9.

35. Jenkins and Munslow, *The New Nature of History*, 13–14.

36. Rosenstone, "Introduction," in *Experiments in Rethinking History*, 4.

37. Mark Poster, *Cultural History and Postmodernity: A Guide for Students* (New York: Norton, 1994), 70–71.

Contributors

John Bale divides his time teaching and researching at the University of Aarhus, Denmark, and Keele University, United Kingdom. His current research interests lie in the fields of sport and postcolonialism, the geographical history of running, and sport and slowness. Among his many books are *Landscapes of Modern Sport* (Leicester University Press), *Imagined Olympians* (University of Minnesota Press), *Running Cultures* (Frank Cass), and *Roger Bannister and the Four Minute Mile* (Routledge).

Douglas Booth is a professor of sport and leisure studies at the University of Waikato, New Zealand. His primary research interests cover the study of sport as a form of popular culture with a particular emphasis on political relationships and processes. Within this broad framework, specific areas of investigation have included racism in South African sport, the olympic movement, and the beach. He currently serves as an executive member of the Australian Society for Sport History and on the editorial boards of several journals including *Journal of Sport History* and *The International Journal of the History of Sport*.

Jeffrey Hill is a professor in historical and cultural studies and director of the International Center for Sport History and Culture, at De Montfort University. He has a longstanding interest in the history of the British labor movement and has also worked on the theme of sport and identity for several years. His most recent book was *Sport, Leisure and Culture in Twentieth-Century Britain* (Palgrave Macmillan, 2002). He is currently working on a book on the treatment of sport in later twentieth-century novels.

Brett Hutchins teaches sociology and media studies in the School of English Communications and Performance, Monash University. He is the author of

Don Bradman: Challenging the Myth (Cambridge University Press) and several journal articles and book chapters that examine the social and cultural dimensions of Australian sport.

Michael Oriard is Distinguished Professor of American Literature and Culture at Oregon State University. He has written five books about American sport and sport literature, including most recently *Reading Football* and *King Football.* He is currently writing a book about American football since the 1960s.

Alun Munslow is professor of history and historical theory at Staffordshire University, United Kingdom. He is the author of several books on the nature of history, most recently *Deconstructing History* (Routledge, 1997), *The Routledge Companion to Historical Studies* (Routledge, 2000), *The New History* (Pearson, 2003), *The Nature of History Reader* (Routledge, 2004) (with Keith Jenkins), and *Experiments in Rethinking History* (Routledge, 2004) (with Robert A. Rosenstone). He is also general editor of the series History: Concepts, Theories and Practice (Pearson) and founding and United Kingdom editor of *Rethinking History: The Journal of Theory and Practice* (Routledge).

Catriona M. Parratt, a native of Lincolnshire, England, now lives in Iowa City, Iowa where she is an associate professor in the Department of Health and Sport Studies at the University of Iowa. Her publications include journal articles, book chapters, and *More Than Mere Amusement* (Northeastern University Press), a history of working-class women's leisure in eighteenth- and nineteenth-century England.

Murray G. Phillips teaches in sport studies in the School of Human Movement Studies at the University of Queensland. His research interests are in the epistemological status of sport history, sport, and gender; the football codes; swimming; and coaching history. He has published journal articles, book chapters, and *From Sidelines to Centre Field: A History of Sports Coaching in Australia* (University of New South Wales Press). At present he is completing the centenary history of swimming in Australia for the national sporting body.

S. W. Pope is a senior lecturer in American history at the University of Lincoln (United Kingdom). He was a Leverhulme Research Fellow at the International Centre for Sport History and Culture, DeMontfort University (United Kingdom) during 2003. He is the author of *Patriotic Games: Sporting Traditions in the American Imagination,* 2d ed., (University of Tennessee Press,

2005) and editor of *The New American Sport History: Recent Approaches and Perspectives* (University of Illinois Press, 1997). He is currently working on a comparative history of motoring cultures in the United States and Britain during the first half of the twentieth century.

Robert E. Rinehart is an associate professor in sport management at Washington State University. His primary research interests are alternative or action sports and qualitative research methods, especially the use of narrative in reporting research findings. He has published in *Qualitative Inquiry, Sociology of Sport Journal, Journal of Sport History, Avante,* the *Waikato Journal of Education,* and *Studies in Symbolic Interaction* and has written one book, *Players All: Performances in Contemporary Sport,* and coedited another (with Synthia Sydnor), *To the Extreme: Alternative Sports, Inside and Out.*

Synthia Sydnor is an associate professor at the University of Illinois where she has appointments in Kinesiology; Criticism & Interpretive Theory; Cultural Studies and Interpretive Research; and the John Henry Newman Institute of Catholic Thought. She has been a National Endowment for the Humanities fellow; book review editor of the *Journal of Sport History;* and assistant editor of *Journal of Sport and Social Issues.* She is the coeditor/author of a recent book (2003), *To the Extreme: Alternative Sports, Inside and Out* that confronts questions about the essences, nature, and origins of sport.

Patricia Vertinsky is a professor of human kinetics and a Distinguished University Scholar at the University of British Columbia in Vancouver, Canada. Her research program focuses upon the history of the gendered body, especially in relation to health and physical activity. She is a Fellow of the Academy of Kinesiology and Physical Education, past president of the North American Society of Sport History, and vice-president of the International Society for Physical Education and Sport History.

She has authored and edited a number of books and articles, including *The Eternally Wounded Woman: Doctors and Exercise in the Late Nineteenth Century, Sites of Sport; Space, Place and Experience* (with John Bale); and *Disciplining the Body in the Gymnasium: Memory, Monument and Modernism* (with Sherry McKay). Her current project is focused on Dartington Hall and a remarkable series of "educators of the body" who passed through there during the 1930s. She is also coediting a book on *Physical Culture, Power, and the Body* with Jennifer Hargreaves for the Routledge series on Critical Studies in Sport.

Index

SUNY series on Sport, Culture, and Social Relations
CL Cole and Michael A. Messner, editors

Helen Jefferson Lenskyj, *The Best Olympics Ever? Social Impacts of Sydney 2000*

Anne Bolin and Jane Granskog (eds.), *Athletic Intruders; Ethnographic Research on Women, Culture, and Exercise*

Ralph C. Wilcox, David L. Andrews, Robert Pitter, and Richard L. Irwin (eds.), *Sporting Dystopias: The Making and Meanings of Urban Sport Cultures*

Robert E. Rinehart and Synthia Sydnor (eds.), *To the Extreme: Alternative Sports, Inside and Out*

Eric Anderson, *In the Game: Gay Athletes and the Cult of Masculinity*

Pirkko Markula (ed.), *Feminist Sport Studies: Sharing Experiences of Joy and Pain*

Murray G. Phillips (ed.), *Deconstructing Sport History: A Postmodern Analysis*

Alan Tomlinson and Christopher Young (eds.), *National Identity and Global Sports Events: Culture, Politics, and Spectacle in the Olympics and the Football World Cup*

Caroline Joan S. Picart, *From Ballroom to DanceSport*